The End of Composition Studies

DAVID W. SMIT
WITH A FOREWORD BY DOUG HESSE

The End of Composition Studies

SOUTHERN ILLINOIS UNIVERSITY PRESS • CARBONDALE

Library of Congress Cataloging-in-Publication Data

Smit, David William.
 The end of composition studies / David W. Smit ; foreword by Doug
Hesse.
     p. cm.
Includes bibliographical references and index.
1. English language—Rhetoric—Study and teaching—United States. 2.
Report writing—Study and teaching (Higher)—United States. I. Title.
PE1405.U6S64 2004
808'.042'071173—dc22
ISBN 0-8093-2585-3 (cloth : alk. paper)   2004007933

Printed on recycled paper. ♻

The paper used in this publication meets the minimum requirements of
American National Standard for Information Sciences—Permanence of
Paper for Printed Library Materials, ANSI Z39.48-1992.∞

Contents

Figures

Foreword

Doug Hesse

SINCE ITS COLLEGIATE BIRTH a century and a quarter ago, composition has led a hard life. Orphaned from rhetoric, a servile Cinderella in the begrudging manor of English-as-literature, composition earnestly began pursuing the research that might win a dance at the academic ball only in the 1960s. But even a closet full of doctoral programs, monographs, professional associations, and journals failed to transform composition's cadre of adjuncts and graduate assistants into a guild of tenured professors. Those who did acquire status achieved it primarily as scholars and administrators rather than as teachers.

So goes one massively abridged version of the history of composition, that singularly American attempt to teach writing directly to all undergraduates, most commonly through one or two required first-year courses. This version focuses primarily on issues of status and working conditions. It longs for a rhetorical paradise now decades overrun by too many students and too few resources, by ill-formed notions of writing and writers, and by the increasingly complex weight of its own self-awareness. This version bears much truth, especially in its sober portraits of who tends to teach writing under what conditions. However, these status issues are ultimately secondary.

More basic are the concerns that Dave Smit engages in the pages that follow, central among them a question both ontological and empirical: is the nature of writing such that the course in composition can be justified at all? Depending on how one answers, the ashen status of composition might be either shameful or fortuitous. I say fortuitous because dismantling a jury-rigged structure is less distressing than breaking one well conceived and made.

Understanding what is at stake begins with the distinction between "writing" and "composition." The two are not synonymous. The former term is the larger and, mostly, loftier. We call people who publish books and articles writers (or authors), reserving composer for musical production. Except for fairly snooty usages (one's "composing a text" is rather akin to one's "penning a letter"), written composition belongs almost strictly to the college freshman classroom. Largely because they point to discursive worlds beyond the academy, technical *writing* and creative *writing* exist, not technical composition or creative composition. Both are courses and programs more advanced, if not always more prestigious, with enrollments restricted to pre-professionals or elective amateurs. Creative writing, further, is historically taught by publishing writers. Such a credential has mattered less to composition, which tradition and necessity suggest can passably be taught by most anyone beyond the bachelor's degree.

I'm partial myself to writing. As program chair for the 2004 meeting of the Conference on College Composition and Communication, I wrestled long before settling on the theme "Making Composition Matter: Students, Citizens, Institutions, Advocacy." The word "composition," finally, respected the origins and emphases of CCCC, and it promised, in concert with the ambiguity of "making matter," lots of acreage for intellectual excursions. There was a productive challenge, too, in the tacit fret that composition might not matter.

Despite these advantages, I was reluctant to use *composition* because the term often tends to designate a narrow and artificial range of writing. This range might be circularly described as "the kind of writing done in composition courses" or, better, as those features of academic discourse that can be (1) abstracted and generalized (albeit thus denaturalized and reduced)—or simply conjectured, and (2) taught somewhat respectably in one or two semesters. At worst, these attempts result in forms seldom produced outside the course. At best, informed by two decades of research, they posit a subtle multiplicity of academic genres cleaving along disciplinary and epistemological lines and richly steeped in content knowledge. In this light, the sufficiency of a composition course as even a pale introduction to academic discourses begins to dim, as Smit articulately demonstrates.

To be sure, academic discourse has hardly been the totality of composition in the past forty years. What is too-handily called expressivism focuses not on composing academic texts but rather on composing selves, what is labeled civic rhetoric on composing the social order through language, and what is called cultural studies on composing (or de- and recomposing) the world itself through interpretation. Pedagogies of process, with their assumptions of generally transferable habits and practices, interlace these orientations in varying proportion. Looming above all, certainly for the broader academic community, is the hope that composition will inoculate students with college-strength grammar, punctuation, and diction.

The presence of so many competing aims undermines faith that a one- or two-semester course of study in composition is definable, let alone doable. It is striking, for example, that the "WPA Outcomes Statement for First-Year Writing" forwards an intelligent but massively ambitious set of desiderata. By the end of the first year, students should "respond appropriately to different kinds of rhetoric situations," use conventions appropriate to those situations, understand and write in several genres, use writing and reading for various purposes, develop flexible strategies (including collaborative ones) for different phases of writing, learn multiple formats, master surface conventions (Council). The statement smartly avoids setting achievement standards for these outcomes, but they constitute a rigorous menu for even a two-semester sequence.

Such is the backdrop against which Smit writes. While I won't preview his subtle translations of "end," grant that the arrow of my essay points less toward thrive than toward demise. Familiar arguments to abolish the required composition course (including for example those by Sharon Crowley) have relied on three broad critiques: that it is unethical to support an inevitably exploitative labor situation; that acting as if the course can teach academic discourse defies current theory and research; and that the inordinate time and energy professionally spent on the first-year course hobbles the broader possibilities of writing pedagogy and scholarship. None of these critiques is settled, in my opinion, although the evidence leans in their direction. Counterbalancing them is the promise that, for all its faults, the course yet does good for its students, occupying a curricular space that has democratizing potential.

What worries me is that composition's center of gravity may slip imperceptibly toward the management of teaching and away from teaching itself. It's historically true that a PhD in composition studies often buys one a career spent at least partly in program administration. The ad hoc traditional preparation for such managerial work, involving a little experience as a graduate student program assistant and a lot of learning on the job, has given way to formalized graduate courses and sequences. "To run a writing program," an unlikely professional aspiration a generation ago, is fairly common today. Some, like Richard Miller, have embraced the *realpolitik* of intellectual bureaucracy. Others, like Marc Bousquet, have decried it. As a past president of the Council of Writing Program Administrators, I see considerable value of thinking programmatically about composition and about its material conditions. Little surprise. And yet, Dwight Eisenhower's valedictory warning about the military-industrial complex resonates for me. If sustaining composition should become its own end because doing so serves vested individual interests, we will have made compromises both intellectual and ethical.

Forces within and without the field now counter this scenario, as colleges and universities develop alternatives to compliment—and replace—composition. Most venerable, of course, is writing across the curriculum in all of its guises, including ones that transfer responsibilities for academic discourses to appropriate departments. Most intriguing is the replacement of composition by topical seminars, especially at prestigious or aspiring institutions. While the motivation is sometimes to curb appeal for prospective students ("our student body surely doesn't need something as basic and blasé as composition"), the topical seminar evinces a fundamental skepticism of the contentless writing course. Beyond these, we are witnessing the slow national rise of writing departments separate from traditional English homes, replete with minors and majors, chartered to grant both undergraduate and graduate degrees, often amalgams of rhetoric, technical communication, creative writing, and journalism. (Some are described in O'Neil, Crow, and Burton's *A Field of Dreams: Independent Writing Programs and the Future of Composition Studies.*) While such units often retain service responsibilities to the campus, they function as destinations in their own right. Tellingly, I know none called Department of Composition.

One prospect for composition, then, is to become writing. By this I mean discarding composition's narrow mission of serving academic discourse, with all of the practices that have thereby accreted. Chief among them is a clutch of forms, formulae, and rump genres specially adapted to and convenient for composition classrooms. Instead of focusing on *students as students* learning to write as students for situations in which students supposedly write, we might better focus on *students as writers* learning to write for extra-disciplinary, extra-academic situations, in the genres practiced there. The recent interest in creative nonfiction—in genres from the memoir, new journalism, the profile, and nature writing to the essay (in the historical tradition out of Montaigne and not the school catch-all)—suggests one turn toward writing, away from composition. Another comes through the pursuit of civic rhetoric.

Alternatively, composition might become *composition*. At root, after all, the term refers to setting elements (notes, colors, shapes, or words) in relation to one another to create works (sonatas, paintings, buildings, or texts). As digital technologies mix word, image, and sound, and "the visual" becomes an important counterpart/constituent of "the verbal," composition has an invitation to transform itself in a fashion that would gain status along with currency. Composition, not writing, offers the best name for this new enterprise.

Either prospect (or variations between and beyond) would cost—and benefit—not only teachers but also composition as field and as profession. More important, either would alter the experiences and abilities of students. How? To what ends? The conventional limits of the foreword conveniently allow me to leave those questions open. However, the author of a book that raises such provocative concerns forfeits this luxury. To his credit and our gain, Dave Smit embraces these issues and others equally vexed, analyzing them in ways thorough and wise.

Works Cited

Bousquet, Marc. "Composition as Management Science: Toward a University Without a WPA." *JAC* 22 (2002): 493–526.

Council of Writing Program Administrators. "WPA Outcomes Statement for First-Year Composition." *WPA* 23 (1999): 59–66.

Crowley, Sharon. "A Personal Essay on Freshman English." *Composition in the University: Historical and Polemical Essays.* By Crowley. Pittsburgh: U Pittsburgh P, 1998. 228–50.

Miller, Richard E. "The Arts of Complicity: Pragmatism and the Culture of Schooling." *College English* 61 (1998): 10–28.

O'Neil, Peggy, Angela Crow, and Larry W. Burton, eds. *A Field of Dreams: Independent Writing Programs and the Future of Composition Studies.* Logan: Utah State UP, 2002.

Acknowledgments

THE MAJOR ARGUMENTS IN THIS BOOK may have begun to take shape in my mind as early as the 1970s, when I attended a workshop on reading for public school teachers conducted by Frank Smith. I had taken a break from teaching, but Smith had just published *Psycholinguistics and Reading,* and his ideas were a hot topic at the time. When my wife offered me the opportunity to attend the workshop with her, I readily accepted.

During the workshop, Smith was very much the neutral, objective scholar and researcher, laying out the theories and models, the studies and evidence, for how children learn to read. His conclusions caused a ruckus among the assembled teachers. For all practical purposes, Smith concluded from his exhaustive research that children teach themselves to read. While he did not explicitly downplay the role of schooling and explicit instruction, Smith clearly implied that instruction in reading was not as important in the learning process as most of the teachers in the room thought.

As the outrage bubbled up in the room, one teacher rose to her feet and asked Smith directly, "What then are we teachers supposed to do?" Smith looked her in the eye and said in all sincerity something like this: "I don't know. I am a researcher. I can only tell you what we know about how people learn to read. Teaching is your job, and I would never presume to tell teachers what to do." My sense was that most of the teachers in the room found this answer infuriating.

Smith may very well have been deliberately disingenuous. In *Psycholinguistics and Reading,* he provides teachers with some broad principles for how to help students learn to read, but his prescriptions are notoriously simple and unprogrammatic. Smith suggests that teachers offer students opportunities to read and that they make the process easy. In two later volumes, *Comprehension and Learning* and *Writing and the Writer,* he would offer the same advice about the teaching of writing.

Since attending Smith's workshop, I have taught in a public middle school, at a community college, and at two major research universities, and at each institution I have been struck by the discrepancy between what we know about learning to read and write and the institutional structures we have in place in order to teach students to read and write. So it may very well be that this book has been lurking in my subconscious for thirty years. I hope that I have captured something of Smith's style in this book: his ability to lay out clearly the evidence of how children become literate and his willingness to promote the implications of that evidence wherever it may lead him.

I wrote much of this book while on sabbatical from my duties as an associate professor at Kansas State University. By the time of the sabbatical, I had done most of the reading, note taking, photocopying, fact finding and pondering about the major issues I deal with here, and I had composed a rough draft of a few chapters. All I needed to complete the project was the time to sit at the computer and sweat blood until the words came. I am grateful to the university and to the College of Arts and Sciences for giving me that time.

I would also like to thank two of the reviewers of this manuscript: Joseph Harris and Stephen North. Both of them gave the book a careful reading and a wonderful mix of praise and criticism. In response to their advice, I cut considerably, added a chapter, and tried to anticipate a number of counterarguments. The book is much better because of their help and advice.

Portions of chapters 2 and 8 were previously published in "Practice, Reflection, and Genre" in *Teaching Writing Teachers of High School English and First-Year Composition,* edited by Robert Tremmel and William Broz. Copyright © 2002 by Boynton/Cook Publishers, Inc. Published by Boynton/Cook Publishers, a subsidiary of Reed Elsevier, Inc., Portsmouth New Hampshire. Other parts of this book—parts of the introduction and chapters 5 and 6—were also previously published, in "Curriculum Design for First-Year Writing Programs" in *The Allyn and Bacon Sourcebook for Writing Program Administrators,* edited by Irene Ward and William J. Carpenter. Copyright © 2002 and published by Longman/Addison Wesley Educational Publishers. And finally, the figure "Structure of the Writing Model" in chapter 3 is from the groundbreaking article by John R. Hayes and Linda Flower, "Identifying the Organization of Writing Processes" in *Cognitive Processes in Writing,* edited by L. Gregg and E. Steinberg and published by Erlbaum in 1980. I gratefully acknowledge the permission of these people and publishers to reprint this work.

The End of Composition Studies

Introduction

OF COURSE, MY TITLE *The End of Composition Studies* is a play on the meaning of "end" and is designed to be provocative, alluding as it does to recent titles such as Bill McKibben's *The End of Nature,* Francis Fukuyama's *The End of History and the Last Man,* and John Horgan's *The End of Science.* Each of these books attempts to define the nature of a large enterprise, to determine its purpose or scope, and to explore several meanings of an "end": a destination or goal; an outcome, result, or consequence; and of course—a meaning that has special resonance for the field of composition and rhetoric—a teleological "reason for being," Aristotle's final cause.

Broadly speaking, the goal of composition studies is to promote the use of writing: to help people acquire the knowledge and skill they need to convey what they want to say when they put pen to paper or fingers to the keyboard. But whether such a goal should be the ultimate consequence of the profession, whether it is the profession's "reason for being," is a matter of serious debate in the field. Some scholars in composition studies conceive of writing as a body of knowledge and a fairly narrow set of skills that people use to communicate with one another. In this view, teaching writing can easily be accomplished in classrooms, where students learn the knowledge and skills they need in order to write in other places and contexts.

Other scholars think of writing as a form of personal liberation. These scholars teach writing "to help [students] develop the ability to think and to write that will give them sufficient self-esteem, confidence, and authority to free themselves, to change their lives" (Holladay 30).

Still other scholars think of writing as part of a larger set of social or cultural practices. They promote writing by introducing novices to the unfamiliar ways of thinking and acting done by various social groups: for example, the academic disciplines or work-related organizations that the novice wishes to join.

And finally, there are scholars who think of writing as a way of participating in a civic culture, a local, national, or even world culture, as part of a literate citizenry with large obligations to participate in and critique forms of social and economic organization for the common good. For these scholars, teaching writing is intimately connected with teaching ways of thinking about social and economic practices and the ways writing can help to promote social and economic justice.

One of the purposes of this book, like those other books concerned with ends, is to look at the purpose or scope of an enterprise—in this case, composition studies—and to determine whether in all its various manifestations that enterprise has an ultimate purpose, a teleological end.

But *The End of Nature, The End of History,* and *The End of Science* share more than an attempt to define a large conceptual field; they also argue that each of the subjects under consideration has reached another kind of "end": a limit or a boundary; a stopping point, a conclusion, a finish. They share an ambivalent tone, sometimes angry, at times resigned, occasionally elegiac, for the conclusion of an era, a sense that the enterprise in question has reached the limits of what it can significantly or usefully accomplish.

I want to make a similar case for the field of composition studies as an academic enterprise, which is now only approximately forty years old, if we take 1963 as the year the profession came of age. I want to argue that the past forty years have seen research and scholarship in the field proliferate in so many different directions that composition studies, which never had a common methodology, has lost touch with its primary reason for being— the teaching of writing—and I want to argue that composition studies needs to go back to basic questions, such as these: What is writing? How is writing learned? Can writing be taught, and if so, in what sense? And if writing can be taught, how should it be taught?

I want to argue that if we take seriously the research and scholarship of these past forty years, we will have to acknowledge the limits to what we will ever be able to say with any confidence about how people write and how they ought to be taught; that in the last analysis our problem is not the limits of what we can know but putting what we do know into practice; that ultimately, the end of composition studies will not be realized through more research and scholarship; it will be realized only through action.

Let me be clear. I am not saying that there is no more important work to be done in the field. We need to know a great deal more about the ways people learn to write and how those ways of learning can be encouraged by various forms of instruction. However, I do want to argue that for all practical purposes, the major concepts, paradigms, and models we have to work with in dealing with these issues are already known and widely accepted, that there is little hope we can reconceptualize writing in startling new ways. Indeed, it strikes me that viable alternatives to current concepts, paradigms, and models are inconceivable, that we do not even know how to *think about* the nature of writing differently than we do now. As a result, future research in the field will be what many scholars characterize as "postmodern": future research will be historicized, contextualized, and contingent, limited in what it may tell us about writing, learning to write, and the teaching of writing to particular groups of people in particular contexts; particular kinds of writing, learning, or teaching; or particular genres in particular contexts.

My argument covers a lot of ground. Let me introduce it further in two steps: first, a brief diagnosis of the "crisis" of purpose facing the profession, and then a specific preview of what is to follow. I realize that the term "crisis" is overused. Often a "crisis" seems to refer to any situation in which people disagree. However, I don't think the term is out of place in describing the current state of composition studies. Lester Faigley and his colleagues have characterized the study of composing processes as being at a stage where all assumptions are questioned (20–21). I would go one step further. It seems to me that every aspect of composition studies is now at a stage where its assumptions are being questioned.

The "Crisis" of Purpose in Composition Studies

Composition studies became a recognizable field after the Second World War, when college teachers and administrators struggled to teach reading and writing to the huge numbers of students who entered college in the 1950s, most of them the first in their families to seek an education beyond high school. A common date given for the birth of the field is 1963, with the publication of Richard Braddock, Richard Lloyd-Jones, and Lowell Schoer's *Research in Written Composition,* a call to base the teaching of writing on empirical research, and Albert Kitzhaber's *Themes, Theories, and Therapy,* which Stephen North calls "the first book-length study of college writing" (14). In addition, 1963 was the year that the meeting of the Conference on College Composition and Communication (CCCC) had as its theme "Toward a New Rhetoric," which symbolized the gradual turn in the field away from semantics and linguistics and toward the history and theory of rhetoric for inspiration in how to teach writing (Young and Goggin). Among the papers from that meeting published later in the October issue of *College Composition and Communication* were Wayne Booth's "The Rhetorical Stance," Francis Christensen's "A Generative Rhetoric of the Sentence," and Edward Corbett's "The Usefulness of Classical Rhetoric."

However, as an indication of the goals and aspirations of composition studies, I think it more useful to go back to the formation of the Conference on College Composition and Communication in 1949 and the first publication of *College Composition and Communication* in 1950 (Gerber, "History"). The articles in the first few issues of *CCC* convey an overwhelming sense of a common purpose and a common mission. In his inaugural article in *CCC*, John C. Gerber, the first president of CCCC, laments that the approximately nine thousand faculty members teaching college courses in composition and communication at the time share the same problems and "the same general objectives," but "we have for the most part gone our separate ways, experimenting here and improvising there." As a result teachers of composition and communication, Gerber says, "have had no systematic way of exchanging views and information quickly. Certainly we have no means of developing a coordinated research program" ("Conference"). Note Gerber's assumptions: that teachers of writing—and communications more generally—have a common objective and that what they need is more information and a coordinated research program. If CCCC meets these needs, Gerber says, "the standards of the profession will be raised."

Just what those objectives were was reported in the entire second issue of *CCC*, which was devoted to reports from the various workshops at the 1950 conference. Workshop No. 3 of "Objectives and Organization of the Composition Course" asserted that the point of a composition course was

> to develop in the freshman the power of clearly communicating facts or ideas in writing to a specified reader or group of readers. All other aspects of the course (such as, skill in reading, the study of semantics, the enlargement of vocabulary, command of mechanics and grammar, introduction to literature) should be considered subsidiary, to be introduced *only to the degree* that they can be demonstrated to serve the end of clear and effective writing. (9)

Some aspects of these objectives might strike us as quaint and even naive nowadays, when reading research and stylistics have demonstrated problems with the concept of clarity and theory in a range of disciplines from linguistics to philosophy and literary criticism has demonstrated the indeterminacy of language and meaning. Still, what I find very contemporary about this statement of objectives is its emphasis on practice in writing and its emphasis on writing for a variety of audiences.

In fact, much of the discussion of teaching writing in the first few volumes of *CCC* is remarkably current. Workshop No. 3 at the 1950 CCCC goes on to recommend a variety of instructional strategies and to address a number of pedagogical concerns that are still major issues today: sectioning by ability, not allowing students to take essay exams to exempt themselves from writing courses, keeping class sizes below twenty or twenty-two, requiring forty-five hundred words the first semester and seventy-five hundred the second semester, having at least two conferences with each student, reading student work together in class, and having no more than sixty writing students in any given semester ("Objectives" 9–10). Workshop No. 3A, whose purpose was also to articulate the objectives and organization of a writing course, recommended that "the main emphasis in the course should be on original writing," most of it expository, and that "if literature *as* literature is to be studied at all, it should be limited in amount; it should come late in the course; and it should be clearly designated for what it is—something apart, essentially, from the central material of the course" ("Objectives" 12). In other words, the unmistakable mission of the Conference on College Composition and Communication at its formation was to promote the teaching of writing, primarily exposition in its various forms. And the recommended pedagogical techniques for doing so were articulated in the first year of the organization's existence, if they were not broadly accepted in practice: an emphasis on student writing, the discussion of students' work in class, and teacher-student conferences.

The question is whether in the fifty years since the very beginning of CCCC the field of composition studies has come any closer to realizing its early aspirations: to foster student writing through an intense focus on the students' own work, to develop a coordinated research agenda, and to raise the standards of the profession. Of course, over the years composition studies *has* developed as an academic enterprise with over seventy graduate programs, a number of major journals and book publishers devoted to publishing scholarship in the field, and a significant increase in faculty in English departments devoted exclusively to the teaching of writing, the history and theory of rhetoric and other related subjects, and training others how to teach writing.

However, despite the heightened status of composition studies in the academy, just what composition studies *is* remains a matter of some dispute. Some people prefer to call composition studies a discipline or a "pre-discipline" or a "mixed discipline"; others refer to it as a field (Gere 3–4). I use the terms "field," "academic enterprise," and "profession." I accept Stephen North's argument that an academic discipline requires some sort of common methodology, point of view, or overarching framework—North cites approvingly Paul Diesing's comment in *Patterns of Discovery in the Social Sciences* that in academia "community and cooperation occur primarily within the boundaries of a method, not a field" (qtd. in North 364–65; see also MacDonald, "Voices")—and as North has convincingly demonstrated, composition studies has no common methodology. However, since composition studies had indisputably found a place in the academy, and "professionalization" is one of the field's major accomplishments, I also refer to composition studies as a profession.

Perhaps composition studies can count professionalization as one of its major accomplishments because it has raised the status of at least one small segment of the population concerned with the teaching of writing—the professoriate, those in tenure-track lines—and it has greatly increased the amount of research and scholarship on the teaching of writing and related topics, such as the history of rhetoric, rhetorical theory, and the nature of literacy.

Besides professionalizing the teaching of writing, the rise of composition studies in the academy has resulted in one other major accomplishment: the promotion of a particular pedagogical approach to writing instruction that was not current at the beginning of CCCC, what is commonly referred to as the "process approach." The "process approach" has focused attention on how students write rather than on what they write, and although there are many different ways of characterizing "process" teaching, most of them conceive of the teacher as a facilitator or coach whose job is to help students work through the various stages of composing: getting ideas, planning and organizing, drafting, revising, and editing.

However, now both of the discipline's profoundest accomplishments—the professionalization of the field and the promotion of the writing process—are being called into question. Our major theorists, the biggest names in the field, are starting to question the price the profession has paid for its "professionalization." Although the profession has an increasing number of graduate programs, which turn out increasing numbers of tenure-track PhDs, there is some question about how many of these PhDs actually teach writing. As Donald Bartholomae puts it, "Composition has produced and justified a career that has everything to do with status and identity in English and little to do with the organization, management, and evaluation of student writing, except perhaps as an administrative problem" (23; see also Connors, "Composition" 10–16). A 1996–97 committee of the Modern Language Association reports that even in English departments at institutions that confer only bachelor of arts degrees, 50 percent of the first-year writing courses are taught by non-tenure-track faculty. In departments that confer the doctoral degree, the proportion is an astonishing 96 percent ("Final" 28; reported in North et al. 242). At best, many PhDs in composition studies take jobs as writing program administrators in colleges and universities, where their primary job is to train and monitor those who *do* continue to do most of the teaching of writing at the college level: graduate teaching assistants and part-time instructors. Theorists such as Jasper Neel write books about the direction the field should go or the traditions the field should hark back to, but creeping into their prescriptions is the lament that the profession has become too institutionalized, too specialized; that the profession has lost its roots in classroom practice. In short, critics suspect that advanced degrees in composition studies are a way to avoid teaching writing.

Also noteworthy is the increasing amount of research and scholarship in the field, much of it based on the history of rhetoric, the sociology of the profession, or critical theories currently popular among literature faculty, much of it only tangentially related to the teaching of writing per se.

This trend raises the suspicion that a great deal of the research and scholarship in composition is not conducted primarily to promote our understanding of the nature of literacy and how people become literate; rather, it is conducted as a means of professional advancement.

No one can doubt that the field has become increasingly divided into narrow areas of concern with little indication that scholars and researchers in one area read, respect, or deal substantively with the work of those in other areas. Since Stephen North's pioneering work *The Making of Knowledge in Composition* classified the work of the field into eight major areas, there have been few attempts to bridge the gaps between those areas. A comparison of the works cited pages in *College Composition and Communication, Rhetoric Review, JAC: A Journal of Composition Theory,* and *Written Communication* reveals some overlap but not much. Hence the need for additional taxonomies, frameworks, and "keys," such as those by James Berlin ("Contemporary"); Richard Fulkerson; and Mark Wiley, Barbara Gleason, and Louise Wetherbee Phelps to explain the various areas of the field. Increasingly, graduate schools offer courses on how to think about the field, the historiography and sociology of the profession, in addition to courses on the nature of writing and how to teach it.

And all the while, scholars continue to argue about what the field should be and what it should be trying to accomplish. On the one hand, Susan Peck MacDonald ("Voices") can call for the field to model itself on the social sciences by accumulating a body of research data on what we know about writing and learning to write so that we can improve instruction in writing; on the other hand, Sidney Dobrin can argue that the field ought to devote itself to theory in the abstract, and that the relevance of theory to practice should not be a major concern of the profession. Such contradictory theoretical reflection is probably the natural "end" of an academic field, but the question remains whether such "reconceptualizing" and "reconfiguring" of the field leads to anything that we might call progress, or whether it is an indication that composition studies is mired in a Hamlet-like ambivalence about what it knows, what it ought to do, and whether it has the means or the will to decide.

Sharp criticism is also being applied to the other major contribution of the discipline: the "process approach." Sharon Crowley argues that most contemporary applications of the process model do not reject the epistemological or rhetorical assumptions of the outdated pedagogy it was supposed to replace, what is commonly called "current-traditional rhetoric"; that process is just a "set of pedagogical tactics" that reify various kinds of heuristic invention strategies and the "stages" in composing. Crowley's primary evidence is from textbooks, which continue to repackage traditional ways of doing things using the jargon of "process": for example, in the third edition of *The Bedford Guide for College Writers,* , outlining is a form of "Planning," and topic sentences and coherence are considered a part of "Drafting" ("Around" 65).

Crowley's criticism is echoed by Joseph Harris, a former editor of *College Composition and Communication.* Harris believes that the proponents of the "process approach" simply instituted "a new sort of formalism" to replace the previous emphasis on "surface correctness": a formalism

> centered no longer on textual structures but instead on various algorithms, heuristics, and guidelines for composing. This new formalism has proven little different from the old, as those versions of process teaching that don't work toward a very familiar set of therapeutic and expressionist goals instead work toward an equally familiar set of technocratic ones. (56)

Even Lad Tobin, a major proponent of the "process movement," admits that "the movement is at a crossroads" because composition studies seems to be reconceptualizing the premises on which process pedagogy is based (9). Tobin admits that perhaps the process movement deserves this reconsideration because its proponents have oversimplified both the premises and the pedagogies associated with the writing process.

Meanwhile, a number of national tests suggest that the teaching of writing is not having much of an effect on the abilities of our students (Campbell, Voelki, and Donahue), possibly because, scholarly surveys tell us, in many ways teachers in the public schools, community colleges, four-year colleges, and universities continue to teach writing much as they did before composition studies *was* so professional; that is, by using "current-traditional" methods (Cuban; Hillocks, *Ways;* Mary Kennedy). Such tests and surveys suggest that whatever the status of composition studies as a field, it may not be as influential as it would like to be, either on teachers outside the narrow confines of the field, even at the university level, or on the world at large.

Whether or not "process" teaching was ever very widespread, books and journals are starting to appear touting such phrases as "post-process" and "after theory" with no indication of what the discipline should teach other than "process" or what it should study "after theory" (Kent, *Post-Process;* Spellmeyer, "After"). Theorists as different as Thomas Kent (*Paralogic*), Aviva Freedman ("Show"), and Joseph Petraglia ("Writing") offer substantial arguments from language philosophy, empirical studies, and classroom observation that writing cannot be taught. What then should writing teachers *do* in the classroom? The answers vary. Some suggest abandoning the designated writing classroom altogether in favor of writing across the curriculum, writing in the disciplines, or real-world experience. Some suggest that teachers should offer practice in "pseudo-writing" that may have some larger application outside the classroom. Some suggest that teachers continue to teach what they have always taught; they should just recognize that it is not writing.

Two major conferences devoted to evaluating the role of English in our culture and the prospects of composition and rhetoric for the twenty-first century have not helped the situation (See Lloyd-Jones and Lunsford; Bloom, Daiker, and White). At neither conference did a consensus emerge about what the field should do about the problems of professionalization and the weaknesses of the "process" approach.

My own diagnosis, as I have already indicated, is that research and scholarship in composition studies have reached a certain limit in their ability to formulate fundamental paradigms, models, and theories about the nature of writing. A number of fields and disciplines, such as psychology, education, philosophy, linguistics, and literary theory have reached a remarkable consensus about how language works, about how we use both spoken and written language to understand one another. At the heart of these current paradigms, models, and theories is the fundamental assumption that the way we understand one another through language is primarily interpretive, a matter of hermeneutics; that understanding is based on a kind of socially influenced psycholinguistic guessing game (Frank Smith, *Comprehension;* Kent, *Paralogic;* Gee, *Social*). We inherit a language used by others before us, a language blended from many sources and echoing many voices, Bakhtin's heteroglossia, and as we learn to speak and write that language, as we try to make it do our bidding, we discover that it often resists our best efforts to bend it to our will, that we often wind up meaning what our language allows us.

Moreover, after a decade of studying intensely the cognitive aspects of writing in the 1980s, composition studies realized the limitations of such an approach and, along with other disciplines concerned with language, took a "social turn" in the 1990s. As a result of this social turn, we now realize much more clearly that our understanding of one another through language depends on context, that general principles and rules of language have to be applied in unique ways in each new social situation in which we find ourselves. In short, we have confirmed that meaning is a matter of interpretation, and that interpretation depends a great deal on matters other than language.

The key tenets of the broad interdisciplinary consensus about how language works are as follows. To the list of tenets, I have added what I take to be the implications of this consensus for the teaching of writing.

- Human beings learn language by actively constructing their own individual mental representation of the world. As a result, instruction in writing will always be constrained by the background and experience, the interest and motivation, that novice writers bring to the classroom.

- Human beings learn language primarily by *acquisition,* by subconsciously internalizing what they hear and read; they do not learn language primarily through formal instruction. As a result, formal instruction in writing will never be able to supply most of what novice writers need to know in order to write well, and the content of writing classes will always be problematic.
- Language is a system of tokens on which human beings project their own meanings; meaning does not "inhere" in language; hence, the meaning or value of any piece of writing will be subject to a range of interpretations, depending on what readers bring from their own knowledge and experience to their understanding of the writing.
- Language users rely on context a great deal in order to interpret the tokens of the language system; hence, the meaning or value of any piece of writing will be constrained by the social context in which it is read and the immediate circumstances and concerns of its readers.

In many ways, composition studies as a field has only tentatively begun to take the implications of these tenets seriously, to grapple with the problem of what writing instruction *means* or what writing instruction should look like, if these tenets are true. And part of my argument will be that there is no one obvious way *to* take them seriously. Writing instruction will always be problematic because of the nature of language and the ways we learn language. Or to put it in philosophical terms, the key concepts of writing and writing instruction will always be "contested."

Rather than argue these tenets again, in the pages that follow I will try to investigate the problems they raise by calling into question two major assumptions of the field: that writing is a global or universal ability and that writing, especially at the college level, is in some sense foundational to advanced learning. My analysis will point out that even at this late date in its evolution as an academic field, composition studies has not adequately conceptualized its object of study: writing. The field continues to talk about writing, to think about writing, and to teach writing, as if it were a global or universal ability similar to the common-sense notion of intelligence. As a result, the field continues to foster writing in generic "writing" courses with no common curriculum or content; it assumes that teaching the "personal essay" or the "research report" or "literary analysis" is tantamount to teaching writing generally, that to teach any genre in classroom conditions is the equivalent to teaching all genres in all contexts. Now, because of recent work in language philosophy, genre theory, and activity theory, scholars are calling this conception of writing into question, and the field must face the fact that writing may not be a global or universal ability at all. Rather, what we call writing ability may be a wide range of knowledge and abilities, many of which are heavily dependent on the context in which the writing occurs. Some of what a writer knows how to do in writing may be applicable to a wide variety of genres and circumstances; some of what a writer knows how to do in writing may be entirely dependent on very particular circumstances. If writing is not entirely a global or universal ability, then it is not at all clear what aspects of writing can or should be taught in generic writing classes.

Another common assumption of composition studies is that writing for students in colleges and universities is in some sense "foundational," that in some fundamental way, knowing how to write is a prerequisite to further learning or at the very least to success in the academy. Hence, the field continues to offer "introductory" writing courses that are supposed to prepare students for more advanced work of some sort or at least to give them some "skills" that may be applicable later in their lives. But if what we call writing ability involves not only broad strategies and general skills but also very specific kinds of knowledge relevant only to particular genres in particular contexts, then it is not at all clear what introductory writing courses "introduce" students to. On the contrary, it may very well be that beyond the sentence level, people learn to write in various ways by learning the conventions of particular genres while they are learning how to respond to various rhetorical situations or while they are trying to join the social groups that use those genres. If writing is not a prerequisite or an introduction to learning but an integral part of learning how to get along in the world, then colleges and universities will have to rethink what they mean by "writing" and "writing instruction" and what they want any particular form of instruction to accomplish.

My own view is that although a great deal of what we know about writing is limited and tentative, what we *do* know suggests some broad principles that the field has yet to act on:

- For writing instruction to be effective, students already need to know and be able to do most of what they are supposed to learn in writing classes.
- Writing teachers get only what they teach for, which is only a very small part of what novice writers have to know and be able to do.
- The primary benefits of formal instruction for novice writers are "tips" from those who already know how to do what the novice writers want to learn how to do.
- The best way to promote a broad-based ability to write is to arrange for novice writers to learn the genres of the discourse communities they wish to join as they become members of that community.

We know the models, the data, the reasoning on which these principles are based. I believe that further knowledge will not greatly modify those models nor add significantly to the data and reasoning on which they are based. Thus, barring a major conceptual breakthrough comparable to the revolutions in linguistics and cognitive psychology in the 1950s; barring, that is, what Thomas Kuhn calls a paradigm shift, I see no solution to the sense of crisis, the sense of questioned assumptions, articulated by so many people in composition studies. Writing and writing instruction will always be confounded by contradiction and paradox, a range of possibilities, or bound by the use of certain concepts that occur over and over again in the thoughtful literature on these matters, concepts such as "complexity," "indeterminacy," "dialogue," "dialectic," "heteroglossia," and "negotiation."

As a consequence, I believe that the solution to the crisis in composition studies will not be more research and more scholarship and more theoretical inquiry into the nature of language and how we become literate, as welcome as that research, scholarship, and theoretical inquiry might be for us as individuals, particularly in helping us solve certain problems in the classroom. Rather, I believe that the solution to the crisis in composition studies will be the result of political action—or perhaps more fancifully, a spiritual reawakening. The solution will involve learning to put into practice what we often teach about language, that to effectively use language we must engage in dialogue and negotiation. It will involve sharpening the focus of composition studies as a field on how to improve writing in this country and engaging in the intensely political process of deciding on common interests, common warrants, for action. Given that the field is so fragmented, given that many models of the field are that it is "postmodern," that knowledge in the field must of necessity be local, historicized, and contingent, reaching any kind of consensus about the teaching of writing will be no easy task. But in that direction I see our only hope for significantly improving the teaching of writing in this country.

My own ideas for a solution involve taking the "end" of composition studies seriously at the post-secondary level. To improve writing instruction we will have to radically restructure the way writing is offered in the undergraduate curriculum. If writing is indeed greatly constrained by context, if we learn to write certain genres by immersing ourselves in the discourse of a community and by using writing to participate in that community, then it makes sense that writing as a subject at the post-secondary level should be taught in those academic units most closely associated with the knowledge and genres students need or want to learn. As a result, I believe that writing instruction should be not be the primary responsibility of English departments and writing programs; rather, writing instruction should be the responsibility of all the various disciplines of the university. In other words, we must put an "end" to the hegemony of writing instruction by composition studies as a field.

Of course, this does not mean that professionals in composition studies will find their work coming to an end; rather, it means that professionals in the field will have to reconceptualize their roles as facilitators whose ultimate goal is to minimize their own importance, even to do away with much of what they do now, and to make writing instruction an integral part of all aspects of university life. Such a radical reorganization of the way we teach writing has already begun at a number of institutions around the country, but I think these institutions need to do more, to go several steps further, to put into practice what we know about how people learn to write.

The solution to the "crisis" in composition studies will also necessitate a reconceptualization of graduate work in the field and the way we train writing teachers. It will mean training scholars in composition studies to live in two worlds of discourse: one world of composition theory and pedagogy and another world of the discourse practices of particular communities. It will mean training compositionists to be writers of the discourses they are to teach and social critics of the discourse communities they will help train novice writers to join. It will mean putting an "end" to composition studies as a distinctive academic discipline.

An Overview

The rest of this book is divided into ten chapters, in two parts. Part 1 is called "Conceptual Limits." It explores what we currently know about learning to write and the difficulties inherent in further conceptualizing six key concepts of the profession. In each of the six chapters in Part 1, I point out the essentially hermeneutic problem at the heart of what I see as a key concept or issue in the field—the nature of writing, learning to write, composing processes, writing as a social practice, writing as thinking, and the process of transferring learning from one context to another—and I argue that for all practical purposes, we are at the "end" of what we can know about these concepts and issues. In each chapter, I also discuss the implications of my analysis for how writing ought to be taught in higher education.

Part 2 is called "Diagnosis and Proposal." It focuses on writing instruction at the post-secondary level. In chapter 7, I offer a model of the way people learn to write, and I analyze the difficulties of teaching writing according to this model in generic introductory classes. In chapter 8, I offer a model for what it means to be a teacher of writing. In chapter 9, I propose an undergraduate curriculum for putting into practice what we know about how people learn to write, a curriculum that takes into account the models put forward in the previous chapters, and I propose a radical restructuring of graduate education in composition studies: I propose that composition studies reconstitute itself as an interdisciplinary field specializing in the linguistic, rhetorical, and ideological analysis of a broad range of genres in a broad range of social contexts. In chapter 10, I put my proposals in the framework of the current discussion in the field about the rhetoric and procedures departments of English need to use in order to deal with the larger "crisis" of English studies generally. In this final chapter, I argue that my proposals provide a compelling rhetoric and rationale for "re-visioning" the profession as truly interdisciplinary, as a field that investi-gates the ways novice writers learn to master particular genres in particu-lar circumstances, as a field that works to put the results of its research and scholarship into practice by promoting writing in those social contexts in which that kind of writing is used. Such a "re-visioning" of composition studies, I argue, may very well be its reasonable and necessary end.

Part One

Conceptual Limits

Think of the tools in a tool box: there is a hammer, pliers, a saw, a screw-driver, a rule, a glue-pot, glue, nails and screws.—The functions of words are as diverse as the functions of these objects. (And in both cases there are similarities.)

Of course, what confuses us is the uniform appearance of words when we hear them spoken or meet them in script and print. For their *application* is not presented to us so clearly.

—Wittgenstein, *Philosophical Investigations*

When we say: "Every word in language signifies something" we have so far said *nothing whatever;* unless we have explained exactly *what* distinction we wish to make.

—Wittgenstein, *Philosophical Investigations*

1   *What Is Writing and Writing Ability?*

THE LIMITS OF COMPOSITION STUDIES begin with its subject: writing. Just what does the word "writing" mean, this word that can refer not only to a set of symbols on paper or computer screen but also to the process of putting them there or even what we have to know, what we have to be able to do, in order to put them there? Is there any single answer to this question? And if there is no single answer to the question of what writing is, how do we know what we are supposed to be teaching when we teach writing?

In general, composition studies has not taken seriously the conceptual difficulties involved in deciding just what writing is in the first place. Historically, the field has conceptualized what we mean by "writing" beyond the sentence level in a number of ways. Each of the following formulations had a certain currency during a particular period and then was succeeded by another formulation: the textual rules and conventions of various forms of discourse; a composing process, a cognitive process, a rhetorical practice—that is, sensitivity to the elements of those exigencies that call for a written response: a particular rhetorical situation or context, the audience or readers the writer must address, the genre forms which seem most appropriate under the circumstances—and finally, the currently most popular concept, a social or cultural phenomenon.

Of course, all of these ways of conceptualizing writing capture some aspect of what we mean by some kinds of writing: all kinds of writing do seem to require a knowledge of rules and conventions, although the rules and conventions of personal diaries and private notes might be difficult to characterize. All kinds of writing do seem to require the ability to compose in a systematic and self-conscious way, although freewriting is designed to bypass conscious thought and help writers put words on the page spontaneously. All kinds of writing do seem to require an awareness of the constraints inherent in a particular rhetorical situation, although scholars have found it notoriously difficult to characterize just what writers know about their purposes, how self-conscious they are about genre conventions, and how much they assume about their audience in any given case. And finally, all kinds of writing do seem to require that writers participate in a larger social or cultural matrix, although many kinds of writing are done for very private reasons.

What I am getting at, of course, is that the term "writing" refers to a great many different kinds of activities, that writing is done in many different ways: general formulations about the nature of writing ignore very real differences in the *kinds* of rules and conventions, composing processes, cognitive processes, rhetorical practices, and social phenomena that may apply in different rhetorical circumstances. The problem is not that these various conceptions of writing are untrue or inaccurate or misleading or unhelpful—nor is it that they contradict one another; they do not—but that they are necessarily concerned with writing at a very abstract level. They all necessarily tend to ignore the fact that people write in many different ways in many different kinds of contexts for many different reasons. When people write, they engage in very specific kinds of thinking and behavior that are very dependent on the particular situations in which they find themselves. The question then is whether all acts of writing do have something in common—whether for example writing may be analogous to the common-sense concept of intelligence, as problematic as that term is—or whether we simply use the term to refer to many different kinds of activities. In the terms of philosopher Ludwig Wittgenstein, the question is what the term "writing" means in its various uses and how these meanings are related to one another; it is a question of how the tools in the toolkit function and whether and how their functions are related to one another.

The foremost limitation to composition studies may well be the very nature of "writing," that when we talk about the teaching of "writing" we are saying, in Wittgenstein's terms, "*nothing whatever;* unless we have explained exactly *what* distinction we wish to make." Moreover, the difficulty of characterizing writing, particularly in a way that will illuminate how it ought to be taught, may be a problem we will always have with us: it may not be solved by greater insight or further research.

In this chapter, then, I will argue that when we talk about "writing" we are saying "*nothing whatever,*" unless we have explained exactly *what* distinction we wish to make," that "writing" as a concept represents such a wide range of knowledge and skill that two examples of writing may have little in common except what linguists call "surface features." I will go on to make the case that any one kind of writing is not typical or representative of other kinds of writing, that different kinds of writing may require different kinds of knowledge and abilities, and that the two main ways we have of conceptualizing writing ability—syntactic fluency and rhetorical maturity—tend to disguise the true nature of writing. I will extend my argument by noting the difficulties in what we can reasonably infer about the ability of writers from a given sample of their writing. Finally, I will note that extensive debate among specialists in literacy have not clarified what we mean when we say that someone is sufficiently literate to write well.

The Many Purposes of Writing

When we say that someone is able to write, what do we mean? Let me begin my analysis of this issue with two observations: First, notice that when we say in ordinary conversation that someone is a writer, we generally are not referring to some overall ability; we are usually referring to the fact that the person in question writes in a specific genre or has a specific profession. We say, "You know Frank; he's a writer," and we are understood to mean, depending on our listeners' knowledge of Frank and the context, "Oh, Frank is a novelist," "Frank is a journalist," or "Frank is a person who writes articles for certain magazines." Occasionally, we will refer to people who are not professionals as writers, but only if these people have made it clear that that is the way they think of themselves. These people may not have published, but they are trying to publish or they take writing seriously as an avocation, or they want to be known as writers, for whatever reason.

Secondly, notice that when we call people "writers," we are using the term in a much different way than we use comparable terms for people who know certain things or have certain abilities. Both of my daughters began to take lessons on string instruments at the age of four and a half from teachers trained in the Suzuki method. The Suzuki method requires that students listen for hours to tapes of the tunes they are learning to play being played correctly and that students train themselves to hear when they are out of tune or differ from the tape. The students do not learn to read music until much later. Within a year or two my daughters had memorized a large number of melodies and were relatively competent at playing them with a certain amount of flair and poise, although they still did not know how to read music.

Now what I find interesting about their experience is that everyone I know who learned of my daughters' accomplishments, not just the parents of Suzuki students, referred to them as string players: they called Rachel a "cellist" and Joanna a "violinist." At the same time, my daughters were doing well in school, and by the fourth grade each of them was fairly competent at writing a passable imitation of a Nancy Drew story. They may not have been able to develop a plot much beyond a page or two, but they had the Nancy Drew style down cold. But despite this accomplishment, no one

I know, not even their proud parents, would call them writers. So it is with many other related situations in which we refer to novices who are relatively unskilled at certain tasks but who take the task seriously. We have no trouble calling unskilled novices "baseball players," "actors," or even "French speakers." But we do not call unskilled novices "writers."

I have no profound explanation of this phenomenon, except to speculate that it demonstrates our unease with the very notion of writing. We are uncomfortable calling people "writers" who write casually or for their own satisfaction or as a secondary aspect of their jobs. Corporate executives can be both vice-presidents and violinists; they are not usually called both vice-presidents and writers, even if they are in charge of drafting the company's annual reports and recognized as being good at it. Perhaps we subconsciously recognize how difficult writing is; perhaps writing has such a reputation for being difficult or it is so generally recognized that people do it badly that we are very careful about attributing the ability to people, even ourselves. However, one thing does seem to be clear in our popular use of the term "writer": we call people "writers" only when they have achieved a generally accepted, socially acceptable level of mastery in a particular genre or social context.

Thus it seems to me that our popular usage of the term "writer" captures both the ambivalence of our culture toward writing and the confusion about what we mean when we say a person is able to write. I suspect that most of us would claim that our most common usage of the term "writing ability" is the ability to write various genres in order to fulfill a variety of purposes. So the question is, what is it that we know or are able to do when we compose in various genres in order to fulfill various purposes? Do our acts of composing in different genres and contexts require the same knowledge and abilities or different knowledge and abilities?

In order to get at this question, consider first of all some of the purposes or uses to which we can put writing. Here is a list composed by Frank Smith of the various uses to which we put language, and by extension, writing: we can use writing to satisfy our material needs; to control the behavior, feelings, or attitudes of others; to interact and get along with others; to express our individuality and feelings; to get answers to questions; to pretend; to convey information; to tell jokes and riddles; to establish and record laws and regulations, as well as to keep records of "how it was" (*Writing* 14; see also Halliday, *Explorations*). Later Smith also mentions that we can use language to talk about language (*Writing* 14)—and in certain cases explained by J. P. Austin and John Searle, we can use language as an act: saying "I name you Ralph" is to perform an action in the world (Smith, *Writing* 218).

Smith goes on to note that none of these uses of language is unique to language: there are always alternative ways of accomplishing the same purposes, achieving the same goals. We can indicate an object we want by pointing at it. We can express our appreciation of friends by hugging them. We can regulate a person's behavior by grabbing him by the arm and shoving him in the direction we want him to go. We can represent our ideas through paintings, diagrams, and maps. The point is not whether language, and in particular writing, is more accurate or more efficient or in some other way better than other means of accomplishing our purposes. In some cases, writing might be better than, say, painting in expressing our ideas; in other cases it might not. The point is that writing always occurs in a specific social situation in which it is one of many means at our disposal to fulfill our purposes. In different social circumstances, certain kinds of writing seem to have little in common.

As a "thought experiment," think about how we might use writing to accomplish two very different goals: to convey factual information and to express our sense of the world by creating a work of art. In the first case we might compose notes or memos and in the second case, we might compose, say, a novel.

Let's limit our discussion of notes and memos to those sent back and forth between people who work in the same office, say a secretary and a boss. The secretary may use memos to remind the boss of appointments or of calls received while the boss was out. The secretary may use memos to provide the boss with certain information needed to make decisions, such as summaries of financial information or reports of sales. In this situation, memos are not designed for anyone other than the two people involved. Should the secretary give the memos to someone else in the office, the second person may not have the slightest idea what certain names or certain kinds of information refer to. The secretary may simply use the nickname of a salesman and note a phone number at which the salesman wants to be called without any further specification of what the call is about or what the salesman may want. Or the secretary may provide an estimate from a contractor without specifying what the estimate is for. In both of these cases, the secretary assumes that the boss knows enough about the salesman or what the contractor is working on so that it's not necessary to elaborate. Moreover, in writing these notes, the secretary may use no elaborate planning or composing strategies; the secretary may simply jot down the information as it comes in over the phone, in a letter or report.

On the other hand, people write novels to express their sense of the world, but mixed in with this purpose may be many other complex goals, many of them not particularly practical. People may also write novels to make money, impress their friends, express a point of view or a moral, or create a unique object, a work of art. The words in novels often do not "refer to" people or objects in the real world. They "express" something, an attitude or point of view towards the characters or subject matter, or on a larger scale, what we commonly call a "vision of life," "a point of view," or nowadays, "an embodiment" or a "critique" of an ideology. Novels can be ordered or plotted in any number of ways, but once again their forms of organization are determined less by reference to what we might call an external practical reality than to the demands of various internal themes or subject matter, what the author is trying to express or capture. And of course novels are composed in many different ways, both physically and mentally. Novelists use all manner of technology, from pens to typewriters to computers. Novelists may compose on a regular basis at a desk or computer terminal or randomly, whenever they have a free hour to spare. Novelists use all manner of plans and strategies: they may rely on elaborate charts and diagrams to organize their plots, or they may use no external plans at all but simply keep track of events in their head. They may meticulously revise their various drafts word for word and sentence by sentence, or like John D. MacDonald, they may just compose quickly and spontaneously, reread later and if they are unhappy with that day's work, simply throw it away and write it all over again from scratch. They may edit their work themselves or give it to someone else to do for them. In other words, novels are composed in so many different ways for so many different reasons, all they may share are the textual conventions—plot, setting, character, and theme—we associate with E. M. Forster's famous definition: a novel is a prose fiction of a certain extent (17).

It would seem, then, that memos and novels have little in common as "writing." People do not compose notes or memos in social circumstances similar to those in which they compose novels. Office memos and novels have different rules and conventions, their own linguistic and cultural grammar. The secretary and the novelist do not think or act similarly when composing their two different genres. As a result, when we call both composing memos and composing novels acts of writing we are presupposing a great deal and in fact we may only be attending to a superficial similarity, that both acts involve the use of language to put words on paper or a computer screen.

However, this "thought experiment" may seem excessive somehow. After all, we may call notes and memos writing, but they are not the kind of discourse we teach in school, except in courses in business writing, and although many of us may read novels, most of us do not write novels, and in any case, the differences between memos and novels may seem like exceptional cases; the differences overly dramatic. We may want to say, "But memos and novels are not *typical* kinds of writing; most writing *does* share a set of conventions; most writing is done for more similar purposes and in more similar circumstances." But then what *is* a typical kind of discourse, and what does that kind of discourse share with one similar to it?

Quite frankly, I cannot answer that question because as deeply as I can reflect on it, I cannot imagine a "typical" kind of writing. I regularly teach students how to write personal narratives and news reports and newspaper feature stories and magazine reviews, as well as researched persuasive reports and literary analyses, and after years of pondering which kind of writing may be typical or what these kinds of writing have in common, I am at a loss.

The various kinds of discourse my students write do not share a set of text conventions beyond the sentence level. My students tend to order their personal narratives chronologically, although they may occasionally pause to reflect on what the experience they are trying to convey means to them. These narratives do not have a formal introduction or conclusion, and the language tends to be colloquial, often even slangy. My students' news stories, on the other hand, begin usually begin with a lead paragraph, which answers the questions who, what, where, when, and perhaps how. Their news stories are organized with all of the important information up front and the story trailing away into less important matters. However, their informational reports, the kind of writing that appears in the Sunday supplements of newspapers, tend to be organized by association or simple lists, interesting information about a local poet or the annual rodeo—although these reports may begin with a colorful anecdote and occasionally proceed more systematically from less important background information to more important issues, an indication of just what makes the subject newsworthy. I can't see that these various forms of organization have any formal characteristics in common: each organizational pattern is simply a different rhetorical strategy for accomplishing different purposes with a different audience.

So it is with how my students compose these different genres. The various kinds of discourse my students write seem to be composed in very different ways and involve very different composing processes. Given that my assignments invite them to accomplish some broad rhetorical purpose using a certain genre, they usually decide on what to do with relative ease. In writing personal narratives, my students' primary problem often seems to be one of structuring what they already know about their experience: how much background information to include, what to summarize and what to dramatize. In writing news stories, their major problem is planning the lead. Everything else in the news story seems to fall in line after the lead is in place. In writing informational reports my students struggle a lot more over choosing a subject and deciding on a broad rhetorical strategy, given that the topic is more "wide-open" than a personal narrative or a news story and the format is less constrained by conventions. They seem to do more conscious planning with the informational report than they do with the other two genres.

In short, beyond the sentence level, I see very little in common among various kinds of writing. Writing each kind of discourse seems to involve very different kinds of knowledge of subject matter and discourse conven-

tions, very different kinds of organizational patterns and rhetorical strategies, very different kinds of thinking and composing processes. I cannot
imagine how one kind of writing is in some way "typical" of other kinds
of writing. Writing is of course a set of textual features—an alphabet, a grammar of syntax, a set of conventions for spelling and punctuation—but these
features seem to function much like Wittgenstein's toolbox. We can understand those features only if we know their larger purpose or function, what
they are being used for.

The Complex Forms of Knowledge or Ability in Writing

What it is that we "know" when we are able to use written language to accomplish a particular purpose is equally problematic. Scholars have com-
piled any number of lists of such knowledge and skills. All of them differ,
and all of them come back to the same fundamental difficulty. Because we
are dealing with mental phenomena that cannot be observed directly, our
concepts are necessarily tentative and highly inferential. In the last analysis, we cannot ultimately know whether the ways we write or the kinds of
writing we produce are based on knowledge or ability or some combination of the two. In any given case, it depends on what we want to call
"knowledge" or "ability."

Take for example the useful taxonomy developed by Peter Smagorinsky
and Michael Smith (see also Alexander, Shallert, and Hare). After survey-
ing the psychological literature, Smagorinsky and Smith distinguish three
kinds of knowledge, with a number of subcategories:

- Knowledge of content: "Factual knowledge of information" and
  "knowledge of one's own personal experiences, of the implications of
  an approaching thunderhead, of the functions of the various buttons
  on one's computer keyboard, and so on—that is, knowledge that one
  can name." (281)
- Knowledge of form: "Knowledge that enables one to distinguish one
  thing from another according to their features—such as knowing how
  to distinguish an alligator from a crocodile, cool jazz from bebop, and
  so on." (281)
- Conditional knowledge: "The knowledge of when to apply knowledge
  of content or form." (281)

To compound the difficulties in thinking about writing even further, Smagorinsky and Smith distinguish among three *other* kinds of knowledge on
the basis of whether such knowledge is necessary for all writing or only for
certain kinds of writing. These additional categories are general knowledge,
task-specific knowledge, and community-based knowledge.

Now this complex system necessarily blurs all sorts of distinctions. For
one thing, knowledge of content seems to include not only "facts" but also
those implications we infer from facts, to say nothing of opinions, beliefs,

and values. We see a thunderhead off in the distance and we "know" that it may signal a storm and perhaps even potentially a tornado, but what we see can be thought of as a different kind of knowledge from what we "know" about what the clouds imply. We "know" that Marlon Brando is or is not a great actor, that God did or did not create the universe, that abortion is or is not murder—all of these statements, no matter which side we take, are things we know, but we know them in very different ways.

For another thing, knowledge of form seems to include not only our ability to distinguish among physical objects—to use Smagorinsky and Smith's example, to distinguish between alligators and crocodiles, which may hinge on our recognizing that alligators have broader snouts than crocodiles—but to recognize a level of abstraction that makes a knowledge of form barely distinguishable from knowledge of content. The difference between a short story and a novel is more than a matter of length; it is also a matter, among other things, of the various ways a plot can be developed. The knowledge of what a novel is, then, could very well be considered content knowledge, in which case, we would label certain things we know "knowledge of form" only when we need to distinguish one concept from another. Is our knowledge of realism and naturalism, love and hate, a democracy and a republic content knowledge or knowledge of form? I don't know.

Even more problematic is that conditional knowledge seems to be a qualitatively different kind of knowledge from knowledge of form and content; we might even call conditional knowledge an ability or a strategy— the ability to apply other kinds of knowledge in certain circumstances, or a strategy we have developed in response to certain circumstances.

The same difficulties exist in trying to distinguish general knowledge from task-specific knowledge and community-based knowledge. Against the notion of general knowledge, Smagorinsky and Smith oppose knowledge specific to particular kinds of tasks and knowledge specific to particular communities. Task-specific knowledge might involve all you need to know about poetry or early modern poetry or T. S. Eliot's poetry in particular in order to write an analysis of "The Waste Land." Community-based knowledge might involve what you need to know in order to belong to the community of literary scholars and critics. But these two concepts are also ambiguous and difficult to distinguish from each other and from general knowledge. At some point, task-specific knowledge about T. S. Eliot and poetry blends in with the ability to use strategies and procedures in order to analyze "The Waste Land." In fact, it could be argued that the only way we recognize what people know specifically is by their ability to use that knowledge in order to accomplish a certain social purpose, that there is no knowledge of T. S. Eliot and poetry outside of our ability to use that knowledge following certain strategies and procedures, from making cocktail party conversation to analyzing "The Waste Land" for a scholarly journal. And it could be argued that there is no task-specific knowledge outside of the social groups we participate in, and the knowledge we have to demonstrate in that group in order to belong. Indeed, it could be argued that the distinction between task-specific knowledge and community-based knowledge is simply a taxonomy of the various uses to which a given piece of knowledge can be put. If we use the opening lines of "The Waste Land" as part of an analysis of the poem, it is task-specific knowledge. If we use those opening lines to demonstrate what we have in common with other literary critics, it is community-based knowledge.

It is then very difficult to characterize the knowledge and skill involved in "writing," except by using a number of different taxonomies. And the difficulty with various taxonomic categories is that they are not mutually exclusive. Often they do not carefully distinguish one kind of knowledge or ability from another. These taxonomic concepts have what Wittgenstein calls "fuzzy borders" and bear only a "family resemblance" to one another. That is, each of the examples of the concept may share features from a list of related features, but no two examples may have the same features (no. 66).

Given that our categories have fuzzy borders and are related by family resemblance, we can characterize broadly what we need to know when we write. We need to know what we are talking about (knowledge of content), but what we need to know about the same subject matter, say T. S. Eliot's poetry, will vary from writing to writing. We need to know the underlying assumptions and presuppositions, the underlying worldview, the deep background against which the subject we are talking about makes sense (general knowledge). We need to know the genre conventions generally used to talk about a particular subject in a particular social context (knowledge of form), but how we use those genre conventions will vary greatly from writing to writing, even when we are using the same genre. That is, we also need to know a host of broad strategies for applying what we know in a particular case, what aspects of our content knowledge apply, what aspects of genre conventions apply (conditional or procedural knowledge). We need to know all about the specific job at hand and its social and contextual implications (task-specific knowledge). We need to know about our audience and the larger social context in which we are writing (community-based knowledge). However, we must constantly remind ourselves that these various kinds of knowledge and ability are not easily distinguished from one another.

It is especially difficult to determine the degree to which writing depends on general knowledge and skill, on broad strategies and procedures, and the degree to which it depends on task-specific or community specific knowledge, on the degree to which we need to know what we are talking about. Most likely, the ability to write in any given case is a complex combination of knowledge and skills from each of Smagorinsky and Smith's categories.

I would argue, then, that writing involves many different kinds of knowledge and skill at various levels of generality and abstraction and that beyond some basic skills in syntax, spelling, and punctuation, there is no single kind of knowledge or skill or no single set of knowledge and skills necessary and sufficient to qualify a person to be a writer. All of this raises the question of the extent to which we can speak at all about generic writing ability.

Syntactic Fluency and Rhetorical Maturity

Now it may be too radical to conclude that the ability to write is really a multitude of subsidiary knowledge and skills. Surely there must be a *reason* that we often talk about writing as a generic concept, as something more unified than a number of more-or-less related features. In the past, scholars have referred to two aspects of writing, which they have taken as general indicators of writing ability. Those two aspects of writing are a full command of all the structural resources of a language, what scholars have variously called syntactic maturity or fluency or complexity, and the ability to adapt what we know and are able to do with language in particular contexts, what scholars have called rhetorical maturity. Because there is considerable evidence that syntactic fluency and rhetorical maturity are an integral part of a person's development and maturation, scholars who study these phenomena often suggest that they are good overall indicators of writing ability. These scholars imply that syntactic fluency and rhetorical maturity are what we really mean when we talk about general writing ability. But the question is: just how do we recognize these attributes and know the degree to which a writer possesses them?

Take first what I am calling "syntactic fluency"—it is also referred to as syntactic maturity or complexity (Mellon 4; Faigley, "Names" 294). A great deal of research indicates that as children and adolescents, we learn syntax in broad stages. By early elementary school, most of us have mastered simple sentences and longer coordinated sentences. An excellent example of the latter is the extended sentences of an excited first-grader explaining his day: "And then we went out to recess, and Miss Reynolds let us play kickball, and Johnny kicked the ball into the swings, and it hit Julia on the leg, and she got mad and stopped swinging and went after Johnny, and . . . and . . . and . . ." By early elementary school the best writers have already begun to use subordination, both adjectival and adverbial clauses, but by middle school the poorer writers catch up. In high school the best writers are no longer making their sentences longer; they are making them denser and more compact, packing more information into fewer words, primarily by using adjectival phrases and clauses—appositives, participial phrases, and other grammatical structures that transformational grammarians trace to deleted relative clauses (Loban; Hunt, *Grammatical* and *Syntactic*).

As a result, we might reasonably infer that good writers, expert writers, mature writers have mastered the syntax of their language and have at their disposal a large repertoire of syntactic forms, especially those forms we associate with longer clauses, which we can recognize simply by their length, or denser sentences, which we can measure by using the T-unit, an independent clause and all related subordination. However, the question that immediately comes to mind is this: Are longer and denser sentences always better, more mature? Can we necessarily infer that a writer who uses longer or more complex syntax in any give case is a better or more mature writer than one who does not? There is good reason to think that this inference may be misguided.

Considerable evidence exists that the length and complexity of sentences varies a great deal from genre to genre; that is, the length and complexity of the sentences in any particular genre may be more determined by the conventions of that genre than by the abilities of the writer. To put it another way, syntactic fluency may require what Smagorinsky and Smith call task-specific knowledge. Kellogg Hunt (*Syntactic*) determined that expository essays in our intellectual monthly magazines, such as *Harper's* and the *Atlantic*, had an average of 20.3 words per T-unit and 11.5 words per clause, which some of his followers have taken as a kind of adult norm. But Lester Faigley looked at recipes in *The New York Times Cookbook* and the "Guide to the Dictionary" in *The American Heritage Dictionary* and found the mean T-unit and clause lengths of the cookbook were below seven words (6.5 and 5.8), while the mean T-unit and clause lengths of the dictionary were much closer to those of the essays in Hunt's study (17.8 and 11.4) ("Names" 293). Faigley notes that although the passages from the cookbook and those from the dictionary are both sets of instructions, they varied considerably in the length of their T-units and clauses because of their different purposes and the different needs of their audiences: cooking instructions need to be short so that novice cooks can follow them in the throes of cooking; dictionary definitions can be less succinct because readers do not need to assimilate them verbatim; readers need only a general sense of words to assimilate their meanings into long-term memory ("Names" 294).

Moreover, Faigley notes that a variety of studies have shown that different kinds of discourse seem to require sentences of different lengths: for his own college class, students wrote both persuasive and expressive pieces on successive days, and "the means for the persuasive sample were nearly five words per T-unit and one and half words per clause higher than the means for the expressive sample" ("Names" 294; see also Seegars; Johnson; Veal and Tillman; Crowhurst and Piché). If, then, the nature of the genre determines the length and complexity of the sentences in that genre, the sheer ability to use long and complex syntax may not tell us much about a writer's overall ability. The question is whether writers can use their mastery of syntax appropriately in particular genres.

It seems then that although syntactic fluency may be a necessary part of what we mean by writing ability, it cannot be the only or even the most important part of that ability. Expert writers may have an excellent grasp of the language, but they still need to know what they are talking about, and they must still need to know how to apply what they know in any given case. Although expert writers may be syntactically fluent, they must be able to apply that fluency using different genres in different situations: different genres and different situations, even different purposes, call for different kinds of language. The test of writers' syntactic fluency can be only whether they adapt their repertoire of structures and techniques to the demands of a particular purpose in a particular context. This means that although syntactic fluency may very well be a general skill that all expert writers share, the only way we can actually know the degree to which a given writer has that ability is to ask that writer to perform in different genres in a variety of circumstances.

"Rhetorical maturity" as a concept has the same difficulties as "syntactic fluency." Susan Miller defines rhetorical maturity this way:

> [Able writers] communicate effectively to a large variety of more or less immediate audiences. They are able to identify with, to use Kenneth Burke's terminology, a variety of people they stand in various relationships to. They are adept in a number of writing situations, and write effectively under various formal, temporal and political constraints. In sum, they are rhetorically mature, able to identify and respond to the various demands for perception, conception, and execution that many writing situations create.
>
> . . . the mark of an able writer comes to be *virtuosity*: not some product-related quality of a writer's prose, but the ability to write with varying degrees of authority and varying senses of an audience's knowledge and prejudices about a subject and a writer. ("Rhetorical" 120–21)

Now there is a great deal of evidence that writers, especially beginning writers, vary greatly in their ability to write certain kinds of discourse primarily because writing different kinds of discourse involves very different knowledge and skills. For example, in a study of five hundred seventh- and eighth-grade students in Ottawa, Canada, Aviva Freedman and Ian Pringle found that almost all of the students—over 98 percent—could write an adequate narrative with some sense of setting and at least one dramatized narrative episode. However, the same students could not write adequate arguments: less than a third had an explicit or implied thesis, and only about twelve percent organized their arguments "within a hierarchic logical superstructure" (74, 76). Freedman and Pringle offer two major explanations for this discrepancy in abilities. First, most students are exposed to narratives at an early age, and most of what they read for pleasure or see and hear on television and in the movies is based on narrative, whereas students are not exposed to arguments early in their lives, nor are arguments a major part of what they read. Moreover, the arguments they are exposed to are primarily oral, and oral argument involves a conversational taking of turns, in which people trade claims and reasons back and forth. Conversational turn-taking does not prepare students for the hierarchical structure of written argument. Secondly, thirteen- and fourteen-year-olds may not have adequately developed the ability to abstract and conceptualize the kinds of claims involved in written argument. The inability of the same students to write two different kinds of discourse is powerful evidence that many kinds of written discourse may require substantially different knowledge and skills. Indeed, Freedman and Pringle assume that such is the case.

In addition, the National Assessment of Educational Progress, which regularly conducts national tests of various academic subjects and abilities, has also found that the ability of students in the fourth, eighth, and twelfth grades varies considerably depending on the kind of discourse they write (Campbell, Voelki, and Donahue). Generally, students at all levels write narratives with the most proficiency; they write informatively with less proficiency, and they find it difficult to write persuasively (Applebee et al. 60–86; see also Engelhard, Gordon, and Gabrielson; see also Wolcott and Legg 15–16 for a short bibliography on the effect of mode on writing ability).

The evidence from Freedman and Pringle and the NAEP does not preclude the possibility that we may possess a generic ability that we can call "rhetorical maturity," what Miller calls "virtuosity," "the ability to write with varying degrees of authority and varying senses of an audience's knowledge and prejudices about a subject and a writer." But as with syntactic fluency, the problem is how we can go about recognizing that ability. There may very well be genres or contexts in which a knowledge of one set of genre conventions and a knowledge of certain audience expectations will be more relevant than others. We may be able to assume, for example, that if a writer can do play reviews well, he might also be able to write political commentary. One person who has made a smooth transition from play reviewer to political commentator is Frank Rich of the *New York Times.* Perhaps Rich's mastery of one kind of rhetorical situation, his knowledge of the genre of the newspaper column and his sense of what the readers of the *Times* want and need, is evidence for a kind of rhetorical maturity. But of course, we cannot overlook that writing play reviews requires an entirely different kind of content knowledge than writing political commentary. Is rhetorical maturity, then, some kind of generic ability that we have in spite of what we know? Or can we account for the apparent ease with which Rich went from one kind of writing to the other to a mastery of two different kinds of subject matter? The answers to these questions are not clear.

What we lack is compelling evidence of just how rhetorically mature expert adult writers are. We do know that expert adult writers tend to think about larger rhetorical issues than novice writers. They think more about their overall purpose, they consider the needs of their audience more, and they contemplate a variety of strategies for meeting the needs of their audience more than novice writers do. Novice writers tend to concentrate more on getting down what they want to say, on getting words on paper or screen in some kind of recognizable order. This research clearly suggests that some sort of fluency, both in the use of sentences and in the various ways that writers adapt to a variety of rhetorical situations, is involved in what we call the ability to write (see Flower and Hayes). But how we go about determining whether writers are "rhetorically mature" and what we would accept as evidence of that maturity is problematic. I have already noted that we tend to identify writers by their ability to write one particular kind of discourse in one particular context. We call a sports columnist a writer because he writes entertainingly and insightfully about sports. And we know from just anecdotal evidence that acknowledged writers do not necessarily write all kinds of discourse equally well. In general, creative writers seem to excel in only one genre. Writers such as T. S. Eliot, who is known primarily as a poet, but who also gained a reputation as an essayist and a playwright, are rare.

However, we might want to say, for example, that the sports columnist we read four mornings a week can write other kinds of things equally well. But how do we know that? Should we assume that the sports columnist can write office memos well? A corporate annual report? A review of the literature in the latest advances in cellular biology? A law brief? Probably not, because in some sense, all writing requires particular kinds of expertise.

But perhaps there is something we might call public discourse, generally shared forms of expression that do not require any special knowledge of a subject matter or a genre—forms of expression, such as letters to the editor in the newspaper or reports of public meetings. To which I would say: Really? And why is it that we often get such a sense of dissatisfaction from reading letters to the editor in our local papers? Why is it that they often seem like mindless ranting, that they often seem to avoid addressing what we take to be the key issues? And why is it that even at club or church meetings when the regular secretary is absent, we do not let just anyone take the minutes of the meeting? Why is it that we have severe reservations about letting Joe or Martha do the job when we consider them to be generally literate, and perfectly capable of writing like an adult? Is it not that, even though we assume Joe and Martha are "rhetorically mature," we know from other acquaintance with them that at times they do not pay attention to detail, that at times they often allow their biases to overcome their ability to report or record accurately? On what basis, then, do we know that Joe and Martha are rhetorically mature in spite of the fact that we do not trust them to take the minutes of a small group meeting?

Still, my argument may not be convincing. Perhaps syntactic fluency and rhetorical maturity may be problematic, but what about other competencies, such as the ability to organize, or a sensitivity to language, knowledge and skills of that sort? Well, yes, I reply: I am perfectly willing to grant such general abilities, but *all* general abilities have the same difficulties as the two previous concepts I have already analyzed. Some people may be able to organize their thinking very well, but if they have no acquaintance with the conventions of writing a research article in history, they will not be able to organize research articles in history very well.

"Sensitivity to language," however, may be a slightly different case. Usually, we use the phrase to refer to the appreciation of literary language—or clear prose in the middle style: an elegant verbal style with a sense of rhythm and metaphor. But not all writing is literary. We don't necessarily expect a person who is "sensitive to language" to be able to write or even appreciate the matter-of-factness of newspaper stories, the precise logic of language philosophy, the technical prose of computer manuals. Each of these kinds of writing has its appropriate uses, its appropriate audiences, its appropriate contexts. Can people develop a sensitivity to language in all contexts? Perhaps. But I doubt if many people do. Nor do we expect them to. Generally, we only expect people to be sensitive to certain kinds of language—generally literary language, or the straightforward no-nonsense prose promoted by Strunk and White or Joseph Williams.

Like syntactic fluency, rhetorical maturity must be demonstrated in specific instances, but our ability to do so must depend on very task-specific and community-specific knowledge.

The Difficulties of Assessing Writing Ability

We make judgments about people's writing abilities all of the time, based on very little information and a great many unstated assumptions about what we mean by writing ability. Usually our judgments are influenced by our own background and experience, our particular tastes and values, what *we* like about writing. There is of course an immense literature on writing assessment, but the fundamental problem of writing assessment is this: what may we reasonably infer about people's writing ability from various samples of their work? Once again, let's get at this problem by analyzing a sample of writing. The following school essay was written under exam conditions and in response to a prompt. While reading it, consider what the essay seems to reveal about what the writer knows or is able to do.

> The author of this questionnaire makes the assumption that, in fact, codes of conduct do exist, although he/she makes no statement concerning the origin of such codes. Since the field is left open to interpretation, I will focus my effort on my personal code of conduct and why that personal code of conduct was created and maintained.
>
> First, what is a code of conduct? To me, a code of conduct represents guidelines for behavior that keep me performing in a manner consistent with my purpose in life. The function of those guidelines then is to provide a framework that keeps me aligned with that which I have decided is most important to me.

Life consists of a seemingly infinite series of moment-by-moment problems to be solved. Without some code of conduct, how do I choose my response to each of those moment-to-moment events?

I know what it is that I want to achieve in life. In my case, I want to contribute to the well-being of those around me, to create more love, health, and satisfaction of those I come in contact with. In order to achieve that I must channel my energy and activities into alignment with those goals. A personal code of conduct then becomes the roadmap for traveling in the direction of contributing to others' well-being, and some of those elements of that road map are trust, co-operation, support, keeping agreements (including societal laws), being consistent in thought, word and deed, being honest, sharing myself with others fully, acting in a positive manner, being loving and caring, and being good-humored. So the first part of the answer to why are codes of conduct created & maintained is to provide guidelines of behavior for the purpose of keeping me moving in the direction I want to go in life.

The second part of the answer to that question is that it works. Having a set of groundrules works. From an experiential level I have definitely proved for myself that when I am consistent with the rules of any given situation, the focus given by my being aligned with those rules gives me clarity of thought, satisfaction and creates positive feelings for myself about myself and about others, resulting in my being more willing and eager to participate with others and share myself, creating value for myself and for them. The result is then in alignment with my purpose, which was to contribute to the well-being of those around me.

In summary, why have codes of conduct? First, to provide guidelines in alignment with purpose. Second, because they work. It's actually quite simple. (Haswell 76)

Now I think it perfectly obvious that to a certain extent this essay demonstrates the kind of syntactic fluency many of us would hope for from experienced writers: the sentences are varied and often rhetorically effective. Moreover, the piece is clearly organized along the lines many of us expect from school essays: it has a recognizable introduction and conclusion, and the analysis directly addresses the issue cited in the prompt with a certain rigor. And of course, it goes almost without saying that the writer has no significant problems with spelling, punctuation, or other aspects of editing. But back to the fundamental question: what can we reasonably infer about this writer's ability to write? Can we reasonably infer that this writer is a good editor? That this writer is syntactically fluent and rhetorically mature? Based on this sample, what can we reasonably expect this writer to be able to write under different conditions? That is, if this sample does illustrate some general knowledge and skill the writer should be able to demonstrate in a variety of tasks and in a variety of contexts, just what are those knowledge and skills?

It may come as a surprise that this essay was not written by a college student but by a writer in the "workplace." It is one sample from a large study conducted by Richard Haswell on how college students and those in the workplace outside of the academy write school essays. Haswell's raters generally considered the essays such as this one by the workplace writers to be far superior to those written by the college students. Haswell's raters found that the essays by the workplace writers were not limited to preconceived patterns of organization, such as chronology or comparison-and-contrast; rather they were what Haswell calls "open-ended," always open to be developed in new ways, "always ready for the evolution of further logical points, patterns provided by inferential arguments, dialectical progressions, or choice among options" (77). The essays by the workplace writers were also more detailed and limited in focus; they tended to zero in on unique aspects of their topics and use "an exact and idiomatic vocabulary" that implied a great deal of expertise. These essays were also longer and more coherent, and they used more complex syntax with more variety and emphasis (78–79).

Haswell uses the evidence of the superior essays by those outside of the academy as evidence of a general writing ability. Although he is not directly concerned with the issue of what constitutes writing ability, Haswell strongly suggests that writing ability is largely determined by the ability to manipulate the resources of language: writing ability is somehow made up of a large repertoire of syntactic and organizational structures or patterns, and the ability to apply those patterns appropriately. What he does not consider is the relevance of context and task-specific knowledge in applying this repertoire of syntactic and organizational structures.

However, we may not be as certain as Haswell and his readers that this essay captures a great deal of what we mean by writing ability. When I first read the piece, I was taken aback by how awkward it is: the writer does not quite seem to know what to do with the material. The content of the piece, the explicit organization, the tone, all strike me as signs of uncertainty. I attribute that uncertainty to the fact that the writer is working in a school genre that has no direct analogue outside of the classroom, and as a result, the writer is unsure of how to address readers and cannot decide what genre conventions to use. That is, the writer does not have enough context to demonstrate what the writer really knows.

The problems begin with the very thing that Haswell admires most about the piece: the way it analyzes the prompt and carefully provides particulars to meet that analysis. Haswell notes that the workplace writers who did this assignment tended to avoid examples and anecdotes, and this essay is no exception. However, most of the writing instructors I know who require similar essays using similar prompts expect the responses to be more literary and expressive, more like an essay from a literary magazine than Haswell's readers apparently do. And so do I. As a result, while I appreciate the writer's analysis of codes of conduct, I am not terribly convinced by the conclusion. The writer has not provided me with any evidence from anyone's life that codes of conduct work and that the way they work is quite simple. I am tentatively willing to accept the writer's assertion that following a code of conduct gives "clarity of thought, satisfaction and creates positive feelings for myself about myself and about others," but I would feel much better about accepting such an assertion if the writer had given me some sense of how the code of conduct managed to achieve these effects.

The tone of the piece also strikes me as uncertain, as if the writer had not quite decided whom the essay was addressing. In the opening line, the writer assumes that the readers of the essay share a knowledge of the prompt, referring to "the author of *this* questionnaire [my italics]" and expecting the readers to know the questionnaire. Given this sense of common knowledge, we might assume that the writer would address the reader directly in a colloquial style, but the writer does not. Although the writer uses the first person, the essay's language is formal to the point of being stuffy, and it is filled with awkward nominal expressions. Overlook for a moment the obvious awkwardness of "he/she" or "to create more love, health, and satisfaction *of* those I come in contact with" or "some of *those* elements of *that* road map [italics mine]." The writer says, "From an experiential level I have proved to myself." It would be more direct and probably more accurate to say, "In my experience I have discovered that." (In what sense do we "prove" things to ourselves?) The writer says, "the focus given by my being aligned with those rules." It would be more straightforward and colloquial to say something like "When I follow those rules, I focus on . . ." The writer says, "the result is then in alignment with my purpose." Why not say, "the result is that I fulfill my purpose"? The stilted diction is at odds with the more colloquial use of the first person, the occasional use of short punchy sentences for emphasis—"Having a set of groundrules works"; "It's actually quite simple"—and the fragment in the last paragraph—"Second, because they work." In other words, the writer seems to be floundering for a tone, a way to address the audience. On the other hand, when the writer does use simpler sentences, a certain amount of rhetorical power results. The last paragraph strikes me as a strong emotional appeal.

Why does the writer have these problems? I think the key to understanding these problems is the rigid overall structure of the piece: an opening that frames the issues, a list of reasons signaled by "first" and "second," and a conventional summary at the end that almost seems like an afterthought. This is the format of a five-paragraph theme, although the writer does use six paragraphs. That limited school format is not really adequate for the writer's purposes, but the writer apparently feels obligated to use it in spite of its difficulties and, as a result struggles to find an appropriate form and tone; the writer tries to imagine a consistent context and a genre appropriate for this task and, failing to do so, winds up with what I would characterize as a strange mixture of the personal essay, an impersonal office memo, and a five-paragraph theme.

Now what I find interesting is that in spite of the objections I have just given, I am willing to grant that this piece of writing demonstrates a "mature" ability to write. But when I try to justify my assessment, I find myself relying more on what I know about the writer—who is in the workplace and presumably has a college degree and a certain amount of experience—than on what I see in the actual writing. Indeed, my natural inclination is to overlook the awkward phrasing, the mechanical organization, the underdeveloped rhetorical strategies and explain them away. I attribute that awkwardness precisely to the fact that the writer has been asked to write a school essay, a genre that does not exist outside of the classroom, and doesn't know how to respond. I am then judging the writer, not the writing. I am assuming that the writer has more ability than I see demonstrated in the writing. If I had to defend my judgment that this is mature writing, I would probably point to all of the things that Haswell has noted and offer excuses for the problems in style and tone, the mechanical organization, the underdeveloped rhetorical strategies.

While I am willing to concede that this essay demonstrates a certain amount of writing ability, I am much less sure of what the essay indicates about what the writer can do in other genres in other contexts. If the writer of this piece asked me for a recommendation for a job that required other writing tasks, I am not sure that I would comply. I would certainly not be confident that this writer could write genres other than school essays with any degree of "maturity." When push comes to shove, I would not want to rely on this piece of writing alone to argue that its author possessed what we call "writing ability." But this raises the question I have been asking all along: what evidence, how many samples and of what kind, *would* I accept in order to be confident that this person possessed an adequate or in some sense a "mature" writing ability?

The field of composition studies is no help: the field has not adequately conceptualized what we mean by "writing ability" or "syntactic fluency" or "rhetorical maturity," and it may be that the field will not be able to conceptualize that ability any better than it already has. People may very well possess writing ability, whether conceptualized as syntactic fluency or rhetorical maturity or some other notion, but because writers can demonstrate their syntactic fluency or rhetorical maturity only in particular contexts, it is difficult to know with any certainty whether a given writer is syntactically fluent or rhetorically mature except by asking that writer to perform in a variety of genres and contexts. And there is always the possibility that the next task in the next context might be beyond the range of the writer's particular knowledge and abilities.

I am suggesting, then, that a commonly accepted definition of syntactic fluency, rhetorical maturity, or some notion of general writing ability may be beyond us, that *any* notion of these concepts will either be intensely disputed, subject to debates about what a writer should be able to do in any given context, or it will result in a very pragmatic decision that we cannot assume anything about a specific person's ability to write, except by asking that person to demonstrate that expertise in a particular context.

The Evidence of Literacy Studies

Scholars in fields related to composition studies have done no better in deciding just what writing is or how to conceptualize it. For example, scholars in the field of literacy studies have struggled for about fifty years to define what it means to be able to read and write. Because their definitions are often used by governments to determine the degree to which their populations are literate, scholars of literacy usually try to define reading and writing at some minimal level of competence, using a "typical" example of writing. According to David Harmon, until the early 1950s, most governments determined the literacy of their populations by relying on UNESCO's definition: people are literate if they can "with understanding, both read and write a short simple statement on [their] everyday life" (227). However, we can legitimately question the degree to which a simple statement about everyday life, a kind of discourse unknown outside of literacy surveys, is representative of all writing, or how much the ability to comprehend or write such a statement tells us about the larger abilities of the surveyed writers.

Our own U.S. Bureau of the Census considers people literate if they can read and write a simple message at the fifth-grade level, although, once again, a simple message does not seem to be what we usually refer to as writing, and just what "the fifth-grade level" means is ambiguous. The U.S. Census Bureau itself concedes that "the completion of no one particular grade of school corresponds to the attainment of literacy" (qtd. in Harvey Graff 58). Harmon notes that since the 1950s, literacy scholars have increasingly debated what it means to be literate, but they have added little to the widely accepted governmental definitions. Nowadays, scholars tend to define literacy in functional terms, as "the essential knowledge and skills which enable [a person] to engage in all those activities in which literacy is required for effective functioning in his group and community, and whose attainments make it possible for him to use these skills towards his own and the community's development" (Harmon 227; Hunter and Harmon 19). This definition seems to assume that writing primarily serves larger social and cultural goals. Hence the use of the term "literacies," the ability to read and write to achieve a variety of tasks in a variety of contexts. However, as Harvey Graff points out, "Crucially, nowhere are the critical concepts of 'effective functioning,' 'knowledge and skills,' or 'development' defined or even discussed" (58). While some scholars have administered various comprehension tests to determine if survey respondents can indeed read as well as they say they can, these reading tests are usually poorly designed, and the scholars conducting them never try to measure writing ability (58–59).

David Resnick and Lauren Resnick point out that our current difficulties in determining what we mean by literacy, the basic ability to read and write, are a result of our very recent high standards—recent, that is, in terms of human history. Nowadays, we expect the general population to achieve levels of literacy that in the past were achieved only by a limited elite, and that as late as three hundred years ago, standards of literacy, even among these elites, were relatively low. In seventeenth-century Sweden, for example, a parish recorded the literacy of its population for thirteen years, and its standard was the ability of the parish members to recite Luther's *Little Catechism,* as well as various confessions and prayers, and to explain selected words from this text. The parish did not require any formal capacity to read or the ability to write as criteria for being literate. As late as the mid-eighteenth century in Europe, a sign of literacy was merely the ability to write one's name. In early twentieth-century America, the U.S. Army found out after World War I that 30 percent of its troops could not understand the written section of the Yerkes tests for general intelligence, but then why should people understand instructions for a series of tasks they are totally unfamiliar with?

In short, just what we mean by literacy has always been a function of the needs of people to fit into various roles in society, and the demand that most people read and write a large range of discourse at a certain level of competence is a fairly recent phenomenon, certainly no older than 130 years, and perhaps no older than fifty years. In trying to conceptualize a broad-based notion of writing, we are trying to conceptualize a fairly recent societal expectation in human history, and we have no empirical norms to go by, no commonly accepted notion of what people at various ages or at various stages of development or at various levels of schooling should be able to do in writing. All we have is our expectations of what we *want* them to be able to do.

Just where these expectations come from and whether they are realistic is almost totally uninterrogated in both literacy research and composition studies. I suspect that such expectations are unrealistic. If writing is not a single ability but a combination of many kinds of knowledge and skill that must be applied uniquely in response to each new exigency, it should not be surprising that people write in many genres and in many contexts that other people will not understand or will misinterpret or will judge unsuccessful.

I would conclude the following from my analysis:

- The features of any particular kind of writing are overwhelmingly determined by the function of the writing, what the writer is using writing in order to *do*. Writing is very task-specific.

- Various kinds of writing involve different forms of knowledge and different kinds of skills, although particular kinds of writing may share certain forms of knowledge and certain kinds of skills with other kinds of writing.
- Competent writers clearly possess some degree of syntactic fluency and rhetorical maturity and some familiarity with a variety of thinking and composing strategies, but after achieving this basic competence, novice writers may simply need to know more: more about their subject matter, more about the possibilities of the genre conventions they want to use, more about the textual practices of the discourse community they want to write for.
- The difficulty with distinguishing various kinds of knowledge is that the only way we can tell whether people possess more generalizable knowledge and skills is to ask them to actually write something. But whatever particular task we give them to write may require such specific knowledge of a genre, subject matter, or context that we cannot separate their more generalizable knowledge and skills from the particular kinds of knowledge and skills required by that particular writing task. No single writing task, no series of writing tasks, can capture unambiguously whatever it is we call "writing ability." The only thing we can know with any certainty is what people can do in specific circumstances.

The larger issue, however, is this: if we find our current concept of writing too schematic and tentative, too underconceptualized, just how would we go about improving it, making it less schematic, less tentative, and more accurately and productively conceptualized? Are there aspects of writing that the field has not considered? Are there other taxonomies that may be more helpful in articulating aspects of writing than those we already have? Are there ways of thinking about writing that we haven't thought of yet? Perhaps. But even if there are, it is difficult to imagine that these future discoveries will radically change what we already understand about writing. It is difficult to imagine what any new conception of writing might tell us that we don't already know or how any new conception might help clarify the concepts we are already grappling with. There may be no way to resolve the ambiguity at the heart of writing and writing ability.

And if the notion of writing in and of itself is difficult to conceptualize, just what then do we teach when we teach writing? Do we try to teach the more generalizable aspects of writing, whatever they may be, or should we focus our instruction on the specific subject matter and contextual background any writer needs to know in order to write well in specific situations? How would we go about teaching a specific kind of knowledge or skill, and how certain could we be that this particular aspect of knowledge or skill would be helpful to the writer in the future? But issues of how to teach writing depend upon how we learn to write in the first place. I deal with that issue in chapter 2.

Language is acquired only by absorption and contact with an environment in which language is in perpetual use.
> —Samuel Thurber, "An Address to English Teachers," 1898, as paraphrased by Judy and Judy

The world that emerges for us is a conceptual world. When we are puzzled about what we encounter, we renegotiate its meaning in a manner that is concordant with what those around us believe.
> —Jerome Bruner, *Actual Minds, Possible Worlds*

2 *Learning to Write*

IF COMPOSITION STUDIES HAS an underconceptualized notion of what writing is, it has an equally underconceptualized notion of how human beings learn to write. Writing is obviously related to speaking—to Walter Ong, writing is a kind of second-order discourse, a formal self-conscious way of recording speech (82)—and a great deal of what we assume about how people learn to write is based on analogies with how they learn to speak. And yet there is a mystery at the heart of how we learn to speak, which also seems to apply to how we learn to write. To get at that mystery, linguists and cognitive psychologists have devoted an incredible amount of time and energy. The results are a host of detailed descriptions of infants and young children in the process of learning to speak and write. And of course these descriptions of language learning have in turn produced a complex web of interrelated models and theories of how infants and young children accomplish this task. The question is, just how successful are these models and theories of language learning, especially in terms of their implications for how writing should be taught? More specifically, since we know much more about how children learn to speak than we do about how they learn to write, how or in what way is learning to write based on or influenced by our ability to learn a native language in the first place?

In the first chapter, I argued the case that the ability to write is a complex combination of many different abilities and of many different kinds of knowledge. Because these abilities are so many and so various and because what we need to know in order to write involves so many generalizations, abstract principles, algorithms, and ad hoc considerations at so many levels of generality—to say nothing of what we need to know about the specific subject matter and context of each unique rhetorical situation— it is very difficult to conceptualize what people "know" when we say that they know how to write.

Of course, the problem is compounded by the fact that most of what we characterize as the ability to write is "mental," an operation of the mind, and of course, the problem in talking about mental life is that we have no direct knowledge of mental operations; we can only infer how our minds work from what we say and do. We *can* use introspection, but introspection is notoriously unreliable (Stich 228–42). Still, we talk naturally about our thought processes all the time; it is part of the way we think about the world and the basis for a great deal of the way we interact with each other. We all have what Wittgenstein calls a "picture" of mental life, a concept of how our minds work, and a great deal of research in composition studies in the last forty years has been to create such pictures and refine them.

The significance of research in learning theory in general and language learning in particular has been to remind us of all the things our minds do or can do when we write, to create a sort of composite portrait of all the possibilities of mental life when we learn all of the many kinds of knowledge and skill we need in order to compose. Researchers in learning theory and language acquisition primarily construct taxonomies of all the things we can do mentally when we learn to speak and write, and then they arrange these lists of possible mental operations into a model that represents a possible relationship between the various concepts suggested by the taxonomy. What these researchers have *not* done is get us any closer to an understanding of how our minds actually function when we learn something about writing.

Most models of language learning are basically elaborate analogies between something we know little about, what Rom Harré calls "the *subject*" of the model (in this case, the mind) and something we do know about, what Harré calls "the *source*" of the model (computers, for example) (38). The problem with models, as Michael Pemberton explains, is that they may oversimplify the complexity of the subject because the source of the model lacks many of the properties of the subject. Think of the many properties of the mind that have no counterpoint in a computer. A model may even misrepresent its subject because the source of the model has properties that the subject lacks. Think of what a computer requires but what the mind does not. The best models suggest things about the ways we speak and write that we may not have thought of before, but none of them even pretends to be a model for how our minds actually work. As Pemberton puts it, "Models are not intended to be thought of as anything more than potential and reasonable explanations for observational data" (46). To which I would add that models help us to focus and refine research questions and provide heuristics for instruction.

However, models are all we have: we don't know enough about mental life to construct a traditional "theory" of the mental operations involved in learning to speak and write, at least in the way psychologists and cognitive scientists use the term, in a way that can be empirically tested and verified. Most of what some researchers call "theories" in linguistics and cognitive psychology are what I call "models." However, there are many testable and verifiable "theories" of various individual aspects of larger models of learning to speak and write.

Now with the "social turn" not only in composition studies but in linguistics and cognitive science in general, with a new emphasis on the social contexts in which we interpret and understand, we seem to be approaching the limits of what models can tell us. More and more, models of learning theory and language acquisition are becoming contextual and asserting that if there are generalizable mental "rules" or "strategies" for how we learn, these rules and strategies have to be applied in particular social circumstances, that in order to understand adequately how infants and children learn language, we have to know the circumstances in which they do so (for a history of this development in relation to composition studies, see Nystrand, Greene, and Wiemelt).

Despite the limitations of our models of language development, there is broad consensus among a variety of disciplines for a primitive model of how we learn to speak. The fundamental basis of most of these models is that we *acquire* our ability to speak; we do not learn to speak primarily in response to formal instruction. I would argue that increasingly, studies of young writers indicate that we develop our ability to write according to the same basic principles as we learn to speak and that for all practical purposes learners must have a fundamental sense of what writing is and how to do it before they receive any formal instruction. Of course, if writing is primarily acquired and not learned in response to formal instruction, the nature and indeed the relevance of formal instruction in writing is very problematic.

My argument in this chapter will proceed in two parts. In the first part, I will briefly summarize the models of how we learn to speak and then show how writing development seems to proceed according to the principles of these models. In the second part, I will provide the evidence that most of what we know about writing must be acquired and not learned from formal instruction. I will end by offering a model of writing acquisition and discussing the implications of this model for how writing should be taught.

Learning to Speak and Write

Learning to Speak

The "pictures" presented by most models of language development are primitive indeed. However, they do share some basic features. Most models of language acquisition are based on the following propositions:

- Children learn various aspects of their native language in regular stages and they progress through these stages by gradually approximating the spoken language of those around them.
- Children must in some sense "imitate" or model their language after the language they hear in the world around them; they do not just imitate that language "directly." Indeed, the language of children is often very different from that of adults, and until they are ready to learn certain aspects of language, children seem impervious to correction.
- Children's language is from the first creative, what linguists call "generative." Children seem to use language according to their own internal rules.

The evidence for these propositions is considerable. Infants and children go through stages of development in all aspects of language. Although they may go through these stages at different ages, and although there is considerable variation among individuals, all infants and children go through all of these stages in the same order: they go through stages of babbling to eventually achieve sentence-like intonation and produce protowords (Sachs 42); they develop morphology and syntax in regular stages, starting with what some linguists call telegraphic speech of one to two morphemes, such as "more car" and "bye-bye baby," through basic simple sentences, until they master such complex patterns as passives, coordination, and relative clauses in early elementary school (Tager-Flusberg 180, 183–94, 179); they also develop a sense of meaning in an orderly way: in their second year they learn words that are intellectually and socially meaningful to them, such as *mommy, daddy, doggy, blanky,* but not words such as *tree, bus,* or *policeman.* These early meaningful words also happen to be easy to pronounce.

Although children seem to develop language in orderly stages, they do not seem to do so by imitating the language of those around them. Usually their early ways of speaking are not at all like those of adults, and they are impervious to attempts to make their language more like adults before they are ready. Consider the case of the child who asked her father, "Want other one spoon, Daddy." Despite the father's repetition of the correct expression, "You mean, you want THE OTHER SPOON," and drilling the child until she mechanically repeated what her father told her, given the first opportunity to speak spontaneously, the child said, "Other . . . spoon. Now give me other one spoon?" (Pinker 281).

In addition, young children constantly use new forms of language that they have never heard adults use. Rather than imitating adults, young children seem to generate original expressions using their own internal sense of how words and syntax work. That is, they often *overextend* or *underextend* the meanings of words: they use words to refer to more things than an adult would, or they use words in a much more limited set of circumstances than an adult would. For example, "they may use 'duck' for birds that swim, 'bird' for those that fly, and 'chicken' for those that don't fly" (Pan and Gleason 134).

Of course, the fact that young children learn spoken language by developing their own internal rules does not mean that their environment is not important. Obviously, children need to hear language spoken in order to know what it is they must learn: a child born in a province of China will learn a dialect of Chinese; a child born in the United States will learn a dialect of English or Spanish. And just as obviously, children need to interact with others who speak the language so that they can observe how language functions in the give-and-take of social interaction and so that they can practice using language themselves.

The standard way of explaining this phenomenon is to say that children *acquire* a language; they are not taught it. James Paul Gee defines "acquisition" this way:

> *Acquisition* is a process of acquiring something subconsciously by exposure to models, a process of trial and error, and practice within social groups, without formal teaching. It happens in natural settings which are meaningful and functional in the sense that acquirers know that they need to acquire the thing they are exposed to in order to function and they in fact want to so function. This is how most people come to control their first language. (*Social* 146)

But of course this definition explains nothing. It simply puts a label on a process we do not understand very well. In conceptual terms, the problem is what Carl Bereiter calls "the learning paradox": "learners must grasp concepts or procedures more complex than those they already have available for application" ("Toward" 202). To put it another way: if we want to explain how children learn the complexities of language by some sort of internal mental process, we have to posit that their internal mental life is just as complex, if not more so, than what they have to learn. After all, how could an organism with a few rather simple mechanisms for learning grasp the complexities of language, indeed the complexities of experience? This conceptual problem has driven many linguistics and cognitive psychologists to posit that our ability to learn language is somehow innate because only a richly complex mental ability—early linguists called it a LAD, a Language Acquisition Device—could make such systematic sense of our experience as children appear to do when they learn a language. On the other hand, many researchers in language acquisition do not want to go so far as to assert that the ability to learn a native language is entirely programmed by our genetic inheritance. Clearly, some aspects of the environment are important, too. These researchers would argue that if we do possess an innate ability to learn language, this ability must be dependent upon other cognitive abilities and many kinds of social interaction. One theory is that language abilities are released or triggered by models. But ascribing much of what the learner acquires to his social context does not solve the learning paradox either. Such a view does not explain how we internalize the complexities of language from our environment.

Models of Learning to Write

Writing, however, is not speech. The texts of writing usually differ significantly from the utterances of speech:

- Written sentences are generally longer than spoken sentences; they also contain more subordination and other complexities of syntax.
- Writing contains more abstractions, fewer self-reference words, and a more Latinate vocabulary. (Chafe; Akinnaso)
- Writing is usually "extended"; that is, at the very least, it contains a number of sentences about a single topic. Even shopping lists can be interpreted as extended lists of items in support of the topic, What I Need to Buy.
- Writing is usually structured hierarchically, often with an elaborate patterning of more general assertions and more specific assertions in support.
- As a result, writing must usually be planned, be self-monitored, and involve consideration of audiences. (Snow and Kurland 191–92; see also Crystal 179; Grabe and Kaplan 61).

Children learn to speak "naturally" by simply listening to others and by gradually building up a repertoire of words and syntax that approximates the language of the people around them. But surely, learning to write is not so "natural" and cannot be simply acquired. Surely, learning to write must depend to some extent on explicit instruction or formal schooling or at least some form of self-conscious reflection. Gee calls this process of explicit instruction or formal schooling or self-conscious reflection "learning":

> *Learning* is a process that involves conscious knowledge gained through teaching (though not necessarily from someone officially designated a teacher) or through certain life-experiences that trigger conscious reflection. This teaching or reflection involves explanation and analysis, that is, breaking down the thing to be learned into its analytic parts. It inherently involves attaining, along with the matter being taught, some degree of meta-knowledge about the matter. (*Social* 146)

Now I think the distinction between "acquisition" and "learning" is clear. However, I have been referring to our overall ability to "learn to write," so it may be confusing to talk about "learning" as opposed to "acquisition" as one of two major ways of "learning" to write. Ross Winterowd calls the process of explicit instruction in writing "drill" (*Culture* 52–56), but that term also has its problems. It calls to mind a certain *kind* of instruction. Consequently, in the hopes of avoiding confusion, I will refer to what Gee calls "learning" as explicit instruction, although like Gee I realize that writers may learn a great deal about writing through their own analysis and reflection, without any outside help.

The most well-known model of learning to write in composition studies is James Britton's *Language and Learning.* Britton's model does not account for any of the ways learning to write may be different from learning
to speak or even for the ways it may be different from learning in general.
I would like to briefly review Britton's model and then discuss the ways the
model would have to be refined in order to be more helpful.

The "picture" of how we learn to speak in James Britton's *Language and
Learning* is one of "active learners" constructing their own individual mental
representation of the world, what Frank Smith calls "a theory of the world
in the head" (*Comprehension* 11). Learners develop this private and unique
mental representation by noting distinctive differences among sensations,
images, ideas, and other objects of thought, and by internalizing and ab-
stracting a "representation" of experience into a complex series of interlocking conceptual hierarchies. In order to adequately represent a concept
mentally, they have to note the similarities between two objects or actions
or ideas and determine what larger class of related objects, actions, or ideas
they belong to. They note the similarities between certain aspects of their
experience—for example, between animals—say, a dachshund and a col-
lie—and they abstract particular aspects of that experience in order to "represent" the concept of a "dog" so as to distinguish it from other similar concepts, say, of a "cat" or of a "cow," all of which have hair, four legs, and a
tail. In Britton's scheme, children seem to construct a conceptual hierarchy,
such as "animals," with subcategories determined by a complex set of interlocking distinguishing features: color, shape, and size, to name the most
basic. Given these complex conceptual hierarchies, children can learn to distinguish between cats and dogs and between breeds of dogs with a high degree of accuracy.

One such conceptual hierarchy related to speaking and writing is syn-
tactical. We tend to think of concepts as a function of the way they are represented in syntax: that nouns represent things, for example; or that verbs
represent action. We also tend to think of concepts as being related the way
they are in the structure of our language—the subject-predicate relation; the
verb-object relation; and the modifying relation (Britton, *Language* 195–201).

In addition, to Britton, learners seem to learn best when what they need
or want to learn makes sense to them; that is, when that information fits
into their previous mental representations. And they appear to learn most
effectively when they are actively engaged in making sense of what is new
and unfamiliar, and when they can be relatively sure that what they are trying to learn will help them accomplish something they value.

Clearly, Britton's model is very basic. It does not even directly confront
the issue of how learning to write may be different from learning to speak.
In order for Britton's model to be more helpful in conceptualizing how we
learn to write, it would have to account for how or in what degree writing—

a second-order language activity—is based on or develops out of our innate ability to learn spoken language. In other words, it would have to account for two things: first, what we currently know about the transition from speech to writing in young children, and secondly, the relative roles of acquisition and explicit instruction in learning to write.

The Development of Writing Ability

More and more research is confirming that we begin the process of learning to write at a very early age, often before school, and that like the development of speech, the development of writing proceeds in stages. However, these stages are not nearly as orderly and sequential as the development of speech. If young children are exposed to reading and writing and if they recognize that reading and writing have a purpose or function that will serve their needs, they will spontaneously begin to develop their own approximations of these tasks without formal instruction, and their approximations will gradually evolve into what we label "literacy." These approximations are what Thomas Newkirk calls "intermediate forms" (*More* 72), analogous to the early stages of oral speech, or what Eleanor Kutz, borrowing from the literature on second-language learning, calls an "interlanguage," a form of discourse containing features that do not occur in the target language (392–93).

There is some dispute among scholars who study young children's first acts of writing whether those efforts are an extension of speech or drawing. Lev Vygotsky interpreted the early scrawls, the "undifferentiated squiggles and lines," of certain three- and four-year-olds as beginning symbols. In a classic experiment, Vygotsky's team of researchers asked children to "write" or mark down a list of phrases in order to help them remember the list later. Most of the children were bewildered by the task and claimed that they could not write. Nevertheless, most of the children made marks of some kind in response to the list of phrases. Afterwards, most of the children did not use their scrawls in order to help them remember the phrases, but a few did. A few seemed to "read" their scrawls as if the scrawls were writing; moreover, they could do so repeatedly and consistently, suggesting that certain specific marks denoted certain specific phrases (114–15). Vygotsky's experiment is evidence that learning to write may begin as a process of differentiating pictures and other graphic signs from symbols of speech (see also Gardner).

Moreover, Newkirk has shown that young children spontaneously draw pictures that can be distinguished as either "descriptive" or "narrative," accompanied by scrawls and early forms of words, an example of what he calls "symbol-weaving" (*More* 37, 44–59; see also Dyson 31–33; Taylor and Dorsey-Gaines 88–89). The fact that children seem to draw different "genres" of pictures and text may confirm Vygotsky's insight that learning to write requires that children distinguish and internalize the differences between the two different symbol systems.

Vygotsky's experiment may also indicate that children have to recognize what writing can do for them, that they need to see how writing can help them accomplish various tasks, what M. A. K. Halliday calls "the functional extension of oral language":

> [W]hat is learning to read and write? Fundamentally it is an extension of the functional potential of language. Those children who don't learn to read and write, by and large, are children to whom it doesn't make sense; to whom the functional extension that these media provide has not been made clear, or does not match up with their own expectations of what language is for. *(Language* 57)

Once they sense what writing can accomplish, once they grasp how it can function in their lives, children begin to use a combination of drawing and writing for a variety of purposes. Often before they go to school, children begin to write in a variety of genres in order to accomplish various tasks. In the spontaneous writing of early childhood, we see examples of stories, lists, notes, plans, and cards and the beginnings of the full range of aims and purposes we associate with writing: to express feelings and attitudes, to inform and explain, and even to argue (Newkirk and Atwell; Gundlach, "Children"; Jacobs).

Scholars have categorized these spontaneous writings in a number of ways, but there is now general agreement that the range of young children's writing represents much of the range of later adult discourse. For example, contrary to the early speculations of James Britton and James Moffett that children naturally write narratives before other genres, a number of studies in the last two decades document that young children use expository and persuasive forms, albeit as exploratory and hypothesis-testing approximations of the target genres. Here is an example by a six-year-old girl of what Suzanne Jacobs calls the "attributive mode": a central topic and several predications of the topic:

> Whales are black and some are gray.
> Whales are big. They can eat you in one bite.
> There are brown whales and there are black whales too.
> There are white whales.
> There are blue killer whales. (422; see also Sowers 832)

Notice that this writer has already internalized the notion that writing is not transcribed speech, that writing is usually done in sentences rather than conversational fragments and that it is more coherent, more directly related to a theme or topic, than the give-and-take of conversation.

And here is an example of a nascent argument in two separate signs that a young preschooler posted on his bedroom door: the first sign is a request or demand followed by a reason for the request; the second sign is a request or demand, followed by a qualification of that request:

DO NAT DSTRB GNYS AT WRK
(Do not disturb. Genius at work.)

DO.NAT KM.IN.ANE.MORE.JST.LETL.KES
(Do not come in any more. Just little kids.)
(Newkirk, "Hedgehog" 597)

Gradually, young writers expand their ways of writing various genres and begin to make them more cohesive and more hierarchical, thereby increasing the ways their writing approximates adult discourse. Here, for example, is a piece by a third-grader about Ralph, the class mouse:

1. Ralph likes to eat Skippy peanut butter. 2. Ralph is in a cage. 3. He has a spinning wheel. 4. He has a motorcycle. 5. It's red. 6. He has a toilet. 7. The first time Ralph was in the classroom Ralph stepped into the box. 8. Ralph likes to climb to the top of the cage. 9. Ralph has two tiny teeth. 10. Everytime Ralph gets down he cleans himself. 11. His tongue is one centimeter long. . . . (Newkirk, *More* 73)

Although we might first think that this piece is entirely associative, it does have the beginnings of a more complex hierarchical structure. Newkirk notes that this writing contains three clusters of related statements: one cluster notes what Ralph has in the cage with him (sentences 2–5); another catalogues what Ralph does in his cage (sentences 7–8), and the last is about Ralph's mouth, what it look like and what Ralph uses his mouth to do (sentences 9–11). Newkirk argues persuasively that this is just one example of how children's writing begins to develop a topic-subtopic structure we associate with exposition (*More* 72–88).

Other genres proceed in the same way: through no set pattern of development, but over time, increasingly approximating the structures of adult written discourse (Graves, *Case* 29; Newkirk, *More* 29–31). George Kamberelis concludes:

[C]hildren's developing understanding and enactment of different genres are emergent phenomena. By this suggestion I mean that development is complex, non-linear, and constitutively related to differential linguistic complexity and abstraction, task conditions, proximal and distal learning experience, and other contextual variables. As with many other developmental phenomena, children seem both to progress and regress as they learn to differentiate and eventually creatively integrate the forms, functions, and contexts of different genres. (448)

(For some examples of the development of writing from the same children at ages eight, twelve, and seventeen, see Loban, appendix D, 112–20. For a list of adult genres across socio-economic groups and races, see Taylor and Dorsey-Gaines 123–90.)

Young children also learn to spell in stages, but again these stages are not necessarily sequential, and any of the early stages may be skipped. According to a study by Donald Graves, the stages are: invented spelling, such as "botafll prnssas" (beautiful princess); words in transition, in which the same word may be spelled in a number of different ways, such as "wuz" and "wsas" for "was"; stable inventions, such as "valin" for "villain" and "neis" for "nice," and finally sight words, the final correct spelling ("What" 314; see also Gentry and Gillet 25).

I might add that the use of invented spelling is analogous to the fact that children often invent words when they forget a word or have not learned the adult equivalent in the first place. For example, they might use *pourer* for *cup,* *needle* for *mend* and *plant-man* for *gardener.* These inventions seem to follow fairly regular patterns (Clark 390).

Finally, children also seem to develop the use of written syntax in an orderly way. In general, over the course of their elementary and high school careers, children's written syntax follows their oral syntax. Both develop toward longer coordinate sentences, then toward more complex sentences using dependent clauses, and then toward denser sentences. The denser sentences primarily result from the use of gerundial, participial, and other syntactic forms that transformational grammarians explain as deletions and transformations of adjectival clauses. Usually, the more complex and denser forms of syntax occur more frequently in the writing of "high proficiency" writers four to six years before they occur in the writing of "low proficiency" writers (Loban; see also Hunt, *Syntactic*). Walter Loban explains this difference in developing abilities as primarily the result of social factors, especially the way language is used in the home, but it may also be the result of "psychological and physical factors" (88–89).

It seems then that writing ability may develop in ways that may be analogous to the development of speech, but not in as orderly a way. In addition, as with speech, different aspects of writing develop in different ways. Written syntax follows the development of oral syntax fairly closely, but the development of conventions specific to writing—spelling, punctuation, and genre conventions—develop at their own pace, apart from speech.

Much of the research in the last twenty years has tried to account for the many factors that contribute to the complexity of writing development, and more complex models than Britton's would have to account for these factors: social background (Heath, especially 190–262); the mentoring of adults (Snow and Kurland; Greenfield); reading (Stotsky, "Research"; Tierney and Leys; Bereiter and Scardamalia, "Learning"); learning styles (Davis; Claxton and Smith; Reiff); gender (Gilligan; Belenky et al.; Coates;

Flynn); identity (Beach 57–59, 67–68); and motivation (McLeod, *Notes* 61; see also 47–64).

So we might conclude that there are good reasons for thinking that we learn to write using the broad principles of Britton's model, the model of an active learner who develops an individual internal representations of the many rules and conventions of written language, who tests hypotheses based on these representations by writing things down and seeing how more literate people respond to them, who modifies internal representations depending on the responses generated. Gradually over time, the writing of the active learner becomes indistinguishable from the writing of those using similar genres in similar social circumstances.

In addition, we might conclude that many aspects of writing proceed in stages, but these stages are not sequential, except in very broad terms. For example, we might say that writing development proceeds in these stages:

- Control over the physical aspects of writing: the ability to hold a pen or pencil and make marks or form letters on paper, or to use a keyboard;
- A sense of the relationship between spoken and written language, the way the alphabet and other written conventions reflect speech;
- A sense of the text conventions for genres more closely related to speech: notes, stories, letters.
- A sense of the text conventions for genres more distant from speech, especially school genres—the descriptive paragraph, the personal essay, the research report;
- A sense of the text conventions for genres outside the classroom.

However, it is much more difficult to specify how novice writers develop particular aspects of writing ability. Much of their knowledge and ability to do certain things in writing seems to leap forward and then regress in ways unrelated to other aspects of writing. Thus, many aspects of writing do not seem to develop at the same rate. Young writers may be good in some things and not in others. They may be competent in the format of a certain genre but not as competent at spelling or punctuation. They may be competent in a few genres and not in others. They may be able to get words on paper in a relatively "correct" manner, but this aspect of writing may so preoccupy them that they don't have the ability to also monitor their writing in terms of their purposes and audience. The picture we have then of novice writers is of many kinds of knowledge and ability in various stages of development, each aspect of writing influenced by all of the factors I have mentioned. This is a messy picture with few neat lines.

The Acquisition of Writing
The Evidence That Writing Is Acquired

Thus, the question arises, among all of these kinds of knowledge and ability, can we distinguish between those aspects of writing that people acquire and those aspects that must be explicitly taught? And the answer is, no. William Grabe and Robert Kaplan baldly assert that "writing abilities are not naturally acquired," but Grabe and Kaplan seem to use the word "naturally" to mean "biologically" as opposed to "culturally": they assert that writing abilities "must be culturally (rather than biologically) transmitted in every generation, whether in schools or other assisting environments." They go on:

> The logical conclusion to draw from this [acquired/learned] distinction is that writing is a technology, a set of skills which must be practiced and learned through experience. Defining writing in this way helps to explain why writing of the more complex sorts causes great problems for students; the skills required do not come naturally, but rather are gained through conscious effort and much practice. It is also very likely, for this reason, that numbers of students may never develop the more sophisticated composing skills which transform information into new texts. . . . Saying that writing is a technology implies only that the way people learn to write is essentially different from the way they learn to speak, and there is no guarantee that any person will read or write without some assistance. (6)

Granted, we may think of writing as a kind of technology, that it is not acquired in the same way that speech is, that it is transmitted culturally and requires practice. Still, a great deal of evidence suggests that in certain circumstances, many young children seem to be able to develop much of their early writing ability—the ability to physically form letters on paper, the ability to recognize certain sound-letter correspondences, the ability to use certain genre conventions—spontaneously, without instruction, if they are immersed in a literate environment and their attempts to act like literate adults are encouraged. Obviously, the degree to which young writers can acquire certain writing abilities will depend on their own abilities and motivation and the degree to which they have been acquainted with some aspect of writing they either want or need to learn. On the other hand and just as obviously, most young children need explicit help in learning their letters or in deciding what to put in the letter to Grandma.

There are, however, reasons for thinking that over time, novice writers need to acquire at least some sense of how any aspect of writing works before explicit instruction in that aspect of writing will be effective. That is to say, children need to have some sense of what letters of the alphabet are and how they function in some familiar genre before receiving lessons in how to print those letters. Otherwise, the instruction in writing the alphabet will make no sense. Likewise, older children need to know what stories are and the various conventions of the genre before they can be asked to write a story in response to a prompt. By the time they reach high school, students need to have a more sophisticated sense of what stories are in order for more advanced instruction to make any sense. For example, they need to know how sensory details function in a story and generally how few details are needed in order to describe a person or scene in order for instruction in being more detailed to make any sense. To put it most paradoxically, in general a writer has to already know how to write before writing instruction can be of any help. Or in the language of current critical theory, novice writers are "always already" inscribed in various writing practices before they receive explicit instruction in writing, and explicit instruction will make sense only if it builds on what writers already know how to do.

However, the most powerful reason for thinking that learning to write, even for older students, is mostly acquired and not learned through explicit instruction is that the conventions of writing, as with speech, are entirely too complex for us to internalize self-consciously, through explicit instruction.

Consider for example how we learn words. By one estimate, by the age of seventeen, we have learned approximately five thousand words per year for sixteen years; that is thirteen words per day. We learn the overwhelming majority of these words in the ordinary give-and-take of conversation with no formal training and outside the walls of schools (Miller and Gildea 94). That is, we acquire our vocabulary; we do not learn it through explicit instruction.

But there is a more interesting aspect to how we learn words, which suggests why learning a language explicitly is inefficient and in many ways counterproductive. Put children in school, try to teach them vocabulary by having them look words up in a dictionary or by having them study the words in model sentences, and then use the words in their own writing, and the likely result is sentences like these:

- Me and my parents correlate, because without them I wouldn't be here. [Correlate: to be related one to the other]
- Mrs. Morrow stimulated the soup. [Stimulate: stir up]
- The blue chair was usurped from the room. [Usurped: taken]

Why do children misuse words such as these? One possible reason is that words are not discrete bits of knowledge; they are tokens with a range of potential meanings, depending on the contexts in which they are used. Given a dictionary definition, children will latch onto one aspect of the definition and simply substitute one term for another: they will use "correlate" as a substitute for "to be related to one another." Given model sentences, they may do better, because with models, they must abstract the meaning of the word from the context. However, in the classroom, even with a great deal of attention to model sentences, if they are asked to use a new word in a sentence, once again they will simply substitute one apparently synonymous expression for another. What the children are missing from dictionary definitions and model sentences is any sense of the range of a word's potential meanings and the contexts in which those meanings may be invoked. In order to really learn a word, children need to hear it used in a variety of contexts over time, so that they can internalize what aspects of the word's meaning is emphasized in each context.

To provide specific drill in this natural process of acquiring words would be extremely complex. It would involve providing instruction in how the word differs in both meaning and application from its synonyms. For example, it would involve explaining and giving examples of the difference between "usurp" and "take":

> When you usurp a title, job or position from someone else, you seize it or take it away even though you have no right to it. In the sentence "The king's brother failed in his effort to usurp the throne" *throne* means not just the piece of furniture the kings sits on; it also stands as a symbol of the king's authority. (Miller and Gildea 99)

In other words, formal instruction would have to make explicit the subtle distinctions between words and their application in a wealth of contexts, which we recognize subconsciously in our natural acquisition of words. Such instruction would be extremely time-consuming and inefficient, which is why we acquire our vocabulary; we do not learn it in school.

But there may be a larger point to how we learn vocabulary: in order to learn how to apply different aspects of a word in different contexts: we *must hear the word in many contexts.* Explicit instruction is simply not rich enough to provide all of the contexts in which words occur and with which we need to be familiar if we are to truly learn how to use a word in all its different meanings and the subtle ways it differs from its synonyms.

All of this calls into question the rationale for explicitly teaching vocabulary development. If whatever words we choose to teach are an insignificant fraction of the total words our students will wind up knowing, then teaching vocabulary in and of itself is totally arbitrary and dependent on the teacher's whim. The only justification for explicit instruction in vocabulary development might be to insure that students know the essential concepts of the subject matter of a course.

Now consider the transition of the conventions of speech to the conventions of writing. We do not necessarily speak in complete sentences. In speech, fragments are common, as when we reply to a question such as "When are you leaving?" with the phrase "Next week." But most written genres, except for transcribed dialogue and literary language that tries to capture the flavor of speech, require complete sentences. How do children learn which elements of their speech are sentences and are thus acceptable in writing? Consider that to describe all of the variations of a simple grammatically acceptable sentence, we would have to note that a sentence is composed of a subject and a predicate, that the subject of a sentence is composed of five kinds of noun phrases (proper nouns, indefinite pronouns, determiners plus common nouns, plural common nouns without determiners, and personal pronouns), that predicates must have at least a verb phrase containing one of five kinds of verbs (intransitive verbs, which can stand alone or take a particle or a complement, such as "sat down," "drowned in the pool"; transitive verbs, which must be accompanied by a noun phrase; "become"-type verbs, which must be followed by a substantive; "seem"-type verbs, which must be followed by an adjective; "have"-type verbs, which must be followed by an noun phrase. In addition, predicates may contain auxiliaries, which include models ("may," "can," "shall") and words that indicate "aspect," such as "have" and a past participle ("had gone") or a form of "be" and a present participle ("was going").

I could go on and on. I haven't begun to mention the various ways adverbials fit into simple sentences or the ways noun phrases function as direct objects of verbs and the objects of prepositions in adverbials. Nor have I mentioned many of the more subtle rules that govern the placement and choice of words in simple sentences: the distinction between count and noncount nouns, for example, or the order of more than one adverbial of different kinds or the function and meaning of tense in verbs.

However, here's the point: clearly the standard ways we have of teaching sentences don't begin to get at the complexity of the subject. Teachers may try to explain sentences by saying things such as "Sentences express a complete thought." Isn't "no" in response to a question a complete thought? Or teachers may say that sentences must have a subject and a predicate. Well, yes. But subjects and predicates come in so many different forms with so many sub-rules that it is very difficult for students to comprehend the terms or recognize them in various contexts.

I know of only one English curriculum that ever tried to introduce students to the full range of grammatical complexity of the English sentence, and that was the curriculum developed by Paul Roberts. Rather ironically, Roberts' curriculum took eight years to teach students the complexity of simple sentences, and thus, Roberts' students were speaking and writing the simple sentences he was trying to describe long before they were taught to recognize the grammatical descriptions of what they were already doing. The fact is that we learn to write simple sentences without formal instruction, or more accurately, we learn to write simple sentences in spite of formal instruction that doesn't begin to make us consciously aware of all the things we have to know in order to write simple sentences appropriately. Indeed, there is good reason to think that formal instruction in simple sentences can succeed only if students already tacitly know in some sense what simple sentences are.

The same could be said for our ability to write paragraphs, a form of language that occurs only in writing. Paragraphs come in so many different forms, with topic sentences in a single clause, "assembled," or implied, at the beginning, middle, and end of one paragraph or a group of paragraphs, that it is difficult to generalize at all about their "structure" or whether they have a structure at all (Braddock; Popken; Meade and Ellis).

Now, anecdotal evidence suggests that writing teachers usually teach paragraphing as a matter of stating a topic sentence and supporting it with details or as a matter of following a number of explicit patterns: comparison-and-contrast and cause-and-effect, to name just two. But clearly, the studies I have just summarized argue that formal instruction in paragraphing does not begin to confront the complexity of how paragraphs are actually written outside of classrooms. Indeed, most of the theorists who have confronted the problem of how we learn to write paragraphs have come to the conclusion that when we compose, we don't structure paragraphs in and of themselves. We tend to write top-down, as it were: we compose in whole discourse, in genres, and paragraphing is a way of breaking up our larger patterns of organization into readable "chunks" (Pitkin; Karrfalt). Paul Rodgers goes so far as to deny that paragraphs have any inherent structure at all, that paragraphing is simply a form of punctuation, a way of drawing attention to the sentences that occur just before and just after the indentation. According to these theorists, any explicit knowledge we have about paragraph structure, such as topic sentence/supporting details, is simply a way of checking our writing in certain situations. If we think we are rambling or not quite getting our point across, topic sentence/supporting details is one strategy among many for making our point more straightforward.

Whatever the particular theory of paragraphing, it seems clear that we must acquire the ability to paragraph, just as we acquire the ability to write in complete sentences. To do so, apparently we *must read paragraphs in many contexts* in order to internalize a complex notion of all the ways paragraphs can be written. Once again, explicit instruction is simply not rich enough to provide all of the contexts in which paragraphs are written in so many different ways.

I could make the same argument for genres, which scholars and critics are coming to realize are more like simple sentences in a natural language than they are rigid forms, such as the Petrarchan sonnet. Genres can be described and codified, but these descriptions are always reductive. It might be more useful to understand genres as part of the patterning of all language, the way human beings develop recurring strategies to use in recurring situations (Berkenkotter and Huckin; Devitt).

Take for example the news story, which is often considered a rigid form with a lead and an anticlimactic structure. However, Janet Giltrow has shown that the opening paragraphs of the crime stories she studied ranged from eight to twenty-three sentences, and while the opening sentence always mentioned the crime and the criminal's sentence, the rest of the paragraphs had no set order, and the only information contained in all of the articles was a description of the events of the crime. Otherwise, the remaining information varied considerably and could be included or not, and be in any order (162). Once again, all the variations of a news report seem to be too rich and complex to be formally taught and learned. I think the same could be said of most genres, no matter how "closed" and conventionally formal they are. Like many other aspects of writing, such as syntax and paragraphing, genre conventions are too complex to be learned by explicit instruction.

Robert Gundlach summarizes the evidence of the effects of explicit instruction this way:

> Becoming literate seems to depend on instructional support and special conditions of language use associated with school. . . . However, while children's writing develops largely in such contexts, there is at best an indirect relation between what children are taught about writing and what they learn. Indeed, some children learn to write with little or no instruction, while others fail to develop as writers, no matter how much instruction is provided for them. ("On the Nature" 134)

A Model of Acquisition and the Role of Instruction

According to Gee,

> The real issue [of writing instruction]—though too little debated directly in these terms, is when and how explicit information can be efficacious. . . . We still have to know what sorts of explicit information need to be given in what form and when in the learning process. And this requires theories of learning, of classroom practices, and of the nature and structure of the sorts of knowledge we want people to acquire. ("Vygotsky" 271)

Exactly. However, the conceptual difficulty here is that if novice writers develop their ability to use different aspects of writing at different rates and through different stages, depending on the novices' own capabilities and experience, and if novices primarily acquire these abilities in the first place, then we may need a different theory of learning and a different theory of instruction for each sort of knowledge we want novices to acquire. A single unified "theory" of instruction in writing may not be very helpful.

Figure 2.1 then is a very abstract model for the acquisition of writing. The central feature of this model is that it tries to capture the way novice writers must internalize representations of a wide range of experience and then practice using those representations over time, often with only partial success.

A Particular Cultural or Social Context

Task Environment		Task Environment	
Representation of target genre $\longrightarrow$	intermediate genre	Modification of presentation of target genre $\longrightarrow$	Intermediate genre

Apply the same developmental stages to each aspect of text

Spelling
Punctuation
Syntax
Generalized Strategies
    Invention Strategies
    Organizational Strategies
    Rhetorical Strategies
    Drafting Strategies
    Editing Strategies

Apply the influence of background/experience

Previous experience with text
Learning style
Gender
Identity
Formal instruction

Fig. 2.1. A Tentative Model of Writing Acquisition

Gee is hopeful that future "theories of learning, of classroom practices, and of the nature and structure of the sorts of knowledge we want people to acquire"—or in my terms, refinements of various models of learning and acquisition—will help us to decide "what sorts of explicit information need to be given in what form and when in the learning process." Perhaps. But over the past decades, many scholars in many disciplines have devised any number of concepts of explicit instruction that might be helpful to novice writers. Unfortunately, the scholars promoting various forms of explicit instruction have failed to convince the profession of their worth. Some of these forms of explicit instruction are: *strategies* or techniques for accomplishing similar tasks; for example, the technique of brainstorming for getting ideas, or the technique of proofreading for one kind of error at a time; *procedural facilitation,* in which teachers describe a certain writing procedure such as revision in concrete terms, and then design a way to make that procedure routine for novices in order to reduce the "information-processing burden of [their] mental operations" (Bereiter and Scardamalia, *Psychology* 254–56); the *environmental mode* and *focus on inquiry,* in which teachers provide clear and specific objectives, select activities to engage students, usually in groups, in "specifiable processes important to some particular aspect of writing"; and then organize discussions or other forms of peer interaction to explore the implications of what the activities have taught (Hillocks, *Research* 122); *distributed cognition,* in which groups work on related tasks and teach each other (Ann Brown et al.); *scaffolding,* in which teachers help novices accomplish tasks without simplifying the task itself, but by simplifying the learner's role in accomplishing the task "through the graduated intervention of the teacher" (Greenfield 119); and a pedagogy of *situated practice, overt instruction, critical framing,* and *transformed practice,* in which teachers immerse students in various experiences that require writing, help them to focus on what is important about these experiences, provide a critical framework for interpreting their experiences, and re-immerse them in the experience "so that the students can demonstrate how they can design and carry out, in a reflective manner, new practices embedded in their own goals and values" (New London Group 35).

The most promising of these ways of conceptualizing explicit instruction might be scaffolding and the pedagogy of situated practice, overt instruction, critical framing, and transformed practice, both of which I will deal with in some detail when I present my analysis of writing instruction at the college level in chapter 7. Here I would simply note that all of these notions have a certain amount of theoretical and empirical justification. And to a certain extent they share a common emphasis on engaging active learners in intellectually challenging tasks that allow the learners to practice skills and to reflect on and generalize from what they have learned from those tasks. I suspect that refinements of these ideas will be severely constrained by all of the factors I have mentioned. Future models of explicit instruction will have to consider the social background and personal experience of the novice; the gender, style of learning, and motivation and goals of the writer; and the degree to which the writer finds writing useful in meeting those goals. As a result, refinements to the model will continue to be more and more contextual studies, such as those by Elaine Chin and by Patrick Dias and his colleagues. These refinements will provide more information, for example, about how people with certain backgrounds and with certain learning styles learn to develop a certain aspect of writing in certain social situations. This new information will be helpful to those of us who are trying to promote similar kinds of writing for similar people in similar conditions. But this research will not significantly alter our current model of the active learner actively constructing meaning.

The evidence that we acquire the ability to write strongly suggests that novice writers need at some point to be, in a sense, *immersed* in various forms of discourse and the contexts in which they are used, so that novices can recognize and internalize a range of sentences, paragraphing, and genre conventions and other aspects of writing and how variations of the elements of writing effect meaning. To be an expert writer means being "fluent" in writing certain genres in a certain social contexts. It means being able to call up all of the resources of writing, both broad strategies and those limited to particular genres in particular contexts, resources the writer has acquired from reading and writing in similar contexts. It means being able to apply those resources as needed. This can occur only if writers have sufficient experience in reading and writing in the social contexts in which they write.

Thus, there is something very limited about the common practice of teaching writing by introducing students to a small number of examples of a given genre; supplying them with a few rules of thumb—when writing narrative, for example, use specific detail; having them go through the writing process—getting ideas, planning, drafting, revising, and editing, even with appropriate feedback from teachers and peers; and then moving on to another genre, especially if these genres are school genres, the academic equivalent of the intermediate forms that young children produce spontaneously as they develop their internal representations of what it means to write a particular kind of discourse. This pedagogical practice in effect institutionalizes the teaching of genres that in young children we recognize as only approximations of real discourse.

The evidence that writing is acquired also suggests that beyond the sentence-level, writing is a process of *socialization,* of novice writers learning to use writing as a tool in order to accomplish particular tasks that they find meaningful and useful or in order to belong to social groups who can use writing as a means of participating in the group. In this sense, much of what passes for explicit instruction in schools may not be directly related to how students actually acquire the ability to write; rather, explicit instruction in schools may be *analogous* to the process of acquisition. That is, in learning the conventions of school genres students may learn to pay attention to the kinds of textual features they will need to learn in order to master the genres they will use outside the classroom. And in learning to write school genres in order to succeed in school or in order to please their parents and teachers, students may learn the power of writing as a means of learning and belonging, and this power may motivate them to unconsciously pay attention to how writing is done outside the classroom.

All this suggests that formal schooling and explicit instruction have a limited role to play in promoting writing, that the appropriate role for teachers and mentors may be to *stage manage,* as it were, novice writers' involvement with reading and writing, to provide occasions for them to be themselves, active learners, and to provide opportunities for them to think about and reflect on what they are learning, to make salient the conventions of writing and aspects of contexts they need to be aware of when they write. All the evidence seems to indicate that we acquire an ability to write through the complex interaction of a large number of factors, such as our own background and experience, our interests and motivation and goals for the future, our familiarity with print, our preferred learning style, our gender, our sense of ourselves as writers. Formal explicit instruction will never be able to adequately compensate for these factors if they are missing. All formal explicit instruction can do is provide a context in which students of any age acquire literacy and a critical or analytic framework for thinking about the learning process. We can never teach writing from scratch. Our students "always already" have to know how to do much of what we want them to do or they would never understand our instruction.

If there are many different kinds of literacy and if we become literate through a long intellectual adventure in which our writing gradually approximates the language of the many different discourse communities we wish to join, then in order to improve our ability to promote writing at the college level, we may have to find ways to integrate instruction in writing into as many different settings and communities as possible and to make classroom practice more relevant to writing as it is done outside the academy. We may have to find ways to connect students to the writing they want to do and have to do for whatever goals they have for themselves. Placing students in those social contexts in which they need to write and want to write may be the best way to develop their sense of target genres, the kinds of writing actually done outside the classroom, and it may also be the best way to motivate them to work through their own intermediate genres and school genres so that their writing approximates more quickly writing as it is actually done in the social contexts in which they want to live.

3 How We Compose

VARIOUS SCHOLARS IN COMPOSITION studies have argued that the one great contribution of the field to our understanding of writing instruction has been the promotion of the "process approach" (see Crowley, *Composition* 187–214 for an overview). After all, the value of the process approach, which began in the late 1960s and early 1970s, seems to have been confirmed by the major research on composing and cognitive processes done in the 1980s: as a pedagogy it provides concrete concepts such as invention and revision techniques for instructors to teach; it provides models to guide instructors in providing feedback and advice to their students (working through drafts, concentrating on only a few major concepts at a time, saving editing until the end); and above all, it is based on what we in the field *know* about how writing is done. The process approach "feels right": it seems to confirm our intuitive sense of how we actually write.

Of course, much of the discussion and application of the "process approach" seems to imply a fairly straightforward linear model of composing—invention, planning, drafting, revising, editing—and we can all cite exceptions to this model in our own experience and in the published accounts of professional writers. There are times when writers do not use invention techniques; they seem to respond "spontaneously" to the demands of a particular piece of writing. There are times when writers do not revise; the first draft seems to be entirely appropriate and need no further tinkering. There are writers who edit as they go and do no major editing when they are at the end of a series of drafts.

And of course, if we become reflective, we must admit that the model implied by the process approach has difficulty accounting for such two widely different composing processes as these:

One evening in the middle of April I had an experience which seems worth describing for those who are interested in the methods of poetic production. It was a sultry spring night. I was feeling dull minded and depressed, for no assignable reason. After sitting lethargically in the ground floor room for about three hours after dinner, I came to the conclusion that there was nothing for it but to take my useless brain to bed. On my way from the arm-chair to the door I stood by the writing table. A few words had floated into my head as though from nowhere. . . . I picked up a pencil and wrote the words on a sheet of notepaper. Without sitting down, I added a second line. It was as if I were re-membering rather than thinking. In this mindless, recollecting manner I wrote down my poem in a few minutes. When it was finished I read it through, with no sense of elation, merely wondering how I had come to be writing a poem when feeling so stupid. I then went heavily upstairs and fell asleep without think-ing about it again. . . . The poem was *Everyone Sang*, which has since become a stock anthology piece. (Siegfried Sassoon, qtd. in Britton, "Composing" 23)

As he writes, Bill engages in numerous revising tactics. He writes a sentence, stops to examine it by switching it around, going back to add clauses, or com-bining it with other text on the same page or a different sheet of paper. For the assigned writing task, he began with one sheet of paper, moved to another, tore off some of it and discarded it, and added part back to a previous sheet. At home when writing a longer paper, he will similarly engage in extensive cut-ting and pasting. (Muriel Harris 183)

What do these two acts of composing have in common? It depends on what we mean. At a very abstract level, we might say that both acts of com-posing illustrate a person getting an idea for something to write and imple-menting that idea with appropriate syntax, organization, detail, and a tone relative to his purpose, audience, and context. In another sense, of course, the two acts of composing have very little in common at all. For Siegfried Sassoon, the idea for the poem seemed to come to him out of the blue, and he found the words, the order, the detail, the tone quite fluently, almost as if the poem had been merely dictated by some inner voice (for an example of a person composing academic prose with the same fluency, see MacNealy, Speck, and Simpson).

Sassoon's experience is evidence for what Stephen Witte calls a "pre-text": "the mental construction of 'text' prior to transcription," "a writer's linguis-tic representation of intended meaning, a 'trial locution' that is produced in the mind, stored in the writer's memory, and sometimes manipulated mentally prior to being transcribed as written text" ("Pre-Text" 397). Pre-texts differ from more traditional planning in that they come close to be-ing the final wording that writers put on the page; planning is more abstract. In his study of pre-texts, Witte found that writers create and use pre-texts in many different ways. Some writers use pre-text hardly at all; others use it a great deal. Some writers create short pre-texts and use them in combination with more abstract outlines and plans; others seem to use short or more extensive pre-texts in various combinations, depending on the task and the context. Witte concludes that "different writers make different uses of pre-text during composing," and "pre-texts can vary considerably with respect to extensiveness and function during composing" ("Pre-Text" 420).

Bill, on the other hand, uses pre-text hardly at all in writing graduate papers. Earlier in her story about Bill, Muriel Harris reports that Bill resists "any attempt at clarification before writing." He starts with a broad topic, so that he can decide what is most interesting about it. He will actually compose four or five drafts, each two to four pages in length, while he thinks through the implications of his material and finally "knows what he will write about" (181). Then he continues his struggle to shape his material, sentence by sentence, paragraph by paragraph, section by section, adding and subtracting material, transposing, combining. Bill claims that he needs to produce "large quantities of text because he needs to see it in order to see if he wants to retain it" and because "the text he generates is also on occasion a heuristic for more text" (183). In other words, Bill needs to *see* most of his writing physically in front of him in order to compose. Harris calls Bill a multi-draft writer with a preference for open-ended exploring. Although Harris did not study Sassoon's composing process, she would probably call Sassoon a one-draft writer with a preference for limiting his choices in composing fairly quickly.

I doubt if we can account for the differences in these composing processes from the fact that the writers are composing in different genres. Not all poets compose fluently in pre-text; not all graduate students need as many drafts as Bill to decide on what they want to say and to work out the structure and evidence of their research papers. In similar circumstances, people seem to compose the same genre in many different ways with different degrees of satisfaction and varying degrees of success.

The fact that writers compose in such different ways might give us pause when we think about how or in what sense the implied model of the "process approach" accounts for the way writing is actually done. And if we look at the various ways that composition studies has conceptualized the process of composing over the past forty years, we will see that our models of composing have become increasingly sophisticated and complex. In the 1960s and 1970s, a great deal of literature in the field was devoted to promoting what Robert Connors and Cheryl Glenn call the *stage model theory* of composing: planning, drafting, and revision in a fairly straightforward linear way (101). Often theorists included invention as an aspect of planning, which was also called prewriting, perhaps because "Prewriting" was the title of an influential research report during the period by Gordon Rohman and Albert Wlecke. Indeed, the popularity of the stage model theory seems to have been based on the work of Rohman and Wlecke, even though they did not study the composing process per se; instead they were interested in creativity: how to stimulate students so that they would write expressive personal essays with more enthusiasm, conviction, and authenticity. The methods Rohman and Wlecke decided upon to increase the creativity of their students were journal writing, meditation, and the study of analogies, and they found that students who studied and used these techniques did in fact write better personal essays.

Rohman and Wlecke's major pedagogical influence may have been to stimulate an interest in journal writing in composition classes. However, their main contribution to theory was that they distinguished between thinking and writing: all of their exercises in journal writing, meditation, and using analogies were designed to help students think *before* they started writing. This was a distinction that later theorists would take vigorous exception to.

The other major influence on the stage model theory was Janet Emig's *The Composing Processes of Twelfth Graders*. Emig examined the composing processes of eight high school seniors, using a case study method to elicit information about their writing behavior. In general, Emig found that when composing aloud, as we might expect, the students went back again and again to certain things they had already written or things they identified as problems. Much of their composing was a self-conscious attempt to put teacher directives, such as to "be direct, concise, and specific," into practice. Although all of the students mentioned "revision," "proofreading," and "correcting," none one of them actually did it—at least for Emig's study.

From these observations, Emig concluded that composing is recursive; it "does not occur as left-to-right, solid, uninterrupted activity with an even pace" (84). Rather, people compose according to their own individual rhythms, which start and stop, ebb and flow, according to what comes to mind as they try to juggle what they want to say in relation to what they have already said, their larger goal, and their accumulated experience of how writing should be done in the situation in which they find themselves.

Emig has received considerable criticism for her methodology, much of which she grants: the small, skewed samples of student writing; the use of compose-aloud protocols; the fact that her results were not correlated with any outside measure of writing ability (North 199–203), but perhaps her major contribution to the literature on composing processes is that she drew attention to composing as an activity, a kind of behavior, indeed a kind of process, and that her study prompted composition studies as a field to develop more significant, more carefully controlled methods of studying composing.

Research in composing processes made giant strides after Emig. Competing models flourished. For example, Carl Bereiter ("Development") listed six different systems of skills we seem to rely on when we write: language fluency, idea fluency, conventions, social cognition, literary aesthetics, and reflective thought. Sondra Perl and Arthur Egendorf conceptualized the ways we discover new things to say in two general categories: retrospective and prospective structuring.

Then in 1980 arrived the most well-known artifact in the history of composition studies: the cognitive model of the composing process by John Hayes and Linda Flower (see fig. 3.1).

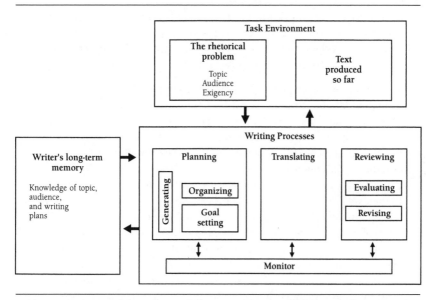

Fig. 3.1. Structure of the Hayes and Flower Writing Model (Hayes and Flower 11)

For the rest of the decade, this model inspired an intense discussion in the field about the nature of the composing process and the significance of empirical research. Much of the discussion was critical. Many scholars pointed out oversimplifications in the model; others questioned the validity of the way Flower and Hayes arrived at the their model—through the analysis of "thinking aloud" protocols (Witte, "Revising"). Interestingly, most of the responses to Flower and Hayes were analytical and critical. Few researchers attempted to duplicate or refine Flower and Hayes's methods in order to determine whether "thinking aloud" protocols would be interpreted in similar ways by different groups of people; more significantly, no one developed an alternative method for devising a more valid model. Alternative models did spring up here and there, but none of them gained much of a following (Bereiter and Scardamalia, *Psychology;* de Beaugrande). By the end of the 1980s, when composition studies began to consider the social context for writing, even Linda Flower had to admit the limitations of mental models of composing and the need for more context-based models.

As a result, our current models are no longer linear and are so recursive that it seems inappropriate to identify the various elements of composing as *stages*. The latest models of composing processes suggest that all composing blends the various "stages" of writing in ways that cannot be accounted for except in the most general terms, and the latest models all accept the fact that a great deal of the composing process is so dependent on a rhetorical context that generalizations about the relative influence of planning, drafting, reviewing, knowledge of the topic and audience, self-conscious monitoring, and revising and editing—to name just a few of the elements of a possible model—tell us very little about any particular act of composing. Patricia Bizzell puts it this way:

> We know that the act of composing through writing is a complex process. Although we are beginning to identify characteristic moments or stages in this process, we cannot say exactly what are the relationships of these stages one to another. We can say that we know such relationships exist, that is, the composing process is hierarchical, and also that they are not necessarily ordered serially, that is, the composing process is recursive. We cannot say that there is one composing processes invariably successful for all writers, for all purposes. Rather, we know that composing processes vary both as the same writer attempts different kinds of discourses and as different writers attempt the same kinds of discourse, and that such variations may be necessary to success in composing. The current state of our knowledge of composing permits the limited generalizations that successful composing results more often from attention to the thinking required by a piece of writing than to its adherence to standard conventions of grammar, spelling, and so on; and that successful composing results more often from a process that allows for rereading, rethinking, and rewriting than from one in which time limitations or other pressures force a rush to closure. I believe that we can also conclude—although this is perhaps more debatable—that "successful" composing results in writing that participates actively in the language-using practices of a particular community, without slavishly imitating them. ("Composing" 66)

Once again, we seem to be facing a conceptual difficulty in teaching writing: if most mature writers do not write in a linear way and do not proceed through recognizable stages; if, as Bizzell says, "composing processes vary both as the same writer attempts different kinds of discourses and as different writers attempt the same kinds of discourse, and that such variations may be necessary to success in composing"; and if successful writers participate "actively in the language-using practices of a particular community, without slavishly imitating them," what then do we mean when we refer to the composing process? And even more to the point, what do we in composition studies mean when we claim to teach the composing process? Why should we teach the writing process in any particular way?

Perhaps we can justify the practice of teaching an explicit writing process by arguing that only mature writers with a certain amount of experience compose so recursively, that novice writers need the structure of an explicit process so that they can more self-consciously develop their own particular ways of composing. Perhaps. But before we deal with this issue, let us look in more detail at two models of composing and see why they may have reached the limits of what such models can tell us.

Models of Composing

Models of composing have all of the conceptual difficulties of models of learning, which I dealt with in chapter 2. Models of composing are necessarily based on what we can infer about mental life from observations of our physical behavior when we write, the written products of that behavior, and introspection into our own mental processes when we write. We have no direct knowledge of what goes on in our minds while we compose. As with learning in general, scholars and researchers of composing mostly construct taxonomies of the things we do mentally when we compose, and then they arrange these lists of possible mental operations into a model that represents a possible relationship between the various concepts suggested by the taxonomy.

The Flower and Hayes Model of Composing as a Cognitive Process

It is easy to get caught up in the early work of Flower and Hayes. They seemed to be onto something. In the unveiling of their cognitive model, they argued strenuously for the reality of the various elements in the model: that the model "identifies not only subprocesses of the composing process, but also the organization of those processes," and that the model could be fine-tuned to "describe individual differences in composing styles" (Hayes and Flower 10). That is, they argued that the model is something more than just a list of the things that the mind knows, such as what the writer may want to write about, the writers' knowledge of the audience, the task environment, and the writer's previous experience writing various kinds of discourse; and what the mind can do, such as generate ideas, set goals, plan, and organize. They argued that their model illustrates how those processes are organized and related to each other: that the writer's long-term memory is a mental function clearly distinct from the writing process per se, and that the writer's long-term memory can be distinguished from the writer's conception of the task environment. In short, they strongly implied that their model bore a powerful resemblance to mental reality, to the way our minds actually work when we compose. If we look at how Flower and Hayes reached this conclusion, we will see the difficulties and limitations of trying to construct any model of composing.

To argue that their model has some kind of reality, Flower and Hayes analyze "thinking aloud" protocols, in which "subjects are asked to say aloud everything they think and everything that occurs to them while performing the [writing] task, no matter how trivial it may seem" (Hayes and Flower 4). In analyzing these protocols, Flower and Hayes concentrate on three aspects of their model: the generating process, whose function is "to retrieve information relevant to the writing task from long-term memory" (Hayes and Flower 12); the organizing process, whose function is "to select the most useful of the materials retrieved by the GENERATING process and to organize them into a writing plan" (14); and the translating process, whose function is "to take material from memory under the guidance of the writing plan and to transform it into acceptable written English sentences" (15). Flower and Hayes's primary evidence of the reality of their categories is the close analysis of one fourteen-page protocol in particular, a protocol they claim "can be divided quite cleanly into three sections," the first of which is dominated by statements indicating that the writer is generating ideas, the second of which is dominated by statements indicating that the writer is organizing, and the third of which is dominated by statements indicating that the writer is translating (21).

Flower and Hayes devised an elaborate scheme to assure that the way they recognized and categorized the textual evidence for each aspect of the composing process was reliable, and they concluded that while many of the items—words, phrases, or sentences identifiable "as being written during a single segment or several contiguous segments"—in section 1 were "complete" or "grammatical," most were not. Items in section 2 typically were part of a systematically indented, alphabetized, or numbered structure. And two-thirds of the items in section 3 were well-formed, and many of them contained interrogatives. Interrogatives did not appear anywhere else in the protocol but in section 3. What is interesting about these results is that from 10 to 15 percent of the content statements in all three sections seem to be devoted to editing.

What to make of all this? Flower and Hayes assert that they have found significant support for the notion that their model goes beyond an intuition that composing involves a number of subprocesses such as planning, organizing, and editing. They argue that their model "specifies the organization of these processes" and that it can "account for individual differences" (Hayes and Flower 29). This seems to be a claim that the model actually describes something the mind does in discrete processes, which are hierarchically arranged: for example, that we can clearly distinguish generating ideas from organizing, which are both subprocesses of planning, and that editing is a subprocess of reviewing, which can clearly be distinguished from planning.

The difficulty with this bold assertion is that Flower and Hayes go on to caution that their model does not suggest that writing proceeds in stages. Writing may generally proceed through a series of stages, but not always: "The model is recursive and allows for a complex intermixing of stages" (Hayes and Flower 29). In particular, editing seems to be intermixed in all of the other aspects of composing. In fact, it is possible to look at the data and conclude that "the whole writing process . . . is a part of an EDITING subprocess. Because EDITING can interrupt any other process, these processes can appear within any other process" (29). This is an extraordinary admission and calls into question the degree to which the model represents the "actual" hierarchical organization of composing processes generally. All Flower and Hayes may have done is document that generating, organizing, and translating tend to occur in order but that they do not do so necessarily. If this is so, all we really have evidence for is a list of things we do while we compose.

Further analysis confirmed that the conceptual categories of the Flower and Hayes model are so blurred that it is difficult to use them to describe in any detail how we compose. In fact, the categories are so blurred that they are difficult to use reliably in analyzing protocols (see Stotsky, "On Planning").

With a new emphasis in the late 1980s and early 1990s on the social and cultural context of communication, Flower herself came to see the problem of creating a model of the cognitive processes involved in writing differently than she had before. To Flower, the problem was that we do not know "how cognition and context do in fact interact, in specific but significant situations"; Flower grants that the model she developed with Hayes "did little more than specify that the 'task environment' was an important element in the process; it failed to account for *how* the situation in which the writer operates might shape composing" ("Cognition" 282–83). Flower notes that early criticism of her work suggested that she and Hayes had not adequately accounted for "people as a social/political aggregate or as members of a discourse community," but Flower argues that such a view does not account for individual differences among members of a social group. The primary difficulty of developing a theory of composing is then, according to Flower, to articulate useful generalizations about composing that are "grounded in specific knowledge about real people writing in significant personal, social, or political situations" ("Cognition" 283).

What Flower assumes of course is that such useful generalizations are possible. But are they? It may depend on what we mean by "useful." Flower offers three broad principles about how context may affect composing. "Principle One: Context Cues Cognition"—that is, our immediate circumstances may give us a reason to write, and our past knowledge and experience may influence how we interpret our circumstances and provide us with criteria for monitoring and evaluating our composing. "Principle Two: Cognition Mediates Context"—that is, writers do not respond to their environment without creating their own internal representation of their task and what they want to accomplish. And finally "Principle Three: A Bounded Purpose Is a Meaningful Rhetorical Act"—that is, writers are in some sense "in control" of what they mean, but that agency is never totally free; it is always constrained by "the assumptions of one's culture, the material realities of the publishing industry, the demands of one's job, or the terms of an assignment" ("Cognition" 292). Flower takes these three broad principles as a way to begin developing a more specific and better articulated theory of how "a big 'C' theoretical Context" and "a big 'C' general theory of Cognition" account for "the small 'c' contexts in which writing is going on" and for "strategic cognition in situ" ("Cognition" 295). What she does not give us is any sense of what such a theory—what I have called "useful generalizations"—would look like, above and beyond her three broad principles. What might such "useful generalizations" look like? I don't know.

Flower constantly implies that in "building" theories of composing we can and ought to do more than all this, that somehow our theories ought to be more "fine grained," that there are some kinds of generalization to be made about composing that are less broad than principles but more widely applicable than individual behavior. What I am groping for is some sense of what those generalizations might be. Could they be some sort of generalizations about the influence of certain social factors, such as race, gender, or class? Some sort of correlation between various kinds of composing behavior and various psychological profiles? Some sort of generalizations about the relevance of common experiences, common environments, or even physical attributes? I don't know, but my natural inclination is to assume that barring evidence to the contrary, composing is determined by such a wide range of factors that no single factor or even small group of factors can help us generalize about how people compose.

Finally, however, Flower admits that all analysis of mental process is hermeneutic, an interpretation, with all of the ambiguity and ambivalence that we associate with the analysis of literary texts:

> But because we cannot *finally know* if the patterns we see [in observational research data] are there, the methods of observational research should be read as *attempts* to test and verify one's claims, as *attempts* to create more precise operational definitions, and/or as *attempts* to rest claims upon multiple, independent observations based on multiple methods. ("Cognition" 303)

Exactly. In the last analysis, all models of composing are just that: models, heuristics for helping us "see" things about composing that we might not have thought of on our own. And perhaps the major contribution of the Flower and Hayes model of the composing process has been to help us "see" the complexity of composing and that there may in fact be a difference between the ways novices and experts compose.

The Nystrand Model

Since the work of Flower and Hayes, a number of theorists have tried to capture the complexity of context in composing. But these models, too, come up against the limit of what we can say, if context is the primary factor in determining how we compose. For example, Martin Nystrand has created a model of composing that takes into account how readers conceptualize their audience and their context, that makes more explicit what Flower and Hayes simply designated as the task environment. Nystrand wanted to know how writers chose issues to deal with, how they decided on the relevant evidence and patterns of organization, or more broadly, the principles that governed "the production of discourse" ("Social-Interactive" 70). And the answer to almost all of these questions, according to Nystrand, is that writers in some sense have their readers in mind: writers recognize that they have knowledge in common with readers, that they have to provide readers with knowledge the readers may not have, and that they are bound to readers through a sense of "reciprocity," an intuitive ability to determine "*what* knowledge they shall exchange when they communicate, plus how they choose to present it in discourse" (*Structure* 53):

> For example, people distinguished by substantial mutual knowledge, e.g., experts such as optometrists or baseball fans, are not bound by reciprocity until they actually collaborate in some joint activity, such as the physicians' attending a medical convention or the baseball fans' attending a game or both mailing a letter. Conversely, individuals who share little or no expert knowledge (e.g., doctors and patients) are nonetheless bound by the terms of reciprocity as soon as they become partners to some particular act (such as doctor-patient consultations). Mutual knowledge alone is neither necessary to nor sufficient for communication though appropriate knowledge is inevitably shared as the conversants uphold their respective ends of the reciprocity principle through communication and comprehension. (*Structure* 54)

In order to account for this sense of mutual knowledge and reciprocity, this sense of what writers and readers share, Nystrand created a model he calls "Social-Interactive." It is based on the idea that writers create a "mutual frame of reference" with readers, what Ragnar Rommetveit calls a "*temporarily shared social reality*," or TSSR for short. Writers introduce the topic of a piece of discourse by satisfying the expectations of readers "vis-à-vis the topic and genre of the text"; in other words, by establishing a clear topic, an appropriate tone, and the other textual elements that serve as a common point of reference with readers, a TSSR. With this common frame of reference, "the discourse is largely structured by the conversants in terms of each other's evolving perspective on the topic and the discourse itself" ("Social-Interactive" 73). Considering the mutual frame of reference they have established with their audience, writers must continuously keep the perspective of their readers in mind in two ways. First, writers need to sustain the discourse by providing readers with additional information that either expands or modifies the original TSSR, always considering what readers may need in order to understand. Secondly, writers need to elaborate on this new information with sufficient definitions, examples, clarifications, and qualifications (for an empirical study that supports Nystrand's model, see Brandt, *Literacy*).

One clear implication of Nystrand's model is that actual words on a page, while not having an "objective" meaning, do have a "semantic potential," which constrains in some ways how readers may interpret them, and that text meaning is determined by a "reciprocity between writers and their readers that binds the writer's intention, the reader's cognition, and properties of text together in the enterprise of text meaning" ("Social-Interactive" 78). Nystrand quotes Bakhtin and Medvedev: "[Message] X is not transmitted from [the writer] to the [reader], but is constructed between them as a kind of ideological bridge is built in the process of their interaction" (152; qtd. in Nystrand, "Social-Interactive" 78).

Clearly, Nystrand makes a strong case that the act of composing is contextually determined in that expert writers compose their texts, in any genre or situation, with an intersubjective sense of how hypothetical readers might construe the words on the page, that the words on the page create a shared context for making meaning. Notice, however, how limited Nystrand's model is in conveying the full implications of writing as a shared reality. The concepts of a mutual frame of reference and reciprocity may give us the tools to talk about how writers and readers interact, but in any given context, the relationships between a certain writer and any two readers may be so different that it would be very difficult to say with any specificity what they share beyond the words on the page. Take one of Nystrand's examples: a doctor-patient relationship. The doctor and patient bring very different backgrounds and experience to the terms the doctor uses in explaining a diagnosis. If the doctor is a good communicator, he or she may use "plain," "simple" language and perhaps a down-home metaphor or two to explain the nature of the patient's disease and how it should be treated. But to a certain extent, as Nystrand admits, these sallies are in a sense projections, best guesses, of how the patient may actually take the words, how the patient will respond, based on very limited, perhaps even stereotypical information. Beyond a certain point, all communication is hermeneutic, interpretive.

Each of the terms of Nystrand's model has its own "grammar," which may vary from genre to genre, discourse community to discourse community, and even from writer to writer. How writers conceptualize readers, how writers determine what readers need to know, what constitutes sufficient support for an assertion, what characterizes an appropriate conclusion, to say nothing of how to apply all of the genre conventions of any particular form of discourse—all of this is beyond the power of a model to convey. And to be fair to Nystrand, it is a problem he recognizes: he notes that "we commit a fallacy . . . if we seek to constitute actual individual cases from structuralist abstractions" ("Social-Interactive" 72).

I cannot imagine how we might go about characterizing composing processes more usefully than Nystrand—or Linda Flower and John Hayes—already have. We might be able to show that two executives writing informative memos to employees on a similar subject engage in similar processes, but the question is whether these similarities are due to similar composing processes or similar constraints. The similarities might very well be due just to the fact that the executives are writing about similar subjects to similar audiences for similar purposes. What we call composing processes may be so determined by contextual factors, such as purpose, audience, and disciplinary knowledge, that we can make no further useful generalizations about composing processes than we already have.

Currently, there is not a great deal of research being published on composing processes, and the reason may very well be that researchers do not know where to go from here. I suspect that future work in composing will be limited to case studies in context, attempts to refine our current models to more accurately portray how various social factors and learning styles may affect the composing process in certain contexts (Chin, Prior). Or researchers in the future may want to explore how a given writer composes differently using different genres in different contexts.

Our models of composing then seem to confirm that composing is so complex and various and dependent on context that we must learn to do it in a very ad hoc way in response to very different circumstances. In addition, people seem to compose in different ways dependent upon their personality and circumstances. This seems to call into question the degree to which writing teachers ought to insist on a certain standard of composing for all of their students. It even seems to call into question the need to help novice writers learn any particular composing strategy or any set of general principles for writing. It suggests that teaching generalizations and principles and processes of writing in the abstract, unrelated to particular tasks, to large groups of young writers is arbitrary, and the success of such enterprises will depend entirely on whether such generalizations, principles, and processes are what any particular young writer needs at that moment. It invites the question, what in the world would be helpful to novice writers above and beyond what they will have to learn for themselves? Perhaps some "tricks of the trade": If you have trouble getting ideas for this project, you might consider this invention strategy. If you are unhappy with a particular draft for a particular reason, you might revise that draft with this in mind.

Such advice is particularly relevant since we cannot claim that a certain kind of composing will necessarily produce better results. For example, learning to revise will not necessarily produce better writing. A number of studies of revision have indicated that the *amount* of revision, at least, bears little relationship to the quality of final drafts (Bridwell; Witte "Revising"; Flower et al., "Detection"). What does make a difference in revision? Flower and her colleagues have a sound answer: the ability of writers to recognize when the words on the page, everything from the spelling of individual words to the overall structure of the writing, do not match their mental goals. Flower and her colleagues demonstrate convincingly the conceptual difficulties novice writers face in detecting when their writing is inadequate and diagnosing what is wrong with it. In doing so, novices must develop a notion of a target text, a sense of what their writing ought to be, so that they have a way to recognize the discrepancy between what they have done and what they could do. But such target texts are complex and cannot be imposed by arbitrary rules about what such texts in general ought to be like. The question is always, in this context, for this draft, what should I be aiming toward? How do writers develop a sense of how everything ought to be on a page, everything from how to spell "receive" to the way a particular structure might work? They seem to acquire such an ability over time—with guided practice and feedback.

The only way to insure that novice writers develop a broad-based ability to compose, then, may be to provide them with a wide range of writing experiences in a wide range of genres and contexts, preferably those social contexts in which they want to participate, and to provide them with a number of composing and revising strategies as they need them. With this kind of experience, they can devise and develop their own composing strategies in context. In other words, explicitly teaching the stages of the writing process as a formula for success may be liberating for students who have been held to rigid standards for school genres such as the five-paragraph theme and who have not been helped to produce those genres. However, students with some experience in writing may find explicit instruction in the composing process, however it is conceptualized, to be beside the point. The composing process may be valuable in teaching writing only as a heuristic for teachers to use when they need it, as a set of strategies to convey to novice writers when they need help in particular situations.

4 Writing as a Social Practice

IN THE LAST TEN OR FIFTEEN YEARS, it has become something of a commonplace in composition studies to argue that writing is in some sense "social." Various composition theorists have called writing "a social activity" or "a social practice"; they have argued that writing is "socially constructed" or "social-epistemic," to name a few varieties of the term. However, none of these conceptions of writing is very well developed.

I have argued thus far that we seem to learn to write primarily by immersion in a variety of literate social contexts, that much of what we know about writing is tacit, an internalization of our interaction with our environment. It seems reasonable, then, that understanding the nature of our interaction with the "social" would help us a great deal in developing our understanding of the nature of writing and how we learn to write. Unfortunately, the very terms that we use to talk about the "social"—context, socialization, discourse communities—are also fraught with difficulty. In this chapter, I would like to briefly survey the way theorists who study writing, or literacy more generally, talk about writing as being social, and then I would like to explore the difficulties of conceptualizing what we mean by the terms "social" and "discourse community."

The Concept of the "Social" in Composition Studies

Of course, writing is obviously social in the sense that we share a language with others, and we share a common set of conventions with which we write certain kinds of discourse. In addition, for most discourse we often write to or for others: writing is social in the sense that it is addressed to audiences. And writing is social in the sense that as children we develop our ability to use language in conjunction with others. As children develop their speaking and writing, their language "gradually approximates" the language of adult or mature speakers. Most scholars in the field of composition studies who promote the idea of writing as a social practice develop these commonsense notions into larger, more comprehensive theories.

For example, Marilyn M. Cooper and Michael Holzman refer to writing as a social "activity." They distinguish their sense of writing as a social activity from Saussure's sense of language as a "communal product"; they want to emphasize writing not as "a common system through which individual minds can communicate" but rather as "a real interaction among social groups and individuals" (ix–x). In addition, Cooper and Holzman distinguish their understanding of writing as a social activity from other theories that emphasize that writing necessarily involves audiences. Rather than focus on the way writers conceptualize readers, which makes writing more of a cognitive process than a social one, Cooper and Holzman prefer to think of an audience as "always present to writers—real people we know and talk with and do other things with": "writing is a way of interacting with others—a social activity"; "it is part of the way in which some people live in the world" (x, xii). Cooper and Holzman cite approvingly the notions of language given by Wilhelm von Humboldt—"language develops only in social intercourse" (36; qtd. in Cooper and Holzman x)—and by M. A. K. Halliday—"language is as it is because of the functions it has evolved to serve in people's lives" (*Language* 4–5; qtd. in Cooper and Holzman x).

Cooper and Holzman's distinctions are interesting but quite problematic. It is not at all clear what a "real interaction" between a writer and a social group is, or in what sense an audience is "always present" to a writer, as we have seen in the theories of the composing process promoted by Martin Nystrand in the previous chapter.

Writing is also considered by various composition theorists to be "social-epistemic." Although the scholars and researchers who espouse this view are many and varied, they may be fairly represented by James Berlin (for a list of possible proponents of social-epistemic rhetoric, see Berlin, "Rhetoric" 488). Berlin first uses the term "epistemic" to refer to a pedagogical theory he otherwise calls "the New Rhetoric." According to the theorists of the New Rhetoric, writing is conditioned by language and its various forms and the social conditions in which that language arose. As a result, Berlin suggests that not only a particular rhetoric or rhetorical theory but all writing, indeed all uses of language, are epistemic:

> truth is always truth for someone standing in relation to others in a linguistically circumscribed situation. The elements of the communication process thus do not simply provide a convenient way of talking about rhetoric. They form the elements that go into the very shaping of knowledge. . . .
>
> Rather than truth being prior to language, language is prior to truth and determines what shapes truth can take. Language does not correspond to the

"real world." It creates the "real world" by organizing it, by determining what will be perceived and not perceived, by indicating what has meaning and what is meaningless. . . .

Truths are operative only within a given universe of discourse, and this universe is shaped by all of these elements [of the rhetorical situation], including the audience. ("Contemporary" 774)

In a later article, Berlin elaborates on his earlier notion of writing-language-rhetoric as epistemic: in this later piece Berlin conceives of rhetoric as ideological and "social-epistemic rhetoric" as "a political act involving a dialectical interaction engaging the material, the social, and the individual writer, with language as the agency of mediation" ("Rhetoric" 488). In the ideology of social-epistemic rhetoric, the writer is a subject who is socially constructed "through the linguistically-circumscribed interaction of the individual, the community, and the material world," and these interactions are all historically and socially conditioned, or constructed ("Rhetoric" 489). To Berlin, who we are, our very selves, our very consciousness, as well as the communities in which we live and the physical world are all limited by "socially-devised definitions," "are all the constructions of an historical discourse, of the ideological formulations inscribed in the language-mediated practical activity of a particular time and place" (489).

As with the concept of the social promoted by Cooper and Holzman, it is difficult to determine the truthfulness of many of Berlin's claims. Clearly, all human beings learn language by interacting with others, but the degree to which our selves, our consciousness, our communities, and our sense of the physical world is "limited" or mediated by language is a matter of some dispute. Indeed, in linguistics, the dispute goes back to the claims of Edward Sapir and Benjamin Lee Whorf that language determines our worldviews (for an analysis of Sapir-Whorf's Hypothesis, see Eastman 75–79; for a critique of social construction see Kent, *Paralogic;* Hacking).

Finally, many scholars think of writing as a tool we use to participate in society or culture. To David Russell, a proponent of activity theory, writing in its many forms is a "material tool" that human beings have developed over time in order to help them meet certain needs or accomplish particular tasks. In order to understand writing, we need to understand the "interlocking, dynamic systems or networks" of human behavior and interaction that "embrac[e] both human agents and their material tools, including writing and speaking" ("Rethinking" 509).

In a similar formulation, literacy scholars Sylvia Scribner and Michael Cole conceive of writing as a range of knowledge and a set of related abilities that allow us to use a symbol system in order to participate in various social practices. They define writing as "a recurrent, goal-directed sequence of activities using a particular technology and particular systems of knowledge" (*Psychology* 236). They elaborate on how social practices involve technology, knowledge, and skills:

We use the term "skills" to refer to the coordinated sets of actions involved in applying this knowledge in particular settings. A practice, then, consists of three components: technology, knowledge, and skills. . . . Whether defined in broad or narrow terms, practice always refers to socially developed and patterned ways of using technology and knowledge to accomplish tasks. Conversely, tasks that individuals engage in constitute a social practice when they are directed to socially recognized goals and make use of a shared technology and knowledge system. . . . [W]e approach literacy as a set of socially organized practices which make use of a symbol system and a technology for producing and disseminating it. Literacy is not simply knowing how to read and write a particular script but applying this knowledge for specific purposes in specific contexts of use. The nature of these practices, including, of course, their technological aspects, will determine the kinds of skills ("consequences") associated with literacy. (*Psychology* 236)

Or to put it more simply, writing is a way of accomplishing some sort of socially recognized task; using a knowledge of written symbols and how to apply them according to linguistic and social conventions, writers get things done.

The view of writing as a social practice is consonant with what we understand about the origins of writing. The earliest examples we have of written symbols, dating from about 3,500 BC, seem to have evolved from very concrete social circumstances. These symbols occur on clay tablets found in various sites in the Middle East, the most famous of which are from ancient Sumer near the Tigris and Euphrates rivers. The symbols on these clay tablets seem to have been part of a system of record keeping for such matters as "land sales, business transactions, and tax accounts" (Crystal 196). Moreover:

Several correspondences have been noted between the symbols used on these tablets and the clay tokens that were used throughout the area for several thousand years before the advent of writing. These tokens, of several distinctive shapes, seem to have been used as a system of accounting from at least the 9th millennium BC. . . . The similarity between the three-dimensional tokens and the two-dimensional inscriptions is striking. (Crystal 196)

A reasonable hypothesis, based on the archeological record, is that writing began as a record of concrete business transactions, and written symbols began as "pictures" of the tokens used in those transactions.

Thinking of writing as a social or cultural phenomenon, as a social activity or practice, as a way of accomplishing a wide variety of tasks using different kinds of knowledge and a set of related abilities conditioned by social and historical circumstances has its advantages. For one thing, the concept of writing as a social phenomenon naturally draws attention to the key question of how we write in any given case: how we vary the recurring features of the social activity or practice—shared text conventions and genre features, similar cognitive processes and composing strategies, and common rhetorical strategies—all for the purpose of accomplishing similar tasks in similar circumstances.

For another, thinking of writing as a social-epistemic activity or practice draws attention to the social, historically conditioned circumstances, the contexts—the immediate circumstances, the discourse communities, the larger social and environmental scenes—in which writing occurs. It helps us to see that writing the way we do is not inevitable but is conditioned by many social factors, some of which we may be able to change.

Thinking of writing as a social practice then forces us to confront the dangers in trying to characterize all writing; it forces us to ask the question, to what degree are large generalizations and broad theories of writing useful. And it forces us to look at writing in all of its overlapping contexts to see how the ways we write, the tools we use, the conventions we follow are a product of larger social forces. However, the notion of writing as a social phenomenon does have its limits.

The Limits of Writing as a Social Practice

The notion of writing as a social practice has few advantages beyond those I have just mentioned. As a concept, it is what philosophers call "opaque." Theories of writing as a social practice are opaque, first of all, because they suggest that we learn to write the way we do through a process of socialization, by internalizing certain aspects of our environment—certain tacit codes or conventions for responding to situations in certain ways or for manipulating text conventions—which can be defined or described and which have a certain amount of causal force; that is, these aspects of our environment can be thought of as the reason, akin to a cause, why people write a certain way. However, social theories of writing are notoriously unclear about what these environmental influences are. When such theories do offer some aspects of the environment that may account for the way people write, these environmental influences can be used to account for very different kinds of writing behavior or very different kinds of discourse.

Secondly, theories of writing as a social practice are opaque because they do not adequately account for how people learn from environmental influences. Theorists of the social use such terms as "socialization" or "internalization" to describe how people learn from the environment, but as we saw with the term "acquisition" in chapter 2, these two terms are very vague. In short, most theories of writing as a social practice are underdeveloped and lack explanatory power.

Let me illustrate by using an argument by Aviva Freedman, a major proponent of the theory that novices can best learn to write particular forms of discourse by immersion in the discipline or professional context of which that form of discourse is an integral part. In one of her research projects, Freedman and her research team observed six undergraduate students in an introductory course in law at a Canadian university. The team observed the students during classes, interviewed them extensively, and analyzed the logs the students kept about their activities related to the law, as well as the notes and drafts the students composed, both for the law course and the other courses the students took that year. Freedman's team discovered from their analysis that over the course of the year, the six students seemed to learn how to write essays for the law course that were distinctive syntactically and rhetorically from the essays they wrote for their other courses. Moreover, in writing their legal essays, the students used forms of argumentation unique to legal situations ("Show" 227–28). What Freedman and her colleagues found interesting about this project, however, was not that the students learned to write a unique genre but that they did so without any formal instruction: the students in the law course were not taught in any explicit way how to write the essays for the course, the students were not given any models to follow, and in follow-up interviews, the students indicated that they had "made no attempt to formulate the rules underlying the genre as they struggled with their writing tasks" ("Show" 229). Freedman attributes the accomplishments of the law students to their socialization in the ways of the legal community, to their natural ability to acquire writing skills tacitly.

In her analysis of how such socialization may work, Freedman offers two different explanations. In an earlier article, she cites Richard Freed and Glenn Broadhead on the existence of "cultural and institutional norms that shape and constrain" genres; these norms "are not perceived because the context is invisible, transparently bound to the ordinary and the everyday" (qtd. in Freedman, "Show" 231). In a later article, she seems to question how normative a social practice may be. She cautions us about "the dangers implicit in reifying genres" and cites a number of theorists, but especially Bakhtin, to the effect that genres are inherently "free and flexible" and that "norms and interdictions are inconsistent with the essential nature of generic creation" ("Genres" 111). And she suggests that what the students in her study have internalized is neither a mental process nor a way of reasoning nor a particular set of conventions nor a number of formats for writing. Rather, what they have internalized is "a certain stance toward reality," a particular way to respond to a particular exigency in a particular context ("Genres" 104–5). But what in the world is "a certain stance toward reality," and how would we go about trying to insure that another group of students would do as well as Freedman's group in learning a particular "stance toward reality?"

Freedman's analysis raises the questions, in what sense and to what degree is a social practice "normative," and if the written responses to a social practice are "free and flexible," how do we go about determining the relationship between the practice and the written response? Freedman asserts that her six students internalized a practice, a way of doing something, possibly a set of norms, but just what that practice is, what those norms may be, is not very clear. The concept of a social practice, a set of social norms, as Freedman and other social theorists use the term, could mean two very different things. On the one hand, theorists of the social often reify the concepts of a practice or a norm so that they seem to refer to these things as if they were objects, with discernible qualities or properties that can cause behavior. On the other hand, these theorists rarely specify what the qualities or properties of these practices or norms are. Instead, they cite evidence from writing samples that people have indeed learned these practices or norms; hence, these concepts could be merely the terms theorists of the social use to describe individual acts of writing with a set of common features. When theorists of writing-as-a-social-practice attribute people's writing ability to their having internalized a practice or a set of norms, they suggest the first definition, and yet often their only real evidence of the concept is the similarities between the writing of people in similar situations.

Thus, Freedman argues that her students write legal essays the way they do because they have worked in the discipline of legal studies sufficiently to internalize a set of practices. This formulation of what occurred with Freedman's students suggests a set of practices that Freedman should be able to describe as some aspect of the environment that caused the students to write as they do. Freedman suggests a number of the characteristics such a practice might have: it uses a distinctive vocabulary, with words such as *statute, common law, equity,* and *sovereignty;* it uses longer and more complex sentences than other practices; and it uses a distinctive rhetorical pattern of issue, rule, application, and conclusion. But the evidence Freedman cites for these practices, these norms, is the writing that the students do. She provides no profile of just what it is about the textbook, the lectures, and the seminar discussions that may have caused the students to write as they did. Of course, she implies that the textbook, the lectures, and the discussions must have used the vocabulary the students picked up; the lectures and the discussions must have used longer and more complex syntax than the students heard in other social circumstances; and the textbook, the lectures, and the discussions must have involved the use of the rhetorical patterns of issue, rule, application, and conclusion.

However, there is reason to doubt the degree to which each of these instructional aids contributed to the students' expertise. Freedman admits, for example, that the textbook did *not* use longer and more complex syntax than the students' did in their arguments, and she is emphatic that although the rhetorical pattern of issue, rule, application, and conclusion was mentioned in the lecture, the students had no models of how to apply the pattern. But if Freedman's students did not internalize their syntactic patterns from the textbook and they did not internalize their rhetorical patterns from the lectures, indeed from models of any kind, from where in their environment *did* they learn these things? Freedman's theory of the social lacks a concrete "picture" of the social practice of legal studies, a picture of the frequency and the manner in which the terms, the syntax, the rhetorical patterns are used, and how the students' work fits that picture. Without such a "picture," it is difficult to say just what it is about the social practice of law that the students have learned.

Clearly, Freedman is uncomfortable saying that they have internalized some kind of norm. People use various terms, sentence patterns, and rhetorical strategies with such a range of frequency, in such a range of contexts, and for sentence patterns and rhetorical strategies, in such a variety of formats, that it is very difficult to determine just how the use of those terms, patterns, and strategies becomes the source of someone else's learning them.

As a result, most of Freedman's argument is devoted to showing that the essays written by her students for the introductory course in the law are remarkably similar to each other and distinctive from the essays written by these same students in their other courses. For example, *on average* the sentences in their writing for the law classes were longer and more complex than the sentences in their writing for other disciplines. Their sentences had more words per T-unit, more finite clauses per T-unit, and more T-units per sentence. Moreover, the students could not have internalized the need for syntactic complexity from their textbook, because in general their sentences are longer and contain more finite clauses per T-unit than the sentences in the text. Freedman attributes this difference to the fact that the students were writing more argumentative pieces while the textbook was primarily informative ("Genres" 117–18).

The rhetorical strategies of the students' law essays were also different from their other academic writing. The essays the students wrote for other disciplines tended to concentrate on providing evidence for claims with the various warrants being only assumed. However, in their law essays the students tended to specify the warrants and argue for them in detail. The warrants in the law essays "were far more highly formalized, precise, and exact than those in other academic essays." Such formality is fitting for a discipline in which there are "precise rules or principles for statute interpretation," and how these rules or principles ought to be applied must be specified ("Genres" 102). Here is an example of the kind of argument the students learned to write in their law classes:

> The defense in this case would presumably argue that the wall is not a building by definition. Using *eiusdem generis* (of the same kind) canon of interpretation, it is evident that "building" as seen in section 4 refers to the list in section 3: a house, shed, barn, or other structure, which infer the membership of those structures that can be occupied. Therefore, the exclusion of members of

the class, fence and wall, imply that they are not included under the meaning of "building." The elements listed that infer building all imply that one cannot occupy them. Since one cannot occupy (in the sense that one cannot enter into it and take shelter) a wall, Brown's boundary marker is therefore not applicable for prosecution under this statute. ("Genres" 102)

This paragraph not only illustrates the explicit justification of a warrant by offering a reason why a particular statute should be interpreted in a particular way; it also illustrates another feature or microlevel rhetorical pattern: "an elucidation of a central *issue,* the presentation of the appropriate *rule,* its *application,* and a *conclusion*" ("Genres" 102).

In all this, Freedman has convincingly demonstrated that as a group, the students' legal essays are different from other kinds of writing in certain ways: the legal essays use a distinctive vocabulary, longer and more complex syntax, and distinctive rhetorical patterns. However, the difficulty with attributing the distinctiveness of the students' legal writing to their social environment remains. Freedman has not illuminated what in the students' social environment may have caused them to write legal essays the way they do, so we do not know what it is that they have internalized.

All theories of writing as a social practice face the problem of how to characterize social practices in ways that show how these practices may have influenced learning. If the only evidence of such theories is the writing that social contexts produce, then theories of writing as a social practice will always be tautological. The argument will be that the social environment influenced the writing, but the only evidence for that influence will be the writing.

Another difficulty with theories of writing as a social phenomenon is that they do not adequately account for how young writers learn the governing principles or norms or chief characteristics of their social environment; that is, they do not contribute to the major model of learning I have already discussed in chapter 2. In Freedman's study, it is not clear how the students learned to write legal essays: all we can say is that to some degree they "internalized" a number of concepts. In order to be helpful, a theory of learning must be able to characterize the way that "learners must grasp concepts or procedures more complex than those they already have available for application" (Bereiter, "Toward" 202). Without a more specific theory of learning, it is difficult to differentiate what Freedman's students learned from their own innate abilities and what they learned from the influence of a social practice or norm, what they learned from hard wiring in the brain or from cultural conditioning.

The Limits of the Concept of Discourse Community

One way theorists of writing as a social practice have dealt with the vagueness of their key concept is to distinguish groups with common writing practices from the larger social environment; these groups are often called "discourse communities." Recently, a number of theorists have also tried to conceptualize how writers use various aspects of writing as tools to accomplish very specific tasks sanctioned by larger groups. These theorists refer to networks of interrelated social groups as "activity systems" (see for example Russell, "Review"; Bazerman, "Discursively"). However, since the conceptual problems with activity systems are the same as those for discourse communities, I will use only the more commonly accepted term. Indeed, I have been using the notion of a "discourse community" all along because it is so useful: it gives us a way to refer to the many different social groups writers participate in when they write. However, just because we must use a certain concept or term does not mean that we are necessarily being clear. Sometimes we are left with the understanding that the language allows us, and with the concept of a "discourse community," we are left with a very uncertain understanding. In many ways, the concept of a discourse community is no improvement over the concept of social practices.

In general, the term "discourse community" refers to what people have in common, what they share, when they use certain kinds of language. The difficulty is in characterizing what that commonality is. Theorists have asserted that discourse communities are unified in different ways. For example, in an early formulation, James Porter defined a discourse community as "a group of individuals bound by a common interest who communicate through approved channels and whose discourse is regulated" ("Intertextuality" 38). Later, Porter substantially revised this definition to account for the way discourse communities are bound together by a system of texts and practices. In this later formulation Porter defines a discourse community as "a local and temporary constraining system, defined by a body of texts (or more generally, practices) that are unified by a common focus" (*Audience* 106). John Swales ascribes six distinguishing characteristics to discourse communities, but his most important is that they have "*a broadly agreed set of common public goals*" (24). Lester Faigley argues that the notion of a discourse community should include people with shared knowledge that may cross disciplinary boundaries, what he calls "issue fields" ("Nonacademic"). Marilyn Cooper thinks of a discourse community in an ideal sense not as a group of people but as a *situation,* in which "people come together in discourse and negotiate what they want to do and what matters to them. It is a community in the sense that it is concerned about each of its members, their goals, their needs, and what they have to offer" (Cooper and Holzman 204). For each of these theorists, a discourse community has as its central unifying force a common interest, a common goal, a common focus, a common knowledge, a common situation, or somewhat more specifically, common channels of communication, common systems of texts and practices, common genre conventions and canonical knowledge, or common needs and desires.

However, there are theorists who think that the unifying element of a discourse community is something deeper. Patricia Bizzell, for instance, begins her analysis of a discourse community by defining it rather simply as "a group of people who share certain language-using practices" (*Academic* 222). But Bizzell quickly gets at what she sees as the heart of a discourse community: the practices of a discourse community involve stylistic conventions, which "regulate social interactions both within the group and its dealings with outsiders," and "canonical knowledge," which "regulates the world-views of members" (222). So too Anne Beaufort conceives of a discourse community as "a dynamic social entity" with "a set of distinctive, yet changeable writing practices," which result from, among other things, "the community's shared values and goals" (522). For Bizzell and Beaufort, what binds a discourse community together is not just a neutral interest, a neutral goal, or a neutral way of communicating but a "world view" and a set of values.

However, as with invocations of the "social" in general, the problem for these designations of a discourse community is that they are quite vague. In any given case, the problem is to characterize more specifically what the members of a discourse community have in common with one another or what they share, at least to the extent that we can distinguish one discourse community from another. But often, distinguishing one discourse community from another is very difficult to do.

Porter provides us with a classic hypothetical case: a group of "Magnavox employees" (*Audience* 106–7). In one sense, the people who work for Magnavox Corporation could be described in sociological terms as members of a business institution with a distinctive identity. We can distinguish between the ways in which the Magnavox workers participate in the workings of the corporation and the ways they participate in other institutions, such as families, clubs, churches, and civic organizations. We can even distinguish between, say, the clerical workers of Magnavox and the clerical workers of other corporations on the basis of the work they do. Clerks at Magnavox may have distinctive filing systems or organizational structures. At a minimum, the clerks at Magnavox work at a different location, in a different building with different colleagues and different managers; they participate in a different institutional structure from other clerks.

But the ways the employees of Magnavox constitute a discourse community is more complex. We may conceptualize Magnavox as one discourse community or as a series of interlocking or overlapping discourse communities. Porter explains:

> On one level, we can see a division between "workers" and "management": workers may operate according to the principles of one discourse community, with a set of assumptions and operating procedures quite different from man-

agement. At the same time, Magnavox is saturated with the conventions of different disciplinary orientations and organizational affiliations: engineers negotiate with business people, people from local headquarters struggle with people from the main office, divisions and departments develop their own discursive habits, lawyers meet with executives to determine corporate policy—and all of this within the corporate boundaries. (*Audience* 106–7)

The problem is obvious. When a Magnavox engineer writes a report for the corporation lawyers working on a particular patent case, just what is the engineer's discourse community—the community of engineers, the community of lawyers, the community of Magnavox employees, or the community of those employees working on the patent case? And how would we go about determining what the engineer's discourse community *was* in this situation? Well, as Porter suggests, we might look at the social circumstances in which the engineer produced the report, the other texts the engineer was responding to, the responses to the engineer's report, and the focus of this web of texts, its stated and unstated conventions, its history. Most likely we would look at the report itself. We would examine the report to see if it most closely resembled the genres used by engineers, the genres used by lawyers, or the memos used by Magnavox employees in general. And most likely, we would find that the engineer's text was to a certain extent a hybrid of these various genres, in which case we might conclude that in writing this report the engineer was participating in all three discourse communities. However, if we had to choose one discourse community over another from the evidence of the report itself, we might choose the group of Magnavox employees working on the patent case. Notice, however, that this sort of reasoning reproduces all of the difficulties involved in determining the influence of the social that I pointed out in connection with Freedman's law students. The definition of a discourse community is largely dependent on a description of texts, and ascribing the features of these texts to the influence of the discourse community is largely tautological.

It is difficult to distinguish among discourse communities more specifically, to clarify the borders between, say, the community of Magnavox employees, the community of Magnavox engineers, and the community of Magnavox engineers writing about a particular patent case. Among theorists who work with the concept of discourse communities, the person who has done the most to make these distinctions is John Swales. Swales's notion of a discourse community has six distinguishing features: "a broadly agreed set of common public goals," "mechanisms of intercommunication among its members," "community participatory mechanisms primarily to provide information and feedback," the use of "one or more genres in the communicative furtherance of its aims," "some specific lexis," and "a threshold level of members with a suitable degree of relevant content and discoursal expertise" (24–27).

Now it is fairly easy to provide examples that test the limits of Swales's notion of a discourse community. For instance, Porter's Magnavox engineers may share a common goal with all other Magnavox employees in trying to make the business more profitable when they communicate through interdepartmental memos and newsletters and e-mail. In doing so, they may also share information using a common vocabulary focused on the day-to-day life of the business, and the degree to which they participate in the system of memos, newsletters, and e-mail may depend on how long they have been employed at the institution and the degree to which they have acquired a knowledge of the institution and can apply their particular expertise to company practices.

However, Magnavox's engineers may share a different set of goals, different methods of communication, different genres, and a different vocabulary with their fellow corporate engineers. They would certainly share an entirely different sort of professional expertise with their engineering colleagues than with other company employees. This means that in Swales's terms, Magnavox engineers belong to at least two different discourse communities. And these two discourse communities are relatively easy to distinguish, although if an engineer writes an interdepartmental memo to a wide variety of employees about matters that primarily concern engineers, we might have to puzzle over just which community the engineer is participating in at the time.

Using Swales's list of features for discourse communities becomes more problematic, however, when we consider the engineer's participation in the patent case. The engineer's report, written with a certain amount of engineering jargon and with a considerable display of professional expertise, is designed to be used by a group of lawyers arguing a patent case in the courts. The report will become part of the evidence that the lawyers refer to in their arguments. However, it is not at all clear in this case the degree to which the engineer is participating in a discourse community distinct from the others the engineer belongs to. We may consider that the engineer and Magnavox's team of lawyers have a distinctive common goal to win the patent case for Magnavox. On the other hand, the engineer's only job is to produce the report; otherwise, the engineer is not directly involved in the case and gives only a cursory reading of the various reports from the lawyers on the progress of the case, if any reading at all. In a sense, the engineer is not directly involved in the patent case and produced the report only as a part of the job of engineer. Is the engineer, then, participating in an "agreed upon set of public goals?" In addition, we may consider the engineer's report as a standard genre and "communicative mechanism" used by the discourse community organized around the patent case to accomplish its goal, or we may consider it as a genre and mechanism used by the discourse community of engineers and merely appropriated by lawyers for a special purpose. We may consider the engineer's special vocabulary, usually a distinctive aspect of the engineering community, as a part of the vocabulary of the discourse community organized by the patent case, or we may consider it as still a distinctive characteristic of the engineering community, which the lawyers have incorporated into their own separate community, much as English has "borrowed" words and phrases from other languages. And finally, we may consider the "threshold level" of knowledge and expertise shared by the engineer and the team of lawyers about various matters surrounding the patent case as distinctive of their discourse community: after all, they may share a common knowledge of what is unique about Magnavox technology and why a competitor's designs may be an infringement of Magnavox's patents of that technology; and they may also share a unique expertise in the ability to understand and participate in the discourse about the case. On the other hand, we may consider the engineer's knowledge of the case to be so limited to the technical aspects of the case—the engineer knows nothing of the expertise the lawyers will bring to the courtroom—that the engineer is not in the same discourse community as the lawyers at all.

One more test case: In composition studies, it is common to argue that introductory writing courses should socialize students to the academic community and introduce them to academic discourse. But in what sense do members of colleges and universities interact with one another, using common textual practices and a common vocabulary, in order to achieve a common public goal? Clearly, the academy is not a single discourse community in terms of the textual practices of the various disciplines. Physics professors do not write about subjects or use genre conventions or publish in journals read by philosophy professors. Faculty and staff in academia may constitute some form of discourse community by using a common system of memos or e-mail in order to conduct university business, but that is hardly what compositionists refer to when they talk about introducing students to "academic discourse." Rather, "academic discourse" seems to refer to the textual practices involved in teacher-student relations. That is, it refers to the school genres—the personal essays, critical analyses, and research papers—that instructors require in their courses. The question is in what sense the teacher and students in Sociology 101 constitute the same or a different discourse community from the teacher and students in Engineering 415. In what sense do the participants in these two groups share, in Porter's terms, "a body of texts (or more generally, practices) that are unified by a common focus," a number of "stated and unstated conventions, a vital history, mechanisms for wielding power, institutional hierarchies, vested interests and so on" (*Audience* 106)? Or in Swales's terms, in what sense do the participants in these two groups share a set of public goals, a mechanism of intercommunication and feedback? (Members of the sociology class do not communicate with the members of the engineering class.) Or share one or more genres? (In what sense is a sociology research report similar to a proposal, design, and plan for an engineering project?). Or share a vocabulary, or a threshold level of members with relevant knowledge and expertise? It seems that if there were an academic discourse community that incorporate a wide range of subject matter, disciplines, and courses, we could characterize it only at a very high level of abstraction. For example, we might characterize an academic discourse community as having the common goal of educating students, especially through school genres, into certain skeptical or critical stances toward reality and the nature of truth, certain broad strategies for considering evidence, or very abstract patterns of reasoning, persuasion, and argumentation. But it is difficult to see how members of different university classes or disciplines communicate with each other or have a common vocabulary (for attempts to characterize academic discourse, see Elbow, "Reflections"). On the other hand, Swales admits that individual university classes may be discourse communities, if the instructor and students agree on goals, the students participate fully and share information, and the class as a whole works on common genres using a common vocabulary (32).

What is problematic about the concept of a discourse community, then, is that its features are so subjective and "fuzzy" that the concept can be used to account for any shared aspects of genres or contexts. The inherent fuzziness of the concept of a discourse community leads Bennett Raforth to question what he calls its "descriptive adequacy" (141). Perhaps because of this fuzziness, the concept of a discourse community has one other major difficulty: as a "picture," it is painted in very broad strokes, and it cannot be used to account for how the forms of discourse within a community differ from one another—that is, it cannot distinguish among variations in genres—or how the community uses textual variations, expertise in using texts, and broader performance and social criteria to determine membership in the community. Raforth calls this a problem in "explanatory adequacy" (141).

Let's go back to the issue of whether or in what sense academia is a "discourse community." As I have already indicated, the primary reason certain composition scholars think of the academy as a discourse community seems to be that faculty across the disciplines seem to write themselves and require of their students a certain kind of discourse, one that has a skeptical or critical stance toward reality, certain common strategies for evaluating and citing evidence, and certain broad patterns of reasoning and arguing. The ability to write this academic discourse helps to determine whether faculty are members of the academy. Consider then, the writing of two scholars in English, Harold and Harriet. Harold is an assistant professor of English at a midwestern state university who has published several critical analyses of literary works using primarily the methods of the New Criticism. His field is nineteenth-century American literature, with a special focus on Walt Whitman. Harriet, also an assistant professor at the same university, has published the same number of articles using critical theory and cultural studies methods. Her field is composition and feminist theory, with a special focus on the status of women in writing programs. If we think of membership in a discourse community as a process of socialization and acculturation, in what sense are Harold and Harriet members of the same discourse community of English, or perhaps just of their particular department? Certainly they participate in the common set of goals for people in their position in the community: they both participate in teaching, research, and service. They both use a common mechanism to communicate, the scholarly journal, but the journals are very different. Harold aims to publish, if he can, in *American Literature*. Harriet aims to publish, if she can, in *College Composition and Communication*. In a sense they both use the same genre, the scholarly article, but in another sense their articles have very few features in common: their articles differ in vocabulary and style, organization, and content. The question is, then, how would we go about using the concept of a discourse community to determine what groups either of these scholars belongs to, and whether they have demonstrated a threshold level of knowledge and expertise in these communities order to qualify as legitimate members, especially when it comes to granting them tenure.

Overlook for the moment two major criteria usually used to evaluate junior faculty for tenure: teaching and service. My analysis will apply to these aspects of academic life, but to include them would be too complicated. Let's concentrate instead on the textual practices of scholarship, research, and publishing. The concept of a discourse community is often used to account for why writers write the way they do: Harold writes the way he does because he belongs to the discourse community of nineteenth-century American literature scholars, or perhaps more specifically of Walt Whitman scholars. The discourse community of nineteenth-century American literature scholars establishes certain norms for discourse: genre conventions, rules of evidence, and the relevance of certain subjects over others. Harold can publish only because his writing meets the norms decided by his community. Since he has published three or four articles in "good" American literature journals, we can consider Harold a member of the community of American literature scholars. The same applies to Harriet: the reason she writes the way she does is that she belongs to the community of feminist composition scholars. The community of feminist compositionists has established certain norms for the discourse of the community, and Harriet can publish only because her writing meets those norms. And since Harriet too has published three or four articles in "good" composition and rhetoric journals, we can consider her a member of the community of feminist composition scholars.

One obvious response to the issue of whether to tenure Harriet and Harold on the basis of their scholarship, then, would be to argue that they belong to very different discourse communities, and their writing can best be evaluated by their peers in the separate communities to which they belong. And in fact, it is a common practice in tenure cases not only in English departments but across the university to submit the publications of

the applicants to outside reviewers with similar specialties, to outside reviewers from the same discourse community.

Still, Harold and Harriet are not being tenured in the community of
nineteenth-century American literature scholars or the community of feminist composition scholars. They are being tenured in a particular English
department at a midwestern state university with particular course requirements and particular professional concerns, and some sense of a common
mission. And since the concept of a discourse community is often used to
account for why writers write the way they do, indeed, since it can be argued that discourse communities provide the norms for textual practices,
members of particular departments may reasonably infer that if their
untenured faculty want to belong to their particular department, their textual practices ought to reflect the particular needs and concerns of their departments or at least some broadly understood standard for what it means
to be an English professor. They may expect for example that the discourse
practices of the faculty will reflect the courses they teach or the institutional
needs of the department or the particular concerns of the local faculty, or
they may expect those practices to meet some standard of style or reason
or relevance; some critical stance toward reality, some use of evidence and
reasoning, and some standard of professional relevance, which apply to all
professors of English. In my example, the faculty of Harold and Harriet's
department might expect their publications to reflect the content of the
courses they teach or they might expect Harriet and Harold to conduct their
scholarly arguments in ways familiar and acceptable to the local faculty. In
this case, Harold and Harriet would be considered to be members of the
same community, and that community would establish the norms for their
discourse practices.

My point is not to take a stand on which discourse communities Harold
and Harriet belong to. Rather my point is this: if discourse communities
establish some sort of norm for textual practices, we can use the concept
of a discourse community to account for both the differences and the commonalties in the ways Harry and Harriet write. At some level, their discourse
practices are very different, reflecting different discourse communities. At
another level their textual practices are the same, reflecting the same discourse community. The same concept can be used to account for very different phenomena. In other words, the concept of a discourse community
lacks the power to explain the differences among various ways of writing
the same genre, in this case the scholarly article. The writing of Harold and
Harriet is the same because they belong to the same discourse community,
but it is different because they belong to different communities.

One way out of this dilemma is to suggest that two people who share a
discourse community but write differently in some way belong to different subgroups of one larger discourse community. In effect, this is to argue that what was one discourse community is really two or three or four

or an infinite number, that people belong to many and overlapping discourse communities. But this argument is eventually incoherent: it leads inevitably to the notion that if a person has a unique way of using language, she constitutes her own unique discourse community of one.

Another way out of this dilemma is to argue that the unique constraints of a particular context account for the differences among people in the same discourse community, but since the number of relevant factors inherent in context are infinite, we must then concede that the notion of people sharing a discourse community lacks adequate explanatory power to account for differences in how they write (see also Beaufort for examples of how two employees in the same office can use radically different memo styles, or the same employee can use radically different memo styles in different contexts).

The concept of a speech community has a similar problem. Linguists usually solve the problem by distinguishing among a language, a dialect, and an ideolect, but these three concepts are difficult to distinguish in practice. It is a matter of some dispute, for example, whether Black English is a distinctive language or a dialect of English. It may be even more difficult to distinguish between a dialect and an ideolect. For instance, in western Pennsylvania and in certain other areas of the country, people say, "These pants need pressed," while most people say, "These pants need to be pressed" or "These pants need pressing." We might then consider "verb + past participle" to be a distinctive dialect. But if certain people use the same grammatical form in areas in which the form is not commonly used—if someone uses "verb + past participle" in northern Wisconsin—we might consider it to be an ideolect of those particular people. How many people using a similar expression not common in the larger area does it take for an expression to stop being an ideolect and become a dialect? Like the concept of a discourse community, the concept of a speech community has inherently fuzzy borders.

The practices of discourse communities, no matter how we conceptualize them, will always be fluid and changeable, depending on social conditions. In addition, membership in discourse communities will also always be fluid and changeable. No one is always fully a member of one discourse community or a member of only one community. People move in and out of discourse communities all the time. Because of the fuzziness of its conceptual borders, all notions of a discourse community become an exercise in Wittgenstein's idea of "family resemblance." The concept of a discourse community may be best understood then to be a hermeneutic "tool" for making certain distinctions among different kinds of discourse produced in different social contexts. The concept of a discourse community is an interpretation of how certain features of a genre or group of genres may be accounted for by the nature of the social context in which the genres are written. But recall the difficulty Freedman had in characterizing what it was about the discourse community of law classes that produced her students' writing about the law. The concept of a discourse community does not solve the conceptual problems inherent in the concept of a social practice.

One final concern: the practitioners of critical pedagogy often worry that the notion of a discourse community as "normative" is inherently exclusionary. Thus, Cooper has pointed out that the term often seems to refer to "a social structure that exists separately from the individuals who are its members" (Cooper and Holzman 204): "as [a discourse community] standardizes rules and expectations and begins to establish a tradition, it makes discourse both possible and necessary" (Cooper and Holzman 211). But such standards can prescribe certain ways of behaving, thinking, and writing— if you don't believe this, if you don't write these genres, if you don't reason like this, if you don't write like this, you can't be part of the group. They can use ways of behaving, thinking, and writing to assimilate newcomers or to distinguish themselves from outsiders to the community. As Geoffrey Chase says, "Discourse communities are organized around the production and legitimation of particular forms of knowledge and social practices at the expense of others, and they are never ideologically innocent" (13).

The degree to which discourse communities set norms for membership in the group is especially an issue for scholars and theorists of basic writing, who question the degree to which the academic community is willing to assimilate and accommodate basic writers, who may write in ways the academic community views as "remedial" or "deficient." Critics of the academy, such an Min-Zhan Lu, Christopher Schroeder, and Rhonda Grego and Nancy Thompson, would like the academic community not only to assimilate and accommodate basic writers, but in some sense to modify its own normative practices, to in effect redefine what it means to be a particular kind of discourse community in the first place. They would like to make basic writing, or the kinds of writing basic writers can do well, more acceptable in the academy.

But of course this is a paradox. Discourse communities can be defined only in the first place by the distinctive writing practices they engage in. All discourse communities must by definition have some sort of border, no matter how fuzzy, and thus in some sense they must be normative. Asking a discourse community to modify its "normative" set of writing practices is asking it to be a different discourse community; to have a different identity. This is a tall order (see Kent, *Paralogic* 112–26).

I suspect that this paradox is a kind of language universal. We will always be able to make some sort of distinctions among groups of people because of the ways they write, and there will always be people who want to belong to the group but who have difficulty mastering the textual practices the group considers normative. As a result, there will always be people both inside and outside the group who will believe that the group ought to modify its textual practices and reconstitute itself as a different discourse community. There will always be a tension between a community's "normal" practices and conventions of discourse and "abnormal" practices and conventions of discourse.

Our sense of what a discourse community is or ought to be will always be a matter of interpretation, and however we conceptualize a particular discourse community, our primary use of the concept will be to make claims about how that discourse community influences writing or how it provides norms for membership in the community, norms that may always be open to criticism and the possibility of change. Part of being literate in the practices of a discourse community may then involve being aware of how "normal" and "abnormal" discourse functions in the group.

My analysis of the concept of social practice and the related concept of "discourse community" suggests that the value of these concepts is largely hermeneutic. That is, theories of the influence of social practice on the acquisition of writing are necessarily opaque and will always be underdetermined. Such theories cannot get us closer to the "reality" of how we acquire our ability to write except to suggest those aspects of reality we should consider when we think about certain aspects of writing.

Likewise, various conceptualizations of discourse communities will always have fuzzy borders and be open to criticism that they are too "normative." The regularities and commonalties of discourse communities allow us to communicate with one another in the first place. But paradoxically, discourse communities also allow for "abnormal" participation in the group— creative and original ways of being in the community.

I see no way to extend our analysis of these concepts to make them more fruitful, no way to make them "deeper" or less problematic. At best, in the future we will continue to conceptualize contexts and genres in ways that may be helpful to particular people in particular contexts who need the insights such concepts provide.

Still, although we may never have a very explicit formulation of what in their social environment people internalize or acquire when they learn to write, although we may never have a very sharply defined notion of a discourse community, perhaps we do not need such explicitness. All we need is a conceptual "tool" to help us think about the social aspects of writing and how writers develop a sense of text conventions and audience, a way to ponder the kinds of discourse communities in which students can most profitably learn particular text conventions or the demands of particular audiences. In colleges and universities, these discourse communities will probably not be generic writing courses but courses designed to introduce students to the genres, audiences, and contexts of more specific discourse communities.

If each language learner actively constructs his own "theory of the world in his head," and if language consists of so many different kinds of knowledge and skill applied in different ways in each new context, then what matters is that speakers and writers use the public aspects of speech and writing in common ways in order to get things done. As Christina Erneling puts it:

> The skills [of using language] need not be the same for everyone but it is only required that they allow effective interaction. It does not matter if my meaning of certain words, or my grammar differs from yours as long as they converge at some point and to some degree, or that language is sufficiently stable to enable us to gather and process information. (156)

This suggests that the primary focus of instruction ought to be immersing students in various discourse communities and providing young writers with "tips" as to how the "public" aspects of their writing may differ from some sense of "convergence," the similar ways other people in similar situations have used similar genres for similar purposes. Such "tips" may also involve advice about the discourse practices of the group and the advantages and disadvantages of writing according to the norms of the group. As novice writers acquire more knowledge of the discourse practices of the group and more skill in writing both "normal" and "abnormal" discourse in the group, they will become more self-conscious about those practices. That is, they will become competent and self-conscious enough to decide how they want their own writing to participate in the community. This is turn suggests that part of writing instruction may involve helping writers develop a self-conscious awareness of the social organization and discourse practices of the communities they wish to join. The New London Group has categorized the various aspects of such a pedagogy as situated practice, overt instruction, critical framing, and transformed practice. I explore these terms in more detail in chapter 7.

Meanwhile, it may be helpful to think of the teaching of writing as more like training than as the conveying of explicit information, more like shaping a practice over time until it fits into some range of public acceptability for some discourse community. Even "abnormal" discourse must be acceptable to some community and be a variation on some previous genre for it to make any sort of sense at all.

I maintain, therefore, that it is a wholly legitimate goal of a composition course to encourage students to think about their thoughts, beliefs, and values, and where those came from—before, during, and after writing. Neither we teachers, nor our students, can ever get the words right until we get the thoughts right.

—Peter J. Caulfield, "Talk, Thought, Writing and Politics"

5 *Writing and Thinking*

I SUSPECT THAT PETER CAULFIELD may be wrong, at least in part, when he argues that we need to get our thoughts right before we can get our words right. It depends of course on what he means, and what he means is not at all clear. His words appear in a book entitled *Left Margins: Cultural Studies and Composition Pedagogy,* in which Caulfield takes exception to an assertion by Gary Tate that most of the essays in the book, which are ostensibly about the application of critical pedagogy to writing classes, do not talk about writing at all; they only talk about making students aware of their own "ideological subjectivity" or of how language works to shape their views of reality. Where, Tate asks, is the writing in these classes? To which I might add, what exactly are the students learning to do? Caulfield's answer strongly suggests that students in writing classes taught from the standpoint of critical pedagogy or cultural studies are learning to think critically—"to think about their thoughts, beliefs, and values"—and that is tantamount to learning to write.

However, the notion that teaching thinking is an integral part of writing instruction is not new to critical pedagogy or cultural studies. There are many different ways to conceptualize what we mean by "thinking," and composition theorists have related them all to writing, either by talking about how to get students to think ahead of time about what they are writing, or about how to get them to think in certain ways while they are writing. Generally, pedagogies that focus on thinking before writing promote various heuristics for getting ideas (invention strategies), various planning techniques, or various ways to think through an issue or problem. Pedagogies that focus on thinking during the writing process, which may include thinking before writing, promote "reflection," "metacognition," or "monitoring." Scholars associated with critical pedagogy and cultural studies often use the term "critical consciousness" to describe a way of thinking about certain problems or issues. In each of these cases, composition scholars assert that teaching students ways of thinking is a way to help them with their writing.

Indeed, many compositionists who promote the use of invention strategies, heuristics, or forms of critical analysis in the classroom seem to imply that the relationship between thinking and writing is direct and even causal. For example, each of the following assumptions seems to underlie a number of currently popular ways of teaching writing:

- Writing is a kind of transcribed thought. (A tenet of much of the process movement and those who promote free writing "just to help students get their thoughts down on paper.")
- Writing improves learning and thinking. (A tenet of writing-to-learn and much of the writing-across-the-curriculum movement.)
- Better thinking will result in better writing; to teach thinking is in fact tantamount to teaching writing. (A tenet of much critical pedagogy and cultural studies pedagogies.)

However, there is a great deal of evidence that these assumptions are overstated, that they claim entirely too much. On the contrary, the evidence suggests that thinking, as a "tool kit" of various kinds of knowledge and skill, can best be understood as those kinds of knowledge and skill that people need to accomplish particular tasks in particular contexts. This suggests in turn that particular strategies for thinking and writing, however we define these terms, may only apply to a limited number of tasks and contexts, that particular strategies for writing-to-learn will aid only certain kinds of learning, and that particular strategies for thinking will aid only certain kinds of writing. And so, contrary to the common assumptions I just mentioned, I would argue the following about the tangled relationship of thinking to writing:

- Writing may in some instances be an *expression* of thought or a *representation* of thought, but writing is not transcribed thinking.
- Writing may also aid learning and thinking, but not necessarily in any clear and unequivocal way. The effects of writing on thinking seem to be local and contingent.
- Engaging in reflection or metacognition or critical consciousness about a certain subject does not necessarily improve our ability to write about that subject in particular social contexts.
- Writing in and of itself, no matter how it is conceptualized, does not necessarily improve "broad cognitive abilities" in particular disciplines or knowledge domains.

Let me argue each claim in turn.

Writing Is Not Transcribed Thinking

The problematic relationship between thinking and writing can best be illustrated with three examples. First, after wrestling with the way to say something and having produced three or four different formulations, none of them acceptable, we toss off one more variation, sit back and read it over, and discover, somewhat to our amazement, that this latest version is in fact what we mean. Second, we often find ourselves saying or writing what we do not mean; we produce slips of the tongue or pen, which is the reason for the slogan, "Take me for what I mean, not for what I say." Finally, out jogging, we may think we have a brilliant idea, but when we get home and try to write down the idea, it may seem much less brilliant, perhaps even incoherent. What these examples suggest is that there is no direct connection between thought and word. Often we find it difficult to put our thoughts into words, and we suspect that the words we choose are not quite what we had in mind. Often our thoughts are those the words allow us. How then can we best characterize the difficult relationship between thinking and writing?

First of all, we need a way to conceptualize the process of thinking. I prefer this simple definition: thinking is what our minds do. Thinking encompasses everything we know and remember, consciously or not; our beliefs and values; our opinions, attitudes, and feelings; and thinking includes every kind of mental activity our minds are capable of: our ability to perceive, distinguish, imagine, evaluate, judge, reason; the list could go on and on. As I noted in chapter 2, our current theories and models of mental life conceptualize the mind as an infinite number of mental representations—Ronald Kellogg calls them "personal symbols" (10)—which we create, manipulate, revise, and refine in response to our interactions with our environment. Kellogg puts it this way: "Thinking involves a set of mental skills that create, manipulate, and communicate to others the personal symbols of mental life" (10). So immediately we are faced with the conceptual difficulty of articulating what that "set of mental skills" is and how we can distinguish among the various skills in a meaningful way, especially as these skills are exhibited in writing.

The standard way for scholars and researchers who study thinking to conceptualize the object of their study is to compose a list of the kinds of things our minds know or can do. These taxonomies are similar to those made for writing: they are generally in the form of lists of various kinds of knowledge and skill. And it strikes me that these taxonomies are themselves of different kinds; that is, these taxonomies illustrate different conceptions of thinking. I see three different kinds of taxonomies about thinking: thinking itself, or perhaps basic thinking; thinking about thinking, and thinking critically. But I would argue that these taxonomies are somewhat beside the point. At their practical best, they are heuristics, ways of encouraging us to further thought. But in and of themselves, these taxonomies are conceptually confused: they draw few clear distinctions, and their many categories overlap and repeat themselves. As a result, I think it would help us all think more clearly about thinking if we relied less on taxonomies of skills and relied more on the notion that thinking can be recognized and contemplated only in concrete tasks in particular contexts, that thinking can best be conceptualized in writing not as a large variety of subskills, but as the knowledge and skill we need to express something or represent something in ways that accomplish certain specific goals.

The Three Taxonomies

Most taxonomies of what I have called "thinking itself" or what we might also call "basic thinking" usually involve a list of skills, such as the ability to define problems and set goals, make observations and formulate questions, encode information and recall it, organize information, analyze that information, and infer and predict things on the basis of that information. These taxonomies might also include skills such as the ability to summarize and evaluate information (see for example Marzano et al. 66).

"Thinking *about* thinking" involves what is commonly called reflection, metacognition, monitoring, or critical consciousness. June Birnbaum calls reflection in writing the ability to pause, rehearse a mental plan before beginning to write, revise extensively, and recognize the "purposeful and more abstract requirements of written language" as opposed to the "extemporaneous, context-bound characteristics of oral language" (31). Lorraine Higgins, Linda Flower, and Joseph Petraglia distinguish two other forms of "thinking about thinking," which may be either synonymous with reflection or a more detailed characterization of it: "*metacognition*, which includes both knowledge of the task and of one's own cognitive resources, and *monitoring*, the ability to control and regulate one's own thinking" (49; see also Flavell). And lastly, when many composition scholars in cultural studies and critical pedagogy talk about critical consciousness, they seem to be talking about something different from reflection and metacognition. They seem to be referring to specific kinds of knowledge or specific kinds of heuristic strategies or frameworks that they want writers to have at their command, specific kinds of awareness they expect writers to exhibit when they consider certain issues in certain social contexts.

A third kind of taxonomy concentrates on "critical thinking." However, just how critical thinking is different from basic thinking or from reflection or metacognition or critical consciousness is unclear. Some scholars and researchers define critical thinking as either a purpose or a method. Thus, Kenneth Hawes characterizes critical thinking as "some kind of reasoned or reasonable evaluation" (47), and Joanne Kurfiss calls critical thinking "the process of figuring out what to believe or do about a situation, phenomenon, problem, or controversy for which no single definitive answer or solution exists" (42). In any case, critical thinking is usually not considered a single discrete mental operation. Rather, it is considered what Barry Beyer calls "a collection of discrete skills or operations each of which to some degree or other combines analysis and evaluation" (272). Beyer provides a useful history of the various taxonomies of skills associated with critical thinking that have been developed in the last fifty years. Beyer sums up his historical review with a list of skills that most recent taxonomies include: distinguishing between verifiable facts and value claims; determining the reliability of a source; determining the factual accuracy of a statement; distinguishing relevant from irrelevant information, claims, or reasons; detecting bias; identifying unstated assumptions; identifying ambiguous or equivocal claims or arguments; recognizing logical inconsistencies or fallacies in a line of reasoning; distinguishing between warranted or unwarranted claims; and determining the strength of an argument (272).

There has also been what Kerry Walters calls a "second wave" of theorizing about critical thinking, associated with the rise of antifoundationalism in philosophy and the rise of cultural studies in the humanities generally. To Walters, this second wave of thinking about critical thinking rejects the notion that there can be some universally accepted standard of rationality and objectivity and posits that we ought to think of critical thinking in much broader terms than simple logic and objectivity. For example, traditional notions of critical thinking ignore the relevance of other cognitive abilities to the process of analysis and evaluation; that is, they ignore "creative imagination, intuition, or insight" ("Beyond" 11). In addition, traditional notions of critical thinking ignore the fact that total objectivity is impossible, that a critical thinker must "at times suspend his skepticism long enough to relate empathetically to perspectives contrary to his own, to accept them in a noncontentious spirit in order to explore their styles as well as content" ("Beyond" 12). Finally, traditional notions of critical thinking ignore the fact that resolving ambiguities and contraries is not always a good thing, that "part of what it means to be a good thinker is to recognize a multiplicity of cognitive approaches and styles, ones that very often are not consistent with one another but are nonetheless complementary" (12).

As part of the second wave, Richard Paul defines critical thinking as the ability to shift from one frame of reference to another, evaluate each one, monitor the process, and be aware of the limits and errors of contingency (183). Thomas Warren distinguishes reasoning from thinking, which he argues may necessarily involve feeling and moral consciousness. Connie Missimer makes the case that critical thinking takes into account other reasoned judgments and is therefore inherently social. Gary Olson and Evelyn Ashton-Jones take these notions of critical thinking to their logical conclusion. They argue that traditional notions of critical thinking are *uncritical* because these traditional notions assume a universal, decontextualized, and unproblematic sense of truth, which they say is simply false. In addition, the pedagogies of traditional notions of critical thinking usually provide nothing more than a set of "cookbook" procedures for analyzing problems. Olson and Ashton-Jones argue for a kind of critical thinking in which people learn to consider the context and ideology of those who are doing the thinking. In the process, they equate critical thinking with a kind of cultural criticism.

Thinking Beyond Skills

Now clearly these different taxonomies can be helpful. We can recognize all of the skills they list as aspects of what the mind can do. But surely in any given context, say the writing of a personal essay, these skills will blend together in ways that make them indistinguishable. Think about writing an essay. Is deciding on the central goal for an essay significantly different from pondering the relevant experiences, generating a plan for relating those experiences, and evaluating how well the project is succeeding as the writer's thinking progresses?

Or perhaps the writer has difficulty deciding how to end the piece and so consciously runs through the options: the writer perhaps remembers the ways he or she has ended previous essays and the ways other favorite essays end; the writer perhaps analyzes some of these previous efforts to see if they might apply to the current effort; the writer perhaps uses these previous efforts to generate some new endings along similar lines. We might call each of these activities an example of self-consciously thinking about what we know, of an awareness of what we have done and what we are doing. But each of these ways of dealing with the problem of how to end an essay also easily fits the description of basic thinking: these self-conscious reflections involve remembering, analyzing, and generating. So how is reflection different from simply thinking? Reflection is difficult to distinguish from simply thinking.

Basic thinking and reflection are equally difficult to distinguish from critical thinking. Strategies for critical thinking, as for reflection, metacognition, and critical consciousness, must depend on a knowledge of the matter at hand and apply new combinations of old skills for different goals in different contexts. Critical thinking is then in some sense yet another variation of basic thinking applied to new purposes in new contexts. For example, "determining the strength of an argument" necessarily involves focusing on the relevant information in an argument, analyzing the argument according to some relevant standard, generating possibilities for strengths and weaknesses in the argument, and integrating the results of the analysis, using particular genre conventions. All of these skills can be viewed as elements of basic thinking.

However, what seems to distinguish most notions of critical thinking is not knowledge or skill, a purpose or a method, but an attitude, an attitude of skepticism, or at least open-endedness, a refusal to accept closure quickly. If we look back at the list of critical thinking skills, we see that every skill on the list assumes that critical thinkers do not accept some aspect of what they are criticizing: they question the verifiability of facts, the accuracy of statements, the consistency of reasoning, the reliability of sources, the bias of arguers, the validity of arguments. In which case, we might say that being able to think critically involves the ability to use various kinds of knowledge and skill to bring up, even confront, and possibly resolve issues raised by a questioning or skeptical attitude. Regarding an essay, the writer may demonstrate critical thinking by questioning the format chosen in the first place: why write an *essay* in this context anyway? Perhaps another genre would be more effective. Or the writer may wonder whether a certain *kind* of example or illustration is appropriate, given the purpose and audience. In these cases, we distinguish between reflection and critical thinking primarily by the degree to which we question what we are doing. Critical thinking often seems to call the very nature of what we are doing into question.

In chapter 1, I made the case that writing is not a single global ability. Rather, writing necessarily involves a wide variety of knowledge and skills that can be used in many different ways in different contexts for different purposes. I would apply my analysis and reasoning about writing to a similar conception of thinking, what the editors of *Thinking, Reasoning, and Writing*—Elaine Maimon, Barbara Nodine, and Finbarr O'Connor—call the "'thinking as' approach" (xvii): we think *as* people in particular social contexts, using particular strategies and particular knowledge to accomplish particular tasks. There may very well be any number of broad cognitive strategies that we use in order to think, call them what we will—basic thinking, reflection, metacognition, critical consciousness, critical thinking—but we can recognize those broad strategies only when they are applied concretely using particular knowledge in particular circumstances. In which case, it might be best to conceptualize thinking as the ability to accomplish particular tasks in a particular way for particular contexts. In this conception, reflection, metacognition, critical consciousness, and critical thinking are not radically different kinds of thinking per se; rather, they are ways of thinking using new information for new purposes in new contexts. To teach novices reflection, metacognition, critical consciousness, or critical thinking is to teach them a different task from what they have done before; it is to teach them to think in terms of a different discourse in a different context.

As John McPeck points out, people we often classify as "independent thinkers" or as those who "think for themselves" are not only "*prone* to question things, but they have the relevant knowledge and understanding to help them do so productively" (103). To McPeck, critical thinkers need to have a wide range of very domain- and context-specific knowledge and skill in order to help them deal with the very different things they are skeptical about; indeed, critical thinkers need a wide range of knowledge and skills in order to be skeptical in the first place. When critical thinkers are skeptical about the tax plan of a particular politician, they bring a knowledge of our tax laws and some sense of economic justice to bear on the issue. When critical thinkers are skeptical about the motivations behind television beer commercials, they bring to bear a knowledge of how alcohol functions in our society and some sense of values about advertising and its role in mass communications. In some sense, then, thinking critically about a politician's tax plan is different from thinking critically about TV beer commercials. The knowledge and skill, the attitudes and values, inherent in the two situations are very different. And recent research regarding the relation of reasoning to emotion and feeling suggests that the two are intimately related at the physiological level (see Damasio).

I would argue that we should apply McPeck's reasoning to all kinds of thinking, not just critical thinking. In terms of pedagogy, the issue is whether we can provide students with the knowledge they need, whether we can help them ponder their interests and values, and whether we can offer relevant strategies and frameworks for thinking through the implications of what they need or want to do. If various taxonomies of thinking skills help us to be thorough, that is all to the good. But in any given case, these taxonomies are relevant only to the degree that they help us help our students accomplish specific tasks. They are relevant only to the degree that they help us help our students express or represent their thoughts in useful ways.

The Effects of Writing on Thinking Are Limited

Writing may aid learning and thinking, but not necessarily in any clear and unequivocal way. The evidence suggests that the effects of writing on thinking are limited; that is, people may use certain kinds of writing to help them learn certain subject matter, but the kinds of writing they do may help them learn only certain kinds of things: note-taking and essay writing, for example, may not promote the same kinds of learning.

The belief that writing aids learning has been a commonplace of writing instruction for quite some time, at least since the rise of the writing-across-the-curriculum movement in the late 1970s. In its simplest formulation, this belief is that students who use writing as part of their classroom activities learn the content of the course more effectively than those who do not.

Such writing is often called writing-to-learn, and its goal is to help us learn new concepts or conceptual patterns or strategies. In writing-to-learn, writing is a way to fix our thoughts, to objectify them, so that we can contemplate concepts, manipulate ideas, ponder what we need to learn.

Generally, the writing associated with writing-to-learn is what Stephen Tchudi calls "workaday writing": it is "short and impromptu" and it is written primarily so that the writer can clarify and ponder what he is supposed to be learning (20). Such short and impromptu writing may include notes, journals, freewriting, or microthemes; that is, "mini-essays," which require students to write summaries, provide support for theses or generalizations, pose questions, or solve problems (Tchudi 21–24).

Despite its widespread acceptance in composition studies, just what writing-to-learn is supposed to accomplish and whether it in fact does so has not been demonstrated. The problem begins with the simple assertion that "workaday writing" of any kind should help students learn any kind of subject matter. This simple assertion assumes that workaday writing produces a generic kind of thinking that should help students learn any kind of subject matter in any circumstances. However, if there is no such thing as generic thinking, and if broad strategies for learning and thinking are severely constrained by both the background and experience of learners and the particular subject matter they need to learn, then we should be suspicious of any large generalizations about the relationship between writing and learning. Whether writing aids learning would seem to depend on the kind of writing and what that writing was supposed to help students learn.

And indeed whether writing does in fact aid learning in some generic way has been called into question. In 1993, John Ackerman reviewed the history of research on the problematic relationship between writing and learning and concluded that the research on the effects of writing on learning is at best a "mixed message" (359). Ackerman looked at thirty-five studies of three different kinds: experimental studies, which used some kind of "controlled comparison"; what Ackerman calls "descriptive-context" studies (that is, descriptions of classrooms modeled after case studies); and what he calls "descriptive-linguistic" studies (descriptions of the "linguistic features associated with learning through writing") (353–54). Generally, Ackerman found that "all of the descriptive studies reported generous gains in learning behavior from writing, although they downplay other variables or biases behind their analysis":

> we have no idea whether other teaching techniques, such as discussion groups, might bring similar results [to pedagogies using journals or other writing-to-learn techniques] or whether the reported gains in performance and attitude transfer to other classes or remain with these students. Neither do we know how the teacher's disposition favored journal writing, disfavored other kinds of classroom behavior, or how the larger institutional context influenced learning. (356)

Of thirty empirical studies Ackerman analyzed, thirteen found a significant relationship between writing and learning; seventeen did not (357, 359).

Nevertheless, one study stood out among those Ackerman reviewed: Judith Langer and Arthur Applebee's *How Writing Shapes Thinking*, which, according to Ackerman, is "unique in that it paid as much attention to classroom contexts and teacher-student negotiation as to writing and learning tasks" (359). I would like to focus on one particular study in Langer and Applebee's book as a kind of metonymy for the research on writing and learning as a whole. Langer and Applebee's conclusions are, I think, representative of what we can currently say with any degree of certainty about the relationship between writing and learning.

Langer and Applebee studied the way six high school juniors in the San Francisco Bay area learned about specific subject matter based on their using three study tasks: "completing short-answer study questions, taking notes, and writing essays" (94). Langer and Applebee gave these juniors two passages to study from an eleventh-grade American history textbook, one about economic expansion after the Civil War, the other about the Great Depression. They met with each student individually for two sessions a week apart. During each session, they asked the student to read one of the passages and then study that information using one of the study tasks:

1. Note-taking: The students were told to read and take notes as they usually do in studying for school.
2. Study questions: The twenty-five study questions were typical of those found in social studies textbooks and worksheets and required the students to fill in the correct responses or to write a brief response of two or three sentences to a particular question.
3. Essay writing: The essay prompted analytic writing: for example, "Given what you learned from the passage, what do you feel were the two or three most important reasons for industrial growth in the late nineteenth and twentieth centuries? Explain the reasons for your choice." (95)

The tasks and the order in which they were done were varied among the students. Each student did more than one task, so that each task was done by four students.

As we might have expected, the writing the students did for each of the tasks followed the format of the task: The students who took notes did so primarily by using fragments: "1920's—prosperity, high wages, large profits, sustained dividends, increasing sales, invest (stock market)" (96). The students who answered study questions also produced writing that was short and often fragmentary: "What were the major manufacturing industries in the United States at the turn of the century? Meat packing iron & steel lumber clothing textiles" (95). Only the essays produced longer, more coherent writing:

> In the United States, between the late 19th century and early 20th century, industrial growth rose to above the highest level of any (other) nation . . . and this made the United States the premier manufacturing nation in the world. A

large influx. *imp. Technology and continuous government aid, and backing, gr helped to create the nation inducstrial growth, which in turn boosted the United States' gross national product.

Great steps in technology were made in the period between. . . . (96)

Undoubtedly, the different study techniques produced different kinds of writing. The question, of course, is whether these different kinds of writing made any difference in what the students learned.

In order to discover what the students had learned, Langer and Applebee did two things. First, they trained the students to think aloud while they were writing, and they audiotaped and transcribed these think-aloud protocols. Then they analyzed the protocols using a taxonomy of "reasoning operations": questioning, hypothesizing, using schemata (noting the ideas being developed or explained in the readings), evaluating, making meta-comments, citing evidence, and validating that a plan had been fulfilled or a decision made. Second, they measured what the students had learned using a free-association test and a scoring system developed by Langer. The free-association test asked students to jot down anything they could think of related to each of the five major concepts in each of the readings. The scoring system noted the amount of topic-specific knowledge students produced in each free-association test. Students took the free-association tests before each read-and-study session and again three days later.

Langer and Applebee's analysis of the think-aloud protocols indicate considerable variation in the kinds of thinking that accompanied each study task. In response to note-taking, students tended to divide the text passages into segments, usually by paragraph, and to use the structure of that segment as the basis for their notes. They did not integrate what they learned from the text into any larger structure that might indicate what the information meant to them or how it related to what they already knew. Students spent a third of their time commenting while they were reading the text; the other two-thirds of the time they were paraphrasing what they had read or thinking about the content of what they had read. Overwhelmingly, most of the students' comments during note-taking involved using schemata, or noting the ideas in the text.

In response to the study questions, students tended to restate the questions in their own terms and then skim over the texts looking for the answers. In general, they did not review the questions or revise their answers once they were discovered and written down. More than 85 percent of the time, the students devoted to answering the study questions were focused on searching the text, looking for information. Students devoted little time to larger cognitive tasks, such as relating what they had learned to what they already knew or to contemplating the significance of what they were learning. As with note-taking, students made about half their comments using schemata, but they also rephrased the questions (24 percent of the comments) and made metacomments (11 percent).

Finally, in writing essays in response to their reading, students tended to consider what they had read in terms of the essay questions, to brainstorm for relevant ideas, and to integrate what they had read into their own personal interpretation and response. Students made fewer than ten percent of their comments while referring to the text. Most of their comments were made while they were generating new ideas, integrating those ideas, or evaluating them. During essay writing, 44 percent of the students' comments used schemata, 19 percent involved hypothesizing, and 12 percent involved making metacomments (97–98).

Thus, we might say that the three different kinds of study tasks focused the students' thinking in different ways. Note-taking tended to focus the students' attention on the main ideas in the text that crossed sentence boundaries, but it did not encourage the students to integrate these ideas into previous knowledge or to make that knowledge their own. Completing short-answer study questions tended to focus the students' attention on discrete ideas in the text, but not in any way that encouraged students to organize those ideas or to integrate them. Writing essays tended to focus the students' attention on reconceptualizing the ideas in the students' own terms, focusing on a few main ideas, and integrating that information in a more complex way than note-taking or study questions. Interestingly, in both note-taking and essay writing, students made more comments about evidence and validation than they did while answering the study questions.

Which study technique produced the most increased topic knowledge as measured by the free-association test? All three techniques produced increased topic knowledge; essay writing produced the most, but not by a great deal. In Langer and Applebee's words, "If we rank the twelve sets of gain scores so that 1 represents the most gain and 12 the least, the average rank was 5.1 for essay writing, 6.8 for note-taking, and 7.6 for study questions" (101).

Now we might be tempted to infer from this study that writing essays about a particular subject is the best way to learn about that subject. And indeed, a number of other studies suggest that writing essays about a particular subject will help us remember many things about that subject, at least in certain ways (see for example Langer, "Learning"; Newell). But there are major reasons we might want to resist this temptation and interpret Langer and Applebee's findings as narrowly as possible. For one thing, Langer and Applebee measured what the students had learned by the students' ability to recall certain facts when prompted by a number of key words, and other studies have called into question the notion that essay writing is better than other study techniques for promoting sheer recall. For example, George Newell also conducted a study closely modeled after the one by Langer and Applebee. However, unlike Langer and Applebee, in order to measure recall, Newell asked his subjects to write down what they remembered immediately after they finished reading and studying the sample passages. Newell found that note-taking, study questions, and essay writing produced about the same overall recall of main ideas, basic content, relationships, and the students' ability to apply the concepts in the reading: "All three writing tasks facilitated (or impeded) recall to the same extent" (275). Essay writing did help students produce a more abstract set of associations for key concepts and to deal with these abstractions in a more complex way than did note-taking or answering study questions (281–82). Ann Penrose also found that when students were allowed to choose their own study and note-taking strategies, rather than follow a given prescription, these personal study and note-taking strategies helped students to recall more information than did essay writing *(Strategic)*.

Another point: Langer and Applebee studied the effect of their three study tasks on only one kind of discourse: factual prose from a social studies text. Might we expect the results to be the same for different kinds of discourse or for texts that are easier or more difficult to read than the passages Langer and Applebee used?

Still another point: Langer and Applebee gave their students a variety of very academic tasks unrelated to the students' own interests or to ongoing learning in a classroom. Might we expect the results to be the same if the students were allowed to choose among various tasks in order to help them learn something they actually wanted to learn? Many studies have shown that learners, given the same assignment, "will, in effect, do different tasks—because they differ in reading and writing ability, in prior knowledge of the topic, in how they interpret the assignment, and in many other ways" (Penrose, "Writing" 56; see also Nelson).

As a result, we might want to be careful about interpreting the Langer and Applebee study and simply say that different kinds of reading, study, and writing produce different kinds of learning and that there is some kind of correlation between the kind of writing students do and what they learn. Or as Ann Penrose puts it, "the value of writing as a means of learning varies according to the type of learning desired," and "the relationship between writing and learning varies with the nature of the material to be learned" and "the nature of the writing task itself" ("Writing" 53–57). In other words, various kinds of writing do not promote the same kinds of learning in the same way.

Thinking Does Not Necessarily Improve Writing

Of course, we write for other reasons than to help us learn things. We also use writing to help us think through issues or concerns, and we use writing to accomplish broader goals, such as to express ourselves or to inform or persuade others. I call these two broad kinds of writing writing-to-think and thinking-to-write. In writing-to-think, our goal is to use writing to discover or invent ideas and to clarify or otherwise explore the implications of what we have already thought or written, primarily to meet standards of logic, reasonableness, or truthfulness. Such writing can provide notation, a concrete record of ideas, concepts, or reasoning, which can in turn be contemplated further for particular purposes: note-takers can use their notes to help them remember or to help them decide whether they truly understand certain concepts. Journal writers can use their entries to reflect on their own experience and evaluate it. Essayists can use their essays to contemplate their ideas and reasoning in the light of new information or additional thought or experience. We think-to-write when we contemplate, reflect on, evaluate, or "monitor" what we have already thought, the written record of that thought, in order to clarify it or revise it or "improve" it on the basis of additional information or according to a framework for thinking through the subject matter.

The goal of thinking-to-write is to think through the implications of every aspect of the rhetorical situation—our own assumptions and purposes, what we do and do not know about our subject, our analysis of the audience and of the rhetorical situation, and how these factors might affect our use of the appropriate genre conventions—in order to affect an audience in a particular way. In short, in thinking-to-write, the act of writing is *rhetorical*. It is always a response to a particular audience in a particular social context, and much of the writing involves shaping the thinking to fit the demands of an audience and a rhetorical situation. In thinking-to-write we conceive of the writing itself as a kind of end product, although it may never be fully "finished," as a particular object shaped in a particular way to meet the demands of a particular exigence, audience, and context.

Obviously, in certain situations, the goals of writing-to-think and thinking-to-write will overlap. We may jot down notes to ourselves before we begin to formally draft our writing on paper or computer screen. These notes may be evidence of brainstorming for ideas or long-range planning or thinking critically about the issue at hand: they may be an example of writing-to-think. However, once we begin drafting we may rethink our earlier notes in relation to our rhetorical purpose, audience and context: in my terms, writing-to-think blends in and becomes indistinguishable from thinking-to-write. Or to put it another way: if our thinking leads us to discard our original purposes and to proceed in new directions, we might call that writing-to-think. If our thinking leads us to reevaluate and refine our current purposes, we might call that thinking-to-write.

I have gone to some lengths to adequately distinguish between writing-to-think and thinking-to-write because I think the distinction is important.

The distinction raises the issue of whether learning particular strategies of writing-to-think necessarily improves thinking-to-write. I would argue that it does not. Learning to think about a certain subject matter in a certain social context, what is often called reflection or metacognition or critical consciousness, does not necessarily help writers shape the results of their thinking to the demands of a particular situation or context. Clear or thoughtful analysis does not necessarily result in better writing, if we think of writing as the ability to go beyond a clear, thoughtful analysis and adapt that analysis to the demands of a particular genre in a particular social context.

Take for example James Berlin's heuristic for helping students to examine "the cultural codes—the semiotic analysis—that are working themselves out in shaping consciousness in our students and ourselves" ("Poststructuralism" 146). Berlin's heuristic invites students to analyze texts broadly conceived—print, film, television—in relation to "the key terms in the discourse and to situate these within the structure of meaning of which they form a part." The analysis is in two steps. The first part of the analysis sets the key terms of the text "in relation to their binary opposites as suggested by the text itself"; the second part places the key terms "within the narrative structural forms suggested by the text, the culturally coded stories about patterns of behavior appropriate for people within certain situations. These codes deal with such social designations as race, class, gender, age, ethnicity, and the like" (146–47).

Berlin applies this heuristic to a 1981 essay written by William Blundell for the *Wall Street Journal* entitled "The Life of the Cowboy: Drudgery and Danger." To Berlin, a key term in the essay is "cowboss," the ranch foreman. In analyzing this term, Berlin sees a number of binary oppositions. On the one hand, a cowboss is a kind of manager who runs a large organization and supervises employees, who happen to be cowboys; on the other hand, in contrast to the office workers in his organization, the cowboss is a cowboy himself in that he works outdoors and engages in largely physical labor. This binary suggests others: cowboys in the country are opposed to union workers in the city; the work of cowboys is overwhelmingly masculine, suggesting that women have a separate domain; other binaries are "nature/civilization, country/ city, cowboy/urban cowboy, and the like" ("Poststructuralism" 148). In teaching this kind of analysis, Berlin claims that students come to see that the binaries are "arranged hierarchically, with one term privileged over the other" but that these hierarchies are unstable; for example, that "cowboy" may be privileged in relation to "union worker" but not in relation to "cowboss."

As part of the next step in his thinking heuristic, Berlin asks his students to consider how key terms function in common "socially constructed narratives": for cowboys, his students come to see that "patterns of behavior involving individuality, freedom, and independence" are "simultaneously coupled with self-discipline, respect for authority (good cowboys never complain), and submission to the will of the cowboss" (149). Berlin then goes on to encourage his students to see similar behavior patterns in "capitalist economic narratives" embodied in the essay on cowboys and "their consequences for class, gender, and race relations and roles both in the workplace and elsewhere" (149). The ultimate point of this analysis is to get students to see that "texts—whether rhetorical or poetic—are ideologically invested in the construction of subjectivities within recommended economic, social and political arrangements" and to help students analyze their own experiences in these terms, to get them to see how their own subjectivities are influenced by given economic, social, and political roles, and how they do not necessarily have to take on the roles assigned to them, that their roles can be negotiated and reshaped "to serve their own agendas" (150). To Berlin, the implications of this analysis for composing should also become clear as students struggle to write essays analyzing various texts. They should also come to see that all writing "is situated within signifying practices and that learning to understand personal and social experience involves acts of discourse production and interpretation, the two acting interchangeably in reading and writing codes" (151).

Clearly, in promoting his form of critical consciousness, Berlin encourages his students to think in ways different from what they have done before. Most novice writers in Berlin's classroom would probably not have learned to analyze key terms using binary oppositions or to contemplate the social, economic, or political influences on their thinking and writing before they arrived. It is equally clear that although the goal of Berlin's heuristic is to create a critical consciousness, his heuristic involves all of the skills of basic thinking. In order to detect key terms, Berlin's students would need to focus on the concept of a key term, "observe" the cowboy essay closely, gather possible candidates for further scrutiny, analyze the collected terms to see which ones might most profitably be used to generate binary oppositions, and evaluate the analysis in order to pick out the one or two most useful terms. We could break down every step in Berlin's heuristic in a similar way. What then has Berlin taught his students to *do* with writing?

As a culmination of their analyses, Berlin's students "analyze in essay form the effect of an important cultural code on their lives" ("Poststructuralism" 150). These analytical essays must "conform to the genre codes of the form of the essay they are writing—the personal essay, the academic essay, the newspaper essay, for example"—or to the codes of other genres the students choose to use, such as short stories, poems, or videos (151). In Berlin's pedagogy, the teacher would also "foreground" the conventions of the genres the students would be using, thereby highlighting "the culturally coded character of all parts of composing" and emphasizing that "all experience is situated within signifying practices," that "the more the writer understands the entire semiotic context in which she is functioning, the greater will be the likelihood that her text will serve as a successful intervention in an ongoing discussion" (150–51).

Now because Berlin devotes the greater part of his essay to an explanation of his heuristic for raising the critical consciousness of his students, he does not describe how he helps students investigate the conventions of the genres they are asked to write or how he helps them explore other aspects of the rhetorical situations in which these genres might be used. His only example seems to be a "personal essay," in which students explore their own thoughts about the importance of a given cultural code in their lives. Berlin never discusses any pedagogical techniques for helping his students shape their essays in ways that will insure their essays "conform to [the] socially indicated formal codes" they must enact in order to participate in some larger discourse community.

Given this lack of attention to shaping writing in certain ways in order to participate in the ongoing concerns of a particular discourse community, I think it is clear that Berlin's pedagogy is overwhelmingly an example of writing-to-think. The goal of his course is to help students analyze texts in ways that will reveal the operation of key terms, to get them to see what their analysis of key terms suggests about the "social construction" of various aspects of society, and the implications of these constructions for race, class, gender, age, and ethnicity. The final essays for the course are primarily a way for students to show that they can use the analytical tools Berlin has given them and a way for them to clarify in their own minds how some aspects of their own lives has been socially constructed.

However, if thinking and writing outside of classrooms is always used to accomplish particular tasks in particular social contexts, we might reasonably ask what sort of tasks Berlin has taught his students to perform. He has taught them to analyze texts and aspects of society using a particular heuristic framework; he has taught them to clarify their own thinking in applying that heuristic. But in what way has he prepared them to write some genre in some social context or discourse community? I do not think we can assume that Berlin's students have learned thinking-to-write.

Nowhere is the discrepancy between writing-to-think and thinking-to-write more dramatic than in persuasion. In order to persuade we need to know not only what we think about a problem or issue ourselves, but how to make our beliefs and values convincing to others. Persuasion is not just a matter of conveying our own thoughts; it is a matter of making our thoughts acceptable, even convincing, to others who may disagree with us. Persuasion involves all kinds of knowledge and ability beyond what we think about a problem or issue ourselves: it involves empathy, patterns of reasoning, and attention to ethical and emotional appeals far beyond what we think, believe, and value ourselves.

James Paul Gee argues that in becoming literate, we learn two kinds of Discourses (with a capital "D"): a primary Discourse, which we acquire through inculturation into the social groups—the family and class, "or the primary socialization group as defined by the culture"—we were born into, and a variety of secondary Discourses, which we learn "in association with, and by having access to and practice with (apprenticeships in)" secondary institutions, "such as schools, work places, stores, government offices, businesses, churches, etc." (*Social* 151). One of the major points of this distinction is that, to Gee, true literacy always involves "*mastery of, or fluent control over, a secondary Discourse*"; that is, true literacy involves not just the acquisition of a primary Discourse, but to a certain extent the self-conscious learning of a secondary Discourse, the learning of particular kinds of meta-knowledge and metalanguage used in secondary institutions, most often of course in school. Thus, according to Gee, a liberating discourse is "a *particular use* of a Discourse (to critique other ones), not a particular Discourse" in itself (153). A liberating Discourse contains "both the Discourse it is going to critique and a set of meta-elements (language, words, attitudes, values) in terms of which an analysis and criticism can be carried out" (156). To Ludwig Wittgenstein, a liberating Discourse is a different language game from a primary Discourse: it has different purposes and different rules; it often functions in different social contexts for different discourse communities.

In Gee's terms, then, Berlin's heuristic may be an example of a secondary liberating Discourse. It provides a framework, a set of concepts and terms, for critiquing other Discourses. Or in Wittgenstein's terms, Berlin's heuristic is another language game from the essays it helps students to analyze. It provides a new "package" of information and new combinations of basic thinking skills in order to accomplish new tasks in new contexts. Berlin's heuristic is in effect a way for his students to *do* something different from what they have done before. Berlin is not preparing his students to write a traditional autobiographical narrative, explaining how they came to certain realizations or epiphanies, for the community of belles lettres, those who read personal essays for wit and character and incident. Rather, he is preparing them to write a much more analytic and theoretical essay, probably organized more by ideas than narrative, for a community of informed citizens who read such essays for their insight into ideology and public issues.

Writing-to-think may be a necessary but not sufficient condition for thinking-to-write. In any given situation, the relationship between writing-to-think and thinking-to-write will depend on how the writer considers his subject and the way that consideration connects to matters of genre, audience, and context. We cannot assume that improving writing-to-think will also improve thinking-to-write.

Metacognitive Thinking Does Not Improve Cognition Generally

People may learn to think in a wide variety of ways, and they may learn to use writing to help with that thinking or to articulate that thinking, but learning to think or write in particular ways may have no broad cognitive effects. Or in more everyday terms, learning to think and write in particular ways may not improve our ability to think in general, whatever that may mean.

Despite a large literature speculating about the positive effects of literacy on our ability to think (see for example Goody; Goody and Watt; David Olson), more recent research indicates that our ability to write allows us to accomplish very particular social goals, but it does not necessarily convey any larger cognitive abilities. The landmark study of the subject is by Sylvia Scribner and Michael Cole (*Psychology*). In their ethnographic study of the uses of literacy among the Vai, a people living in northwestern Liberia, Scribner and Cole found a high correlation between certain kinds of literacy and certain very specific social practices. Males of the Vai are often literate in three languages: Vai, which has a written script the men do not learn in school but informally by teaching one another, often in their teens or early twenties; Arabic, which they often learn as children from tutors in classes of six to twelve; and English, which they learn in schools.

Vai men generally learn Vai script for social reasons: they want to write letters or to participate in particular social groups in which the ability to write Vai is common. Once they learn the script, they often continue to use it to keep records or family histories (*Psychology* 65–69). They learn Arabic at the prompting of their parents, who want to foster their religious life: being able to read and recite the Qur'an is considered a sign of devotion among the Vai; many of Scribner and Cole's respondents commented that learning the Qur'an was a sign of discipline and obedience (68–69). Surprisingly, the Vai use written English in much the same way they use Vai script—to write letters and keep records—perhaps because the rural economy does not allow for a more extensive use.

In comparing the way the Vai use these three different forms of writing, Scribner and Cole found that literacy in and of itself did not confer any "higher order intellectual skills" and that the effect of literacy among the Vai was generally limited to helping them accomplish fairly concrete social tasks (*Psychology* 132). On certain tests that measured the ability to sort items according to abstract concepts, the ability to retain information, and ability to reason verbally, Scribner and Cole found that improved performance on the tests was "associated with years of formal schooling," not with literacy in and of itself. That is, formal schooling seems to promote the ability to generalize from particular instances in a wide variety of knowledge domains. However, "Vai literates [without schooling] were not significantly different from nonliterates on any of these cognitive measures, including the sorting and reasoning tasks that had been suggested as especially sensitive to experience with a written language" ("Literacy" 453).

Such evidence suggests that reading and writing have few larger effects than those we associate with the ability to accomplish concrete tasks. We write personal narratives because we want to capture our own experiences for our grandchildren or to share our experiences with others. We write critical analyses because we want to convince others to change their minds about a particular point of view. We write business memos because we have to communicate the latest company policies to our fellow employees. We write scholarly articles because that is what scholars *do:* they conduct research and share their findings with interested parties. We write in these ways because we have a particular purpose in a particular social context, and we have learned the particular conventions that people use in these contexts.

The relationship between thinking and writing will always be problematic. Of course, in the future we may discover new taxonomies of thinking and new ways of conceptualizing the relationship between thinking and writing. However, it is difficult to ponder what such future taxonomies might be like or what difference future conceptualizations of thinking and writing would make in terms of what we already know.

In all likelihood, future studies will confirm that thinking and writing are related in very local and limited ways; that in particular contexts, certain heuristics, strategies, and frameworks for thinking may help certain kinds of writers and thinkers achieve certain purposes with certain kinds of knowledge.

Let's now reconsider Caulfield's claim from the epigraph of this chapter that we cannot "ever get the words right until we get the thoughts right." If Caulfield means that clear thinking involves being able to articulate to ourselves in writing what we mean by a particular claim, belief, and value, he may very well be right. Being able to articulate a thought or belief or value may be the only way we can demonstrate what in fact our thought or belief or value *is.*

But that does not mean that clear thinking about our beliefs and values or about a problem or issue necessarily results in good writing to an audience other than ourselves. It is entirely possible that we may be able to clarify our own thoughts, to have a clear sense of what we believe and value, of what we think about a particular problem or issue, and still not express those thoughts very well to some audience other than ourselves for some larger social purpose. Being able to articulate to ourselves why a particular episode in our lives is dramatic and interesting is not the same thing as being able to write a good story about the episode. Being able to write a good story means being able to master the conventions of the story genre. Having a clear vision of what the long-term goals of our business or company should be is not the same thing as being able to explain that vision clearly and coherently to our superiors or to stockholders. Being able to write a vision statement for a business means being able to master the conventions of an office memo or annual report in ways that account for the particular concerns of those who will be affected by that vision.

So when we talk about teaching thinking in its many guises, we ought to ask ourselves just what it is we are asking students to do. It seems most helpful to conceptualize thinking not as a list of context-free skills but as those skills that people need in order to accomplish particular tasks in particular contexts. Overwhelming, it seems to me, composition scholars who promote a particular kind of thinking are teaching a very narrow range of writing or even thinking. And given the limited amount of writing students do during their college and university careers, we ought to ask ourselves whether this is the only kind of experience we want them to have or whether this is the kind of experience they would choose to have if we were more explicit about what we mean when we teach writing.

One way to deal with the problem would be to find a way to insure that students had a range of experiences in writing-to-learn, writing-to-think, and thinking-to-write as part of their college experience, a way to insure that they were introduced to a wide repertoire of knowledge and thinking strategies across a range of disciplines and knowledge domains. Thinking is always a matter of thinking about a particular subject in a particular way with the "relevant knowledge and understanding" in a particular context for a particular reason, just as writing is always a matter of writing in a particular way about a particular subject with the "relevant knowledge and understanding" in a particular context for a particular reason. We have serious reason to question whether generic thinking and writing strategies are helpful in specific contexts. It depends on whether thinkers or writers can use the generic strategy—or indeed whether they can even see the relevance of the strategy—given the new knowledge and the new issues they confront in each next context. I will deal with this issue more specifically in the next chapter, where I deal with the problem of transfer.

6 Transfer

NOW WE HAVE ARRIVED at what I take to be the heart of the matter in learning to write. If writing is a complex number of related abilities that rely on very different kinds of knowledge, depending on the writer's purpose and context, when writers learn any particular piece of knowledge or when they learn how to put a particular skill into practice, just what have they learned? Have they learned a general skill that can be applied any time they write again, or have they learned something that can be applied only in very limited circumstances similar to those in which they learned that knowledge or that skill in the first place? In psychology and learning theory, these questions are part of a process called "transfer": in what sense can various kinds of knowledge and skill be transferred from one situation to another, or learned in one context and applied in another?

And overwhelmingly, the evidence suggests that learners do not necessarily transfer the kinds of knowledge and skills they have learned previously to new tasks. If such transfer occurs at all, it is largely unpredictable and depends on the learners' background and experience, factors over which teachers have little control. If learners *do* transfer the appropriate knowledge and skills from one context to another, they do so because they see the similarity between what they have learned in the past and what they need to do in new contexts. The only way teachers can help students with the process of transfer is to help them see the similarities between what they have learned before and what they need to do in new contexts.

The implications of these claims for the teaching of writing are radical. In effect, the evidence suggests that writing teachers can claim only that students have learned what teachers have taught and evaluated, that in effect, writing teachers get what they teach for, instruction in particular kinds of knowledge and skill and not broad-based writing ability. If we want to promote the transfer of certain kinds of writing abilities from one class to another or one context to another, then we are going to have to find the means to institutionalize instruction in the similarities between the way writing is done in a variety of contexts.

I am going to present the evidence for these claims in the following order. To set the context for the empirical evidence, I will begin with David Russell's Wittgenstein-like analogy comparing writing with games that use balls and then make a distinction between strong and weak strategies for learning. Then I will present the evidence of a number of case studies and ponder their implications.

An Analogy

> Many different games are played with a ball. The originators of each game have appropriated this tool for the object(ive) of each, the "object of the game." The kind of game (activity system) changes the form of the ball (tool)—large, small, hard, soft, leather, rubber, round, oblong, and so on. The object(ive) and the history of each game also condition the uses of the ball. One could play volleyball by using the head, as in soccer, but it is much less effective in achieving the object of the game than using the wrists and hands. (Russell, "Activity" 57–58)

When we teach someone to use a ball, just what are we teaching? If we teach young people to use a ball in one kind of game, would we expect those people to use any kind of ball in any game? Well, we might say, it depends on the ways the balls are used in the two games. Exactly. We would expect people taught to throw a small hard ball overhand in baseball to be able to throw other round balls overhand as long as they could grip the ball with one hand. We would expect people skilled in throwing baseballs to also be able to throw softballs, for example, but we would not expect them to necessarily be able to pitch underhand or to throw basketballs or soccer balls or volleyballs with two hands. We would expect people trained to dribble and kick a soccer ball to be able to also control a basketball or a beach ball if it were used in a pick-up game of soccer, but we would not expect the skill of being able to control a soccer ball with the feet to carry over to an ability to dribble a basketball with the hands or the ability to set up or spike a volleyball. In each case, the ability to use a ball is a particular skill to be used in a particular manner in a particular context, and we would expect the skill of being able to use a ball in a certain way to be transferred only to other similar uses: throwing overhand, pitching underhand, tossing with two hands, dribbling and kicking with the feet, setting up and spiking.

The same may be true of a wide range of mental abilities. Barbara Rogoff puts the problem succinctly: "cognitive skills seem to fluctuate as a function of the situation, which suggests that skills are limited in their generality" (1). She goes on:

This is not to say that cognitive activities are completely specific to the episode in which they were originally learned or applied. In order to function, people must be able to generalize some aspects of knowledge and skills to new situations. Attention to the role of context removes the assumption of broad generality in cognitive activity across contexts and focuses instead on determining how the generalization of knowledge and skills occurs. (3)

This suggests that some aspects of a writer's knowledge and ability are broadly based, something the writer can apply in any context, and some aspects of that knowledge and ability are dependent on things the writer needs to know and is able to do only in particular contexts.

In Russell's terms, learning to write is a matter of learning how to use similar tools, such as language, discourse conventions, composing strategies, and problem-solving techniques in radically different contexts. We do not use the word "book" to mean the same thing—it is not even the same part of speech—in different contexts. We tell someone near us to "hand us that book" in one context. Playing the role of a detective in another context, we say, "Book him." Mastering the word "book" means being able to use the word in all its different meanings appropriately in different contexts. We do not write "introductions" using the same conventions in informal essays as we do in research articles. Our ability to write introductions depends on our knowing the conventions of many different genres and when to apply them appropriately. We do not plan the writing of laboratory reports the same way we plan the writing of movie reviews. Being able to plan in writing means that we know about many different kinds of subject matter and genres and how to organize that knowledge appropriately for a variety of purposes and audiences. We do not think through a proposal to change the undergraduate curriculum in an English department the same way we think through a proposal to a city council to add a stop light at a city intersection. Our competence to solve problems depends on both broad analytic strategies and very specific kinds of domain-specific and context-specific knowledge. All of these examples call into question what we mean when we say that writers have learned "vocabulary" or "introductions" or planning strategies or problem solving. The question is the degree to which our ability to use a word, an introduction, or a problem-solving strategy in one context will carry over into another context.

In chapter 1, I suggested that we can evaluate the ability of writers to accomplish a specific task only by asking them to show us what they can do in a variety of circumstances, that we cannot assume that writers know many different meanings of "book" unless we actually hear them use the word to mean many different things. We cannot assume that writers know how to plan a movie review if they have only had experience planning lab reports. We cannot assume writers know how to put together an effective proposal to a city council just because they can write effective proposals to change an English department's curriculum. In each case, there is a reason to think that what the writer knows or is able to do is something that can transfer from one situation to the next, and there is a reason to think that what the writer knows or is able to do is very local and context-dependent and will not transfer to another situation.

Weak and Strong Strategies

James Voss distinguishes between *weak* and *strong* problem-solving strategies. This is a distinction that may be helpful in thinking about the knowledge and skills we use when we write. To Voss, even though certain problem-solving strategies apply to a variety of domains and contexts, these strategies seem to be *weak* because "they lack power rather than generality, that is, they are not applicable for the more specific problems within the respective domains" (74). One weak problem-solving strategy is what Voss calls "decomposition"; that is, dividing a problem into a number of smaller subproblems and solving the larger problem by solving each subproblem in turn. The paradox of weak problem-solving strategies is that a knowledge of the strategy may be helpful as a way to approach a problem or as a way to begin to solve it. On the other hand, weak strategies are so general that they are not much help in thinking through the particulars of a problem.

Strong problem-solving strategies, on the other hand, "tend to be domain-specific and usually are not applicable to other domains" (74). Most concepts and formulas in mathematics—say, subtraction or "distance = rate × time"—are strong strategies and can be applied only in situations that clearly call for them.

Now we might be able to use the concepts of "weak" and "strong" to think about the knowledge and skill we use in writing, although the distinction does not apply exactly. Many dedicated writing teachers offer their students opportunities to think about and acquire a metacognitive sense of how writing varies from purpose to purpose, genre to genre, and context to context. For example, Gene Krupa has designed a series of related assignments that requires students to use the same experience as the basis for writing for different purposes in a different genre. In one such series, Krupa invites his students to write about a job they have held. In the first assignment, the students express how they feel about the job as if they were talking to a friend. In the second assignment, they write a set of instructions to help others who work at the job overcome some problems associated with it. The third assignment is to write a letter of recommendation for someone who might want the job (30–35, 67–73, 116–22). The point of this series of assignments, of course, is to help students see that their knowledge and experience about a single subject can be the basis for many different kinds of writing, which use different genre conventions, depending on the writer's purpose and audience, and to help them develop a strategy, a way of thinking, about the many aspects of writing they must control: a sense of style and voice, a sense of the variability of genre conventions, a sense of audi-

ence, what I have called rhetorical maturity. Peter Elbow has a similar series of assignments ("Reflections" 150–51). But the strategies promoted by
these assignments are necessarily "weak" strategies: they apply to a wide
range of genres and contexts. We might formulate one such strategy this
way: "Be stylistically formal or informal depending on your purpose, genre,
and audience." And in order to help implement this strategy, teachers might
introduce students to various genres that use in varying degrees first-person pronouns, the passive voice, and types of jargon, and give students practice in altering their style or voice to the occasion. Such practice and the
self-conscious awareness it is designed to promote is all to the good.

But there are limits to such weak strategies. Sooner or later, after they
have graduated from the writing classroom, novice writers will find themselves in social contexts in which they have to write in genres and for audiences that are new to them, and their self-conscious awareness of weak strategies—"alter your style to the demands of the context"—will depend
entirely on their ability to determine what those new demands are. Take for
example the supposedly simple demands of writing a research paper for a
history class, a genre I never mastered as an undergraduate, at least to the
degree that I could earn A's on my papers. In this case, does the novice writer
use first-person pronouns and the passive voice? The professor of the course
hands out no sample papers and, in his assignment sheet, states only that
the papers should be written in standard academic prose. And how does
the novice go about determining the particular jargon of the field and the
key concepts for the period and subject of the paper? Without models, how
does the student go about determining how history papers are organized?
Does the student model the paper after articles in *American Heritage* or
more specialized academic journals? Little the student has learned in introductory writing classes will help accomplish these tasks, which require
strong strategies, a knowledge of where to look and how to discover particular discourse conventions at work in history—or at least in particular
history classrooms.

The same paradox of strong and weak strategies applies to all of the many
kinds of knowledge and skill we associate with writing: spelling, punctuation, usage, and other text conventions; patterns of organization and discourse formats and other genre conventions; strategies of invention, planning, drafting, revising, and editing, or any other aspect of composing; and
heuristics for analyzing audience and context.

Ross Winterowd asserts that most of the skills we associate with writing
are transferable: skills such as syntactic fluency, control of diction, a sensitivity to audience, organizational ability, and "mechanics," such as punctuation and spelling. What is not transferable, according to Winterowd, is what
he calls a local skill, the ability to use a particular genre or "special form"
such as the scientific report, with its particular requirements for footnot-
ing, vocabulary, style, and tone ("Transferable" 1). But perhaps Winterowd

is oversimplifying. Consider "organizational ability." Of what does such an ability consist? In Voss's terms, it consists of a number of related strategies for organizing different sorts of discourse, some strong, some weak. Suppose a novice writer has been primarily taught the five-paragraph theme or a thesis-and-subpoints strategy as a way of organizing writing. Still, this novice reads popular novels and the local newspaper, both the news section and the editorial page, and has come to realize that not all discourse is organized by an introduction, a number of explicit major points, and a conclusion. In other words, despite instruction in the five-paragraph theme, the writer knows that writing can also be organized by chronology or by the anticlimactic structure of news stories, or by a complex number of persuasive strategies. In other words, this writer knows a number of weak organizational strategies. The novice writer's problem is knowing under what circumstances these strategies may be strong, under what circumstances they can be applied directly with some degree of appropriateness.

Now our novice writer may very well see the relevance of a thesis-and-subpoints strategy to most of the writing required for college coursework—may realize that for most academic writing, a thesis-and-subpoints strategy seems to apply. But in particular cases—for example, in a second semester introductory writing course in persuasion—the novice writer may have to use certain genres or practice writing in certain hypothetical situations in which the thesis-and-subpoints strategy may not apply. Assigned to persuade an audience of peers, perhaps in the college newspaper, that the honor code used by the college ought to be abolished, the novice may not know how to proceed. Having never written a persuasive editorial before, the writer must decide whether any of the known strategies is relevant and, if they are, how to use them in some appropriate combination. In this context, it is not at all clear whether a generally broad but weak thesis-and-subpoints strategy will be strong; that is, whether it will be sufficiently domain- or context-specific to be helpful.

In addition, as I pointed out in chapter 5 on thinking, the novice writer needs to see the similarity between what's been learned in the past and its relevance to the new writing task. The writer has to see that a thesis-and-subpoints strategy taught, say, for literary interpretation and final exams may also apply to persuasive editorials, although perhaps not in quite the same way. As a result, the degree to which our novice writer can transfer organizational strategies from one situation to another is not at all clear.

A Few Case Studies

As far as I know, there are no research studies that concentrate directly on the nature of transfer in writing. Most of what we know about transfer comes from studies of problem solving or chess playing or the ability to recall factual information (Gick and Holyoak). These studies are often the basis for theoretical articles in composition studies on the nature of expertise in writing (see for example Carter, Foertsch). However, a major study by Barbara Walvoord and Lucille McCarthy of the writing required in four different college courses does deal with the problem of transfer. The courses that Walvoord and McCarthy studied were these: a mid-level business course in production management (Business 330); an introductory history course in modern civilization (History 101); a low-level psychology course in human sexuality (Psych 165); and a mid-level writing-intensive biology course introducing students to the range of writing in biology as a field (Biology 381).

In each of these classes, students were required to write in response to what Walvoord and McCarthy call "good/better/best questions." That is, students were asked to evaluate something or to solve a problem in a way that dealt with one of these questions:

> Good: Is X good or bad?
> Better: Which is better—X or Y?
> Best: Which is the best among available options? What is the best
>   solution to a given problem? (7)

Walvoord and McCarthy's goals in analyzing the writing done in response to good/better/best questions included answering the following questions: (1) What difficulties did students have meeting their teachers' expectations? (2) "How did teachers' methods and students' strategies appear to affect, contribute to, or help overcome these difficulties?" (3) What were the similarities and differences among the four classes in these areas?

Now it might seem that Walvoord and McCarthy's study would be an ideal way to look at how students learn to transfer what they know about a certain kind of thinking and writing—in this case, their ability to think about and write evaluations—in new and different contexts. But immediately, we run into the problem that I have been pointing out all along: just what kind of knowledge or skill is involved in writing evaluations? Of course, at a high level of abstraction, all the forms of good/better/best questions are related to each other, and once writers learn a particular strategy or set of strategies to use in evaluation, we might expect them to be able to apply these strategies regardless of subject matter or context. For example, a common evaluation strategy taught in many introductory writing texts, especially those that emphasize persuasion, is what John Ramage, John Bean, and June Johnson call a criteria-match strategy: developing a set of criteria for making an evaluative judgment, analyzing the characteristics of the object to be evaluated, and determining how well those characteristics match the criteria (290–99). In addition, Walvoord and McCarthy note that the students in their study often referred to "models they had learned elsewhere, such as the 'term paper,' 'reflection paper,' 'thesis and subs,' or the model of the streetcorner debate" (233). For example, in writing their evaluations, the students in the business and history classes, both of which were offered in the same college, often seemed to rely on a common organizational strategy—the "thesis and subs" strategy or "organize by thesis and subthesis"—which had been taught in the introductory writing courses at the college.

As a result, we might expect criteria-match and "thesis and subs" strategies to be what Voss calls weak strategies: they apply to a variety of contexts and domains of knowledge, but they are not particularly helpful in dealing with the specifics of different contexts and domains. Thus, the problem is how helpful these strategies may be when students are "asked to apply discipline-based categories, concepts, or methods *to new data and new situations*" (Walvoord and McCarthy 7). That is, in Voss's terms, how helpful are these strategies in situations seeming to call for *strong* strategies, those with a great deal of power to help in specific contexts that call for specific knowledge.

Consider how different each of the good/better/best questions was in subject matter, evaluative criteria, and relevant evidence for each of the four classes. In Business 303: Production Management, students were expected to write three evaluations of various kinds, one of which the instructor called an "analytical assignment": evaluating the layout and work design of two fast-food restaurants, McDonald's and Popeye's, in terms of the restaurant's overall goals. For this assignment, students had to determine the restaurant's goals and then develop criteria for evaluating those goals. For example, one student determined that the goals of both restaurants were to promptly and efficiently serve a large number of customers. In order to evaluate how well each restaurant did so, the student looked at how each restaurant distributed work among its employees so that they were constantly busy and could move the products as fast as possible.

In History 101: Modern Civilization, students were expected to "use historical material as evidence to argue questions of concern to citizens involved in the public life of the nation," such as the value of political stability, the meaning of economic growth, and the degree to which nations should arm themselves or go to war (Walvoord and McCarthy 100). For one such assignment, students were given a hypothetical situation in which the dictator of the mythical country called Loyoliana asks for advice about whether he should implement certain reforms because in many ways, his country resembles France before the revolution of 1789. In order to help the students develop their thesis, criteria, and evidence, the instructor explicitly stated that

> the students' opinion should be supported by specific, accurate facts/opinions found in the primary and secondary sources students read. These facts and opinions should be used as evidence—that is, the student should connect the historical material to his/her own opinion by stating warrants and by using subtheses. . . . In the argument, the student should acknowledge alternative solutions/outcomes and should raise and answer the counterevi-

dence or counterarguments that would be expected from course readings or common sense. (101)

Notice that in this assignment, much of the problem of developing criteria for determining the best advice to the dictator is only implied in the directions to connect the historical evidence to the students' opinion by using warrants.

In Psychology 165: Human Sexuality, students were expected to write a number of pieces in the role of a counselor, giving advice to a client. The last assignment was to write "a letter to a friend who is about to marry, advising him or her 'how to have a good marital sex life'" (Walvoord and McCarthy 150). As in the history class, this assignment immersed students in a hypothetical situation and listed a number of factors for the students to address in their writing: their role and audience (friend to friend), the form of the piece (a letter), the theme (any of the topics addressed in the course, supported by at least one outside source, such as a magazine or journal article or a book). Notice, however, that as in the history assignment, the instructor did not formally involve the students in evaluative reasoning per se; that is, the instructor did not help the students to develop criteria for evaluating the best possible advice to give the friend although the instructor did implicitly expect the students to note counterarguments and address them.

In Biology 381: Biological Literature, students were expected to write a research report comparing two commercial products, using original scientific research modeled after the kind of research done in companies located in the area around the university where the course was offered, companies where many of the graduates of the program found jobs. These companies analyzed such products as facial creams and spices. For this assignment, students were expected to formulate a hypothesis as to which product was better, define "better" operationally in terms of measurable factors such as the degree of acidity in pickles, design an experiment that controlled a number of variables, interpret the data, and then write up the report in a standard scientific format. In this case the scientific format included the following categories: title, abstract, introduction, review of the literature, methods and materials, results, discussion, and literature cited. In this assignment, students *were* explicitly taught to address the issue of criteria in the development of their definitions of "better."

In their analysis of these four kinds of evaluative writing, Walvoord and McCarthy note how similar they are in terms of a "thesis and subs" format, even though the instructors who designed the assignments use very different terms for each aspect of the assignment and put different aspects of the criteria-match evaluation strategy in different categories. Notice in figure 6.1 that developing a set of criteria is part of the process of articulating a definition or thesis in the biology class, but it is part of the process of analysis in the history class (see also Walvoord and McCarthy 181). These observations raise two questions: How much of what the students wrote for each of these classes was similar to what they wrote in the other classes? And to what degree could we expect them to transfer what they had learned from one task to the other? (For a similar conceptual problem with defining problems in various academic disciplines, see MacDonald, "Problem.")

	Thesis/ Purpose	Criteria	Evidence/ Match
Business	Evaluate goals of two restaurants	Distribution of work among employees	Work loads
History	Support advice to a dictator	Implied criteria for implementing reforms	Facts and opinions about the value of reforms
Psychology	A letter offering advice to meet client's goals	Implied criteria for a good sex life	Facts about sex
Biology	Evaluate two products with an "operational definition of "better"	Define criteria in measurable ways	Interpretation of research results

Fig. 6.1. Good/Better/Best Reasoning Across the Curriculum

One of Walvoord and McCarthy's major conclusions is that in trying to fulfill these assignments—despite their similarity—the students had difficulties in six areas:

1. Gathering sufficient specific information
2. In the paper, constructing the audience and the self
3. Stating a position
4. Using appropriate discipline-based methods to arrive at the position and to support it with evidence
5. Managing complexity (i.e., avoiding what the teacher considered overgeneralization or oversimplification; considering various aspects of an issue; discussing alternative solutions to problems; acknowledging and answering counterarguments and counter-evidence; in science, designing an experiment with appropriate operational definitions and control of variables)
6. Organizing the paper. (14)

Walvoord and McCarthy insist that they saw examples of students transferring knowledge from one class to another and that in their writing for a particular class students often relied on examples of thinking and writing that they had learned elsewhere. But overwhelmingly in their case studies,

Walvoord and McCarthy cite example after example of students who have difficulty with such transfer. They cite example after example of students who try to apply knowledge and experience that is inappropriate or in ways that are not helpful.

Here is one case. For the business assignment to evaluate the layout and work design of two fast-food restaurants, 30 percent of the students used a two-columned comparison-and-contrast chart they very likely learned in an earlier writing class. We might consider this an excellent example of transfer of learning, of applying a broad but weak strategy effectively in a new context. However, Walvoord and McCarthy's one case study, a student named Kurt, had difficulty moving past his comparison-and-contrast analysis to an evaluation. In fact, the comparison-and-contrast format may have actually hindered his analysis because it did not help him to see how the differences between the restaurants had to be evaluated in terms of the goals of the restaurants.

Walvoord and McCarthy speculate on why a significant number of students had difficulty doing more than simply comparing and contrasting the two restaurants, despite the fact that the instructor recorded in his teaching log that "he emphasized his expectations that mere comparison/contrast was not enough. He told students that they needed a theme that would evaluate the layout and work design in terms of the restaurants' goals" (84). Perhaps the reason the students did not follow the instructor's oral admonitions is that his assignment sheet used the phrase "compare and contrast," and the students immediately associated that phrase with a model of writing they had learned elsewhere. Walvoord and McCarthy conclude: "Once again, models from other settings . . . may be powerful influences on students' writing and thinking strategies, overriding other instructions from the teacher" (85).

Or take one more example: in the history class, a student named Bonnie had difficulty responding to the following assignment:

> In a one-paragraph essay, state which solution to the problem of 17th-century anarchy—French or English—*you* personally find more realistic and attractive. Try to explain why you feel the way you do, and to back your feelings with some evidence. (132)

According to Walvoord and McCarthy, Bonnie's paragraph had a clear thesis statement—"I find the English solution to 17th Century anarchy to be more realistic and attractive than the French solution"—but in documenting this assertion, she reverts to what may have been a strategy she learned earlier: thesis/subs. She merely lists three good things about the English solution: "it established a Bill of Rights, it built a system of checks and balances, it lasted a long time" (132). She makes only one passing reference to how the English system was a "solution to anarchy," and she never addresses the main point of the assignment: her own feelings about why the solution she chose was more "realistic and attractive."

Walvoord and McCarthy point out a number of reasons why Bonnie goes awry in her response to the assignment. The major difficulty of course is that Bonnie never addresses the major issue of the task. Perhaps she did not do so because the instructor, responding to difficulties that students had with the assignment in previous classes, overly stressed the importance of defining what an adequate solution might be and did not emphasize sufficiently the need to link the reasons to why the chosen solution was personally "realistic and attractive." Or perhaps Bonnie simply overrelied on an earlier thesis-subtopic strategy she was familiar with and did not develop sufficiently the new strategies the instructor was teaching: the need to personalize evidence and develop counterarguments. It is fascinating that in her planning sessions for writing the paragraph, Bonnie explicitly addresses the problems of how she should "feel" about the English solution and tests her position by thinking of counterarguments, but neither of these ideas survives the composing process. Bonnie's final paragraph does not deal with her feelings; neither does it develop counterarguments in any significant way (132–35).

The conclusion I draw from Walvoord and McCarthy's study is fairly commonplace in the literature on transfer; indeed, it follows from the models of learning I discussed in chapter 2 and applied to thinking in chapter 5. The ability to transfer knowledge and ability from one context to another is what we mean by learning in the first place. However, we cannot assume that writers will transfer the kinds of knowledge and skills they have learned previously to new writing tasks. Such transfer is unpredictable and depends to a great degree on the student's background and experience, over which the instructor has little control. Whether writers do transfer the appropriate knowledge and skills will depend on whether they see the similarity between what they have learned in the past and what they need to do in a new context (Perkins and Salomon, "Teaching"). Often, however, novice writers do not see the relevance of what they have learned before to new tasks (see also McCarthy).

Here is an example of a woman who reports that she transferred the knowledge of a particular kind of specific detail, the conversational anecdote, from one context to another without any formal instruction at all: Carol—not her real name—was a secretary for the vice president of a company that produced Catholic missionary films. One of the vice president's additional jobs was to produce a magazine for a national civic organization. Carol typed and proofread letters and magazine articles for her boss, and in the process, she picked up a "rhetorical strategy":

> [My boss] didn't just write to write. He wrote in a way to make his letters appealing. I would have to write what he was writing in this magazine too. I was

completely enthralled. He would write about people who were in this [organization] and the different works they were undertaking and people that died and people who were sick and about their personalities. And he wrote little anecdotes. Once in a while I made some suggestions too. He was a man who would listen to you. (qtd. in Brandt, "Sponsors" 180–81)

Thus, when she began to go door-to-door for the Jehovah's Witnesses, Carol adopted her previous boss's strategy and used colorful anecdotes as part of her presentation. She also transferred the strategy to preparing demonstrations on how to live a life faithful to Biblical principles, which she and other women perform at their weekly congregational meetings (Brandt, "Sponsors" 181).

Another example: A week or two after designing and collaboratively revising a sequence of questions for a survey of opinion about a junior-level writing proficiency exam, a student named Priscilla reported that she had applied what she had learned about designing a questionnaire to designing a test for her middle-school students on *Huckleberry Finn:*

From that paragraph [stating the purpose of the test], I discovered that the usual format of a literature test (vocabulary, followed by objective questions, followed by essay questions) not only did not get at what I wanted to find out, but our discussion of what questions to use as an opener for our questionnaire showed me that the students probably would not be too interested in the test either. (qtd. in Mansfield 79)

As a result of her experience revising questions in order to clarify the purpose of the questionnaire, Priscilla decided to begin her test with an essay question, which would give her students "a chance to use their imaginations and to 'personalize' the test," something they would not do as well if the test began with questions about vocabulary (Mansfield 79; for an analysis of the problems of transferring skills from school to the workplace see Anson and Forsberg; and Freedman, Adam, and Smart).

Lucille McCarthy mentions a number of factors that may interfere with a novice writer's ability to transfer knowledge and skill from one context to another. They include the function the writing serves personally to the writer, the role of the writer in relation to the subject matter, the task at hand, and the teacher. To her list I would add one more item: the individual ways that writers interpret the tasks that have been given them in the first place. There is a large literature on how writers can interpret the same task in very different ways (Penrose, "Writing" 56–64; but see also Langer, "Effects"; Flower et al., *Reading-to-Write;* Nelson). McCarthy concludes:

school writing is not a monolithic activity or global skill. Rather, the contexts for writing may be so different from one classroom to another, the ways of speaking in them so diverse, the social meanings of writing and the interaction patterns so different, that the courses may be for the student writer like so many foreign countries.

. . . writing development is, in part, context-dependent. . . . In each new classroom community, Dave [the subject of her case study] in many ways resembled a beginning language user. He focused on a limited number of new concerns, and he was unable to move beyond concrete ways of thinking and writing, the facts of the matter at hand. Moreover, skills mastered in one situation, such as the thesis-subpoint organization in Freshman Composition, did not, as Dave insisted, automatically transfer to new contexts with differing problems and language and differing amounts of knowledge that he controlled. (260–61).

The problem is that although people seem to learn to write by transferring knowledge and abilities from one discourse to another, from one kind of discourse to another kind, from one situation to another situation, all the time, they do so at all levels of abstraction, and we cannot say much about this phenomenon except that it indeed occurs. That is, we know little about the mental processes involved and can generalize very little from what we can observe. In addition, we have to distinguish among all the different kinds of knowledge and skill writers possess, and entertain the possibility that transfer will occur at different rates and in different ways, depending on the kind of knowledge and skill. The only principle we have is that transfer can be taught if the similarities of the knowledge and skill needed in different contexts are pointed out (for an explanation of this phenomenon from the perspective of literacy theory, see Scribner and Cole, "Literacy").

It is difficult to see how we could learn more about the nature of transfer. Consider this thought experiment. Suppose we want to discover with greater certainty just how students in the Walvoord and McCarthy study go about evaluating various situations and presenting their evaluations in an organized way. We already have the samples of writing from a number of students in the Walvoord and McCarthy study. Would we require a larger sample of their writing? If so, how many samples? Suppose we collected another writing sample from each student the following semester, this one from a class in sociology in which they had to summarize and evaluate a research article on the relationship between poverty and education. Suppose we analyze the summary/evaluation and find that the paper does seem relatively well organized around three or four major points, but that at key moments, usually dealing with some statistics correlating socio-economic status with educational attainment, the organization of the papers breaks down and flirts with incoherence and that the students' evaluations tend to lack specificity. Would we then be able to say with some confidence that the students had learned how to transfer a knowledge of how to evaluate from their previous experience to new situations? How so? And how do we account for the sections in which the organization breaks down and the evaluations become vague? Is it that the students had difficulty understanding the sociology statistics as they had difficulty understanding certain concepts in their other courses and that they do not summarize well what they don't understand? Or did their general transferable ability to summarize and evaluate "disappear," as it were, because in this instance they did not see the relevance of their thesis-sub strategy to the statistics? Can we then say, well, the students *generally* know how to summarize sociology papers of a certain kind? And could we reasonably infer from our four samples how well the students might be able to summarize other kinds of information in other genres in the future? That is, can we infer that because the students seem to evaluate poems well, they would do equally well evaluating the plots of novels and plays, that because they can evaluate sociology research articles, they would do equally well evaluating a work of philosophy? Could we reasonably infer that because they can use a thesis/subs strategy in writing academic discourse for university courses that they will be equally proficient summarizing business transactions in a memo format? I suspect that I have made my point. It is difficult to say just what kind of evidence would demonstrate sufficiently whether a person is capable of transferring certain kinds of knowledge and ability from one situation to another.

Implications for Teaching

Writing involves a variety of general and specific knowledge and a variety of physical and mental abilities to use a system of written symbols based on the rules of a language system and other discourse conventions in order to accomplish a specific task in a specific social setting. In one sense, writing is a tool for getting things accomplished. In another sense, writers must always use to some extent a previous form of discourse and modify it to fit an analogous situation. Which is to say that writing involves the application of regular patterns, rules, conventions, formats, and strategies in circumstances that may be new and even perhaps unique but also bear some analogous relationship to previous circumstances.

For these reasons, the degree to which any kind of knowledge or any given skill in writing is generalizable—that is, transferable from one context to another—will always be problematic. It is so problematic, in fact, that beyond a few general principles, there may be little we can say about how novices develop the broad knowledge and skills it takes to write. What might those few general principles be? Here are some possibilities:

First, writers may very well possess a kind of knowledge we might call "general," a kind of knowledge about many different things independent of particular contexts: knowledge of syntax, for example, or a general ability to adapt generic knowledge to particular rhetorical situations. The difficulty is that we can recognize this knowledge only in specific contexts. As David

Perkins and Gavriel Salomon put it, echoing Barbara Rogoff, "There are general cognitive skills, but they always function in contextual ways" ("Are" 19). Or to put it another way: sooner or later, depending on the particular context, all weak strategies become less helpful, and only strong strategies dependent upon particular "domain-" or "context-specific" knowledge will help improve writing.

Second, writers seem most obviously to apply general knowledge in situations in which they need to write outside the realm of their expertise, that is, when they need "global strategies" to write in areas "outside of the domain of local knowledge" (Carter 279), as when Kurt relied on his previously learned strategy to compare and contrast when confronted with the task of evaluating two restaurants using similar criteria.

Third, expert writers learn to see analogies, to see similarities and differences between old and new genres and old and new contexts; novices don't often recognize the similarities between old and new genres and contexts in order to apply what they do know (Rogoff 96; Perkins and Salomon, "Are" 20; Foertsch 371). If these analogies, similarities and differences, are not obvious, they must be taught.

And last, writers seem to learn the general and specific together, uncovering relevant generalizations, principles, and strategies, and applying them and justifying that application in new contexts (Foertsch 378). For this reason, the most effective pedagogical methods for teaching writing may be those that immerse novices in particular social contexts, give them the opportunity to use writing to accomplish very specific tasks in those contexts, and promote a sense of how what they are doing has been shaped by what they have learned before and how it might be used in different contexts in the future.

The bottom line for writing instruction may be this: We get what we teach for. And if we want to help students to transfer what they have learned, we must teach them how to do so. That is, we must find ways to help novices see the similarities between what they already know and what they might apply from that previously learned knowledge to other writing tasks.

It strikes me that the implications of what we know about transfer are very significant, even radical, not only for the ways writing might be taught but for the writing curriculum as a whole and the way courses relate to or "talk to" one another. It is rare in college and universities that we explicitly teach the transfer of knowledge and skills from one course to another or from one discipline to another. The question is how to construct a writing curriculum so that such instruction in transfer is commonplace, indeed a major feature of the curriculum.

PART TWO

Diagnosis and Proposal

7 What Is Writing Instruction and Why Is It So Problematic?

IN 2001, GARY TATE, AMY RUPIPER, and Kurt Schick edited a collection entitled *A Guide to Composition Pedagogies.* The collection included twelve chapters, each devoted to a different pedagogy used in the teaching of writing: "Process Pedagogy," "Expressive Pedagogy," "Rhetorical Pedagogy," "Collaborative Pedagogy," "Cultural Studies and Composition," "Critical Pedagogy," "Feminist Pedagogy," "Community-Service Pedagogy," "The Pedagogy of Writing Across the Curriculum," "Writing Center Pedagogy," "Basic Writing Pedagogy," and "Technology and the Teaching of Writing." These chapter titles give us a fair indication of the many different ways writing is taught in our colleges and universities.

Now what I find interesting about these twelve different ways of conceptualizing writing and writing instruction is that they have very little in common; they do not agree on the kinds of writing that should be taught or the methods to be used in writing instruction. Even more interesting, they do not agree on what courses in writing should ultimately accomplish. Process and collaborative pedagogies seem to be based on a *method* of instruction whose primary goal is to make people sensitive to audience and to give them practice in revision. Likewise, writing centers focus on a particular method of instruction—tutorials—whose ultimate goal would seem to be helping students accomplish any writing task they find themselves engaged in at the college level, and pedagogies that use technology focus on what we might call a "delivery system" for instruction that has no specified subject matter or content and can be used to promote any other philosophy or theory of instruction.

The remaining pedagogies are not so "neutral" about their ultimate goals. Expressive pedagogies seem to use a variety of strategies whose ultimate point is to unlock students' inherent insight and knowledge. Rhetorical pedagogies also seem to use a mix of methods but for a different purpose: to make students aware that writing varies according to the constraints of the rhetorical triangle. Cultural studies and critical pedagogies use a variety of critical strategies to help students analyze a variety of content and genres, everything from literary narratives to artifacts of popular culture; the ultimate goals of these pedagogies seem to be to promote "committed citizenship" and democratic power-sharing. Feminist pedagogy uses many of the techniques associated with process and collaborative teaching to further its "investment in a view of contemporary society as sexist and patriarchal, and of the complicity of reading, writing, and teaching in those conditions" (Jarratt 115). Community-service pedagogy involves students in studying and working with and for community service organizations, in order to make students more aware of how writing works outside the classroom and to promote, if possible, some concrete social good in the world. And finally, writing-across-the-curriculum pedagogies promote both writing-to-learn and the use of particular genres in particular disciplinary contexts.

This cacophony of voices in writing pedagogy has necessitated a new area of study for the field of composition studies: the development of taxonomies to account for all the conflicting assumptions and points of view. Perhaps the three most well known are by James Berlin ("Contemporary"), Richard Fulkerson, and Lester Faigley ("Competing").

In many ways, the essays in *A Guide to Composition Pedagogies* epitomize the kind of conversation that has been going on in composition studies for the past few decades about how writing should be taught. In general, the participants in the conversation have not made their case by arguing how people learn to write and then citing relevant evidence. Rather, they have aligned themselves with a particular theory or philosophical position focused on a particular kind of discourse or a particular epistemology, and argued the merits of the theory. As a result, all of the discussion of "theory" and "philosophy" has tended to obscure the fundamental questions I have been trying to raise. The essayists in *A Guide to Composition Pedagogies*, for example, make their case entirely by *asserting* that the pedagogy they advocate is good for students. Although they offer reasons for the teaching methods they favor, the reasons they give are entirely theoretical and, in a sense, self-evident: it is obvious that students will be better writers, better people, better citizens if they can revise substantially or critique patriarchal society or write well in a particular academic discipline. These essayists cite no evidence as to the efficacy of their particular pedagogy; they in effect use the device of exhortation to rally supporters of their particular point of view to their side.

In many ways, this kind of argument by assertion and appeals to theoretical values does not get us very far. I would frame the issues of how writing can be taught, if it can be taught at all, this way: in teaching our students to write, what is it that we want them to know, what is it that we want them to be able to do, and how should we go about helping them to learn what they need to know and practice what they need to be able to do? And what sort of evidence would we accept in order to demonstrate the efficacy of a particular kind of instruction? To begin, let me summarize what I take to be the major points of my argument in the first six chapters:

- Writing is the use of written symbols, involving many different kinds of knowledge and ability in order to accomplish particular purposes in particular social contexts. Because people always write in specific contexts using specific kinds of knowledge and ability, it is very difficult to determine the degree to which writing involves broad strategies for thinking and composing.
- People learn by paying attention to what is salient to their lives and by internalizing what they want to know or what they may need to know in the future. They learn by recognizing significant differences among concepts and organizing those concepts into interlocking hierarchies. They learn by fitting new knowledge into old knowledge. They learn *to write* by being immersed in the social practices of the discourse communities they wish to join. They learn to write by working on the tasks in those discourse communities that require writing and by getting help in doing so. Over time the various aspects of their writing will gradually approximate the writing of others in the groups they wish to join, but their level of competence in using different aspects of writing may vary considerably.
- People have always learned to write in ways that are largely independent of any particular form of instruction or even independent of any instruction at all; that is, people learn what they need to know and do when they write primarily by acquisition, not by explicit instruction. However, schooling, which immerses students in a literate environment, is a major factor in how people learn to write. The primary benefit of school instruction in writing may not be the "content" of the instruction but that it gives young writers tips about what to pay attention to when they must write outside of school.
- Because writing as a "social practice" is opaque, we have only the broadest notion of how people learn to write through immersion. However, even in immersion, novice writers need help in accomplishing their purposes. Put another way, novice writers do not need to have writing tasks simplified for them; they need help in accomplishing writing tasks in all their complexity, and over time they will learn to write on their own.
- Thinking is not writing, although thinking may be both a prerequisite to writing and a part of writing itself. One way of thinking about the relationship between thinking and writing is to distinguish among

the purposes to which thinking can be put in writing. Writing can be used to facilitate learning; writing can be used to aid reflection and critical thinking; thinking can be used to clarify and shape writing. I have called these broad goals writing-to-learn, writing-to-think, and thinking-to-write. For each of these kinds of writing, we might think of instruction as a way to help young writers accomplish certain goals or tasks rather than as a series of skills to practice.

- In order to apply old concepts in new contexts, people learn to recognize the relevance of the old concepts to new situations. People best learn this kind of "transfer" by receiving help in noticing the similarities and differences between certain aspects of writing in certain contexts and in applying their knowledge and abilities in similar contexts. However, we know if people can write in a particular genre or situation only if they in fact do so. We cannot necessarily assume any kind of transfer of learning from one kind of genre or situation to another, unless it is explicitly taught and we see the results of that instruction.

If we accept these propositions as a fair summary of what we know about writing and how people learn to write, how would we go about conceptualizing the conditions under which writing might be best learned or taught?

A Model for Learning and Teaching Writing

The model would be primarily one of acquisition, not explicit instruction: giving students what they need to know in meaningful contexts, providing "scaffolding." Following Patricia Greenfield, I take "scaffolding" to refer to a specific pedagogical strategy in which teachers do not simplify tasks for learners; rather, they maintain the difficulty and complexity of the task, whatever it might be, and simplify the learner's role in accomplishing the task through "graduated intervention" (119). This means, for example, that in the teaching of written sentences, paragraphing, or genres, teachers would not try to simplify the complexities of written sentences or paragraph and genre conventions through arbitrary rules or unrealistic models. Rather, teachers would offer guided practice in accomplishing certain rhetorical tasks through writing, tasks with the actual intent to express, inform, or persuade, to use Kinneavy's list of aims, and they would introduce "tips" only to help novices write whole discourse in all its complexity, gradually pushing them to accomplish these tasks on their own.

However, sooner or later, novices also need to be able to step back and analyze what they have been learning using a variety of metalanguages and critical frameworks, not only linguistic and rhetorical metalanguages and frameworks, but also social and cultural ones as well. That is, novices need to become self-conscious about their writing and how it participates in the discourse practices of various communities, so that they can "creatively extend and apply [what they have learned], and eventually innovate on their own, within old communities and in new ones" (New London Group 34). As a result, novices also need help in what the New London Group calls overt instruction, critical framing, and transformed practice.

In the following analysis, I am going to focus primarily on what most people outside composition studies mean by writing, what I have called thinking-to-write, but my analysis will also apply to writing-to-learn and writing-to-think. The basics of a model for learning to think-to-write beyond the sentence level might be this:

- Novice writers want to join a particular social group or they want to accomplish a particular social task, and they see learning to write a particular genre in a particular context as a way to achieve these goals.

- Members of a particular social group are aware of how discourse functions in the group, they are aware of the assumptions underlying the group's practices and can analyze and critique them from a variety of critical frameworks, and they are aware of the genres the group uses and how the conventions of those genres may vary from situation to situation. They are eager to share their knowledge with new members of the group.

- Novice writers acquire a general sense of how writing is done in the group from simply being in the group, by participating in the discourse practices of the group, but when they have to produce a piece of writing on their own and they are unsure of how to do something, they go to experienced members of the group for help, for "tips."

- The "scaffolding" provided by the experienced members of the group occurs "naturally." That is, the novices are so integrated into the social group even from the beginning that they are given important writing tasks at once, but they are also given a great deal of help. Increasingly, the novices learn to write on their own, and help from the more experienced members of the group becomes less necessary. Increasingly, the novices learn how the group functions and how the discourse of the group contributes to that functioning, so that the novices achieve the ability to analyze and critique the group's practices and write in "alternative discourses."

- If experienced members of the group see that particular novices have not been able to learn various aspects of how to write for the group— they have not mastered certain genre conventions; they have failed to notice a particular way the group reasons or conducts its affairs—the experienced members provide extra help, pointing out similarities and differences between what the students have done and what is accepted practice and inviting the students to submit new versions of the work they have done.

In other words, the kind of pedagogy that would seem to best account for the writer as an active creator of meaning and writing as a means of accomplishing specific social tasks is the tutorial or a master-apprentice relationship. I realize that many of the names we give to people with a great deal of knowledge or expertise have negative connotations. The terms "tutor," "master," "expert," and "mentor" each have their disadvantages. The same is true for the terms we use to refer to those on the other side of the relationship: "tutee," "novice," and "apprentice." With no unproblematic choices, I have been using the terms "expert" and "novice" because I think they come closest to expressing what I take to be the basis of the relationship I am trying to describe. I use the term "expert" to refer to someone who has not only mastered the conventions of a particular genre or a number of genres but who also has the experience of a particular social context and the necessary sensitivity to apply those conventions appropriately. I use the term "novice" to refer to someone who is still learning the conventions of the genres used in a particular social context and who needs to acquire experience in applying those conventions.

In an ideal expert-novice relationship, the two participants share a set of goals and values and a worldview. The novice does not resent being a beginner: the novice is working in a discipline, profession, workplace, or public forum, a discourse community that the novice has freely chosen and wants to join. The expert does not need to persuade the novice about the importance or relevance of what is to be learned. The expert welcomes the novice into the community and freely gives attention and advice to the novice as needed. The expert in effect models what the novice wants to be.

Now of course in the real world, this ideal state does not exist, but as a model it may best account for all of things I have noted about writing and how we learn to do it: the need for a real social context for writers to be immersed in so that they can work at developing a sense of how things are done in that community and apply what they know and learn along with their ability to write about it in accepted genres. Indeed, ideally writers would become so integrated into the discourse community and so master the assumptions and conventions of the group from a variety of critical perspectives that they would be free to write about and for the group using genres and formats not sanctioned by the group.

The Problem of Mass Education

If our model for teaching writing is the tutorial or an apprenticeship, one of an expert guiding a novice through the intricacies of applying particular genre conventions in a particular social context, with all that implies about the expert knowing the needs of the novice, the novice wanting to learn what the expert knows, and the expert and novice agreeing on what the novice needs to know and be able to do, then it is obvious that it would be very difficult to put the model into practice in colleges and universities, which must teach large masses of students. Even with the class sizes and number of students per instructor recommended by the Conference on College Composition and Communication—twenty students per class, no more than sixty students per instructor—it is difficult to capture the close relationship of an expert and a novice.

This is not a recent problem. Both Robert Connors *(Composition-Rhetoric)* and Sharon Crowley *(Composition)* have shown how composition as an academic subject arose in the nineteenth century as a way to enforce certain standards of literacy across the university. However, in the nineteenth century, scholars tended to view the problem only in terms of a large number of students. They conceived of writing as a kind of unitary ability—to teach one kind of writing was to teach all kinds of writing—and they envisioned higher education as the production of an educated upper class, or at least an educated upper middle class for whom the personal belles lettres essay was an expression of intellectual ability and insight. They felt no need to teach any other kind of writing than the "theme," an academic version of that belles lettres essay.

Nowadays, we have no consensus about what the purpose of higher education is. True, there are still people who believe that it is the primary duty of colleges and universities to produce the best and the brightest minds they can, but there are also widely held competing views that the primary role of higher education should be to produce students with the skills they need to survive in the marketplace or to produce students who are socially well adjusted, work well with others, and have a sense of civic commitment. As a result, there is no consensus about what students should be learning when they learn to write. Indeed, the question of what it means to be able to write often does not even get asked. Writing is, after all, just writing.

The problem of applying the tutorial or apprenticeship model to mass education, then, involves more than the difficulties of dealing with a large number of students. It involves the problems of genre, context, instructional focus, and transfer.

The Problem of Genre

What kinds of writing are students to be taught? In a tutorial or expert-novice relationship, this question does not come up. Novices learn the genres of the discourse community they are joining, the genres they are in fact using as they become integrated into that community. But as they are usually constituted, college and university writing classes reflect no particular discourse community outside of the school. As a result, what kinds of writing college and universities should teach is and must necessarily be in dispute. The range of options is quite diverse: "academic discourse," whatever that may mean; the discourse of particular disciplines in the university or of professions and workplaces outside the university; expressive writing; writing-to-learn; and various public genres, such as the newspaper editorial or reports and proposals for various civic organizations.

The rationale for teaching each of these kinds of discourse varies widely. Academic discourse is usually justified as a way to prepare students to write the kind of essays their professors will require of them during their stay at the university. The discourse of particular disciplines, professions, and workplaces is justified as a way to prepare students to write as professionals in their choice of career. Expressive writing is justified as a way to help students articulate their own thinking and to master a kind of stylistic eloquence. Writing-to-learn is justified as an aid to learning and thinking. And public genres are justified as a way to prepare students to participate in larger civic life.

As a result of these various rationales, there is a certain arbitrariness about what colleges and universities offer as writing instruction. Consider all of the different subject matter found in standard introductory courses with such titles as Writing about Literature, Writing and Popular Culture, Writing and Critical Thinking, Writing Persuasion, Writing and Cultural Studies, Writing and Diversity or Multiculturalism, and Writing Expository Prose. Quite often, these courses are justified by the importance of their subject matter rather by any indication of what the students are supposed to learn about writing, thereby once again conveying the impression that writing is writing, and writing anything is preparation for writing anything else.

The lack of any coherent rationale for why writing should be taught in connection with a particular subject matter explains, I think, the popular conception among certain constituencies of the university that writing classes are often governed by people with particular political agendas. Consider the uproar over English 306: Rhetoric and Composition, a course proposed by Linda Brodkey and the members of the Lower Division English Policy Committee at the University of Texas in 1990. English 306 was designed for students to study "the *structure* of arguments," through the reading of "opinions in discrimination suits, some of which are from the Civil Rights Act of 1964, the Educational Amendments of 1972, and the Bill of Rights" (Brodkey 228). The proposed course created a storm of protest, primarily from conservatives, who thought, often without ever reading the course proposal, that it was an example of political correctness run amok. Liberals tended to defend the course on the grounds that thinking, writing, and arguing about discrimination is just what college students need to do in these troubled times.

That is, they tended to defend the course in terms of its content. Lost in all of the debate, the accusations and counteraccusations, however, was any sense of English 306 as a writing course, just what aspects of writing the course was supposed to teach, and why those aspects of writing would be best taught in conjunction with legal texts about discrimination and affirmative action.

Brodkey's purpose for the course was "to recreate [for "students who for years have been learning *not* to write"] the circumstances under which others have turned to writing": "While it is not the only reason, a good many literate people write when speech fails, that is, when something they have decided is worth reflecting on and asking others to contemplate is sufficiently complex that writing about it seems more promising than just talking it over with someone" (224–25). And since most people have an intense interest in discrimination and often have uninformed opinions about the subject, Brodkey and her committee created a course that aimed "to develop informed opinions on complex issues raised in the aftermath of civil rights law" (225). That is, Brodkey and her committee chose the topic of discrimination as the focus of the course primarily as a motivational device for teaching argument, and because discrimination is a good topic to argue about. The topic of discrimination offers students what Brodkey considers

> the quintessential academic experience, the often exhilarating and at times even liberating experience of making a sustained analysis and critique of unexamined assumptions, an intellectual privilege tantamount to an academic right, founded on the willingness to lay out a *candid* argument in support of a position. (229)

Brodkey goes out of her way to offer "no apologies" for wanting to require beginning writers "to read law or cases or essays." After all, they are young adults, surveys indicate that they believe discrimination is a problem, and "while student attitudes are not in themselves sufficient grounds for a course, they suggest topics of interest and, in their turn, topics amenable to writing" (230).

However, the issue that haunts Brodkey's proposal is the issue that haunts all generic writing courses. If writing is a generic ability, or a series of related generic abilities, such as syntactic fluency or rhetorical maturity or the ability to argue, and such generic abilities can be taught with any content, then there is no reason why it should be taught in conjunction with any particular content. Why teach writing through the study of discrimination? Why not teach it through the study of foreign policy or abortion rights or any other argumentative topic? Any content will do. Brodkey does not state what reading and writing about case law on discrimination is supposed to teach about writing except argumentation, broadly construed. If the rationale for choosing the topic of discrimination is primarily one of motivating students to want to write arguments, why wouldn't any socially contested topic do?

A more serious objection to introductory or generic writing courses is that because they lack content, they do not go beyond broad generalizable skills such as syntactic fluency, rhetorical maturity, or various heuristics for thinking or composing. They do not provide students with specific knowledge and expertise in a particular discipline, domain, or subject matter. And if introductory courses *do* offer students practice in a specific content, they are immediately subject to a further objection. If the introductory or generic course does have a specific content, there is the real question of where it should be offered in the curriculum and who is best qualified to teach that particular content. In the case of English 306, the question is why instructors in English are teaching the reading and writing of case law. Why isn't that being done in the law school? In addition, the expertise students would gain would be in a very esoteric kind of knowledge, although that expertise would have implications for their views on a topic of crucial interest in American life today. Would this expertise be primarily in discrimination law or in argumentation? Is arguing for the law comparable to arguing generally? Is it comparable to arguing in other disciplines? Brodkey does not say.

Neither does Brodkey indicate what genres the students would be writing in for their potential audiences. Would they be writing legal briefs? Rebuttals to legal opinions? From several comments she makes, I assume that the course would focus on writing the standard school essay, with an emphasis on argument. That raises the issue of school genres that I will deal with shortly. My point here is simply that the problem of English 306 is the problem of writing courses generally. If writing is just writing, then a writing course can be about the writing of anything. If writing involves domain-specific knowledge, then a writing course ought to be about writing specific genres in the context of specific disciplines. If writing is some combination of generic skills and more domain-specific knowledge, then we need to justify writing courses on much more complex grounds than that they are motivational and involve students in some sort of practice in a generalizable ability.

The most common rationale for introductory writing courses in colleges and universities is that they prepare students to read and write academic discourse, the kind of writing required of students in various disciplines of the university. Rather ironically, however, academic discourse is a genre unique to school, a variation on the personal essay, which in many ways is a holdover from the old nineteenth-century theme and which bears no relationship to most of the writing done by the practitioners in the various disciplines of the university. True, occasionally a professor from history or engineering may write an essay for the alumni magazine or an article about the profession in a journal devoted to administrative issues. But few professors of history or engineering or any other discipline in the university actually report the results on their research or scholarship using the conventions of the essay. Instead, they use the highly constrained genres unique to their disciplines.

Considering what I have said about transfer, this raises the interesting question of what we are teaching when we teach the academic essay. Mike Rose studied "445 essay and take-home examination questions as well as paper topics from seventeen departments" and was able to articulate only a very general sense of what the academic essay entails. Most essay prompts called for some form of exposition or argument, but a form of argument unique to academia, "a calculated marshaling of information, a sort of exposition aimed at persuading" (111; see also Elbow "Reflections"). Most of the assignments also called on students to incorporate "large bodies of information garnered from lectures and readings" (111). In addition, academic essays are not usually taught as an actual response to a personal need or a real exigency or for possible publication in a journal or magazine with actual editorial guidelines and the need to appeal to a designated audience. Rather, academic discourse is usually taught as an exhibit of students' ability to think seriously about a given topic and report on their reflections in clear and organized prose. As such, it is usually taught as writing-to-think, as a way to foster personal reflection on an issue or topic and as a way for students to demonstrate that they know enough about the subject matter that they *do* have a point of view about it. However, there is a real question about what the writing of personal essays teaches about thinking-to-write.

After all, without a larger rhetorical context, personal essays are not used to convey information to someone who needs to know that information, and they are not designed to persuade anyone to a particular belief or course of action. Joseph Petraglia puts it this way:

> In transactional contexts (those outside the formative context of the rhetorical-writing classroom) writing generally entails accomplishing something beyond the production of writing itself. Put simply, transactive writing is a means to an end. We write to get something done, be it to "make things happen" or to alter an attitude. Conversely, pseudotransactions required by assignments do not have to result in any action being taken, any attitude being changed; they need only appear to have that *potentiality* in the teacher's opinion. ("Spinning" 24)

Academic essays and other school genres do not exist to allow students to do the work of real writing; they exist to allow students to demonstrate their knowledge and abilities; they provide what Susan Miller rather savagely calls "a consciously established menu to test students' knowledge of graphic conventions, to certify their propriety, and to socialize them into good academic manners" (*Textual* 66). School genres are, in short, a kind of exam.

Other school genres include personal essays, research reports, and analyses. The personal reflective essay is a classic example used in English departments; so is the traditional term paper or the literary analysis of a poem or story. Such genres may give students practice in certain skills, such as syntactic fluency; they may even introduce students to the conventions of certain kinds of disciplinary discourse—for example, the standard literary analyses of poems and stories may prepare students in some way to write the sort of professional interpretations done by their teachers, if they are required to survey previous scholarship on a topic and to explain how their arguments fits into a larger scholarly conversation. Or persuasive essays may give students practice in such skills as the ability to summarize and synthesize other points of view and to use various persuasive and argumentative strategies.

However, the major question about school genres generally is the degree to which they are helpful in giving students practice in the kinds of considerations they will have to confront outside the classroom. That is, if school genres lack sufficient context to help students grapple with all of the rhetorical constraints they will confront in the world at large, just how useful are they in preparing students to write for that world? At best, school genres may be justified as examples of the intermediate genres that students should practice on their way to mastering genres outside the classroom. The question to ask then is this: what sort of "real-world" genres are writing classes supposed to be training students to write? Or what sort of skills are school genres supposed to be honing that will transfer to writing outside of the classroom? What evidence do we have that such transfer may actually occur?

The Problem of Context

Can classroom instruction adequately capture the kinds of contextual considerations that writers face outside the classroom? In the expert-novice model, the question doesn't come up, because novices face the full range of contextual considerations as they participate in their discourse community. Novices are immersed in a social system; they learn genres and how to apply them through reading these genres as an integral part of their daily life and producing them themselves as the need arises. They receive help in writing as they need it or want it, or it is forced on them. If they have a particular problem with writing, they will find out about it all too quickly and "naturally." They will not accomplish with their writing what they set out to accomplish. Their boss will send back their memos for revision because they have not adequately addressed the issues they were assigned. Their editors will reject their essays because they have not been sufficiently literary or insightful. The city commission will reject their petitions because they have not been sufficiently persuasive. The members of their community will provide the responses, the feedback, the criticism they need. They will learn how to write because they want to, because they have to, for the same reason that young children gradually learn to talk. Like learning to talk, learning to write means learning to gradually approximate the written language of the social group you wish to join.

The question, as I put it in chapter 2, is whether this process of acquisition can be imitated or aided by explicit instruction and formal schooling.

In general, scholars and researchers in composition studies answer this question in a wide variety of ways, but let me address the issue by juxtaposing two recent bodies of theory and research on the opposite ends of a spectrum. On the one side are those who argue the case for acquisition and immersion. They argue that writing is simply too dependent on particular contexts to be taught effectively, that all we can do to further writing is to put novice writers in social situations that require certain kinds of writing and provide a mentor to give them occasional "tips" about how to do certain things as the need arises. These theorists tend to discount a great deal of what passes for instruction in most writing classes.

Those who argue that writing cannot be taught generally have a very narrow definition of what writing is. Thomas Kent *(Paralogic)*, following the philosopher Donald Davidson, defines writing as the application of a passing theory, which is entirely unique and dependent on the context of each distinct rhetorical situation. Because, according to Kent, writing is *by definition* the application of certain kinds of knowledge in specific contexts, it cannot be governed by previous knowledge, broad conventions, or general rules. Each writing task is unique to the exigency that called it forth. Like Kent—although he does not rely on Kent's philosophical arguments— Joseph Petraglia ("Writing") defines writing as "ill structured problem solving" that cannot be mastered by learning generic strategies and rules, and as a result he argues that general writing skills instruction (GWSI), courses organized to teach concrete rules and strategies for writing, may serve little or no useful pedagogical function. Elsewhere, Aviva Freedman, drawing on Carolyn Miller's "Genre as Social Action," defines writing as the application of genres, "typified rhetorical actions based on recurrent situations" (Miller 159, qtd. in Freeman, "Show" 222), which are too rich and complex to be reduced to a series of rules. As a result, these theorists seem to favor a kind of pedagogy in which novice writers are immersed in "real" social contexts outside of the classroom. In these contexts, the only explicit knowledge the novices need to receive are tips given to them by experienced writers in that social milieu.

The arguments and evidence used by these and other scholars and researchers against certain pedagogical practices take many forms, but the major points seem to be these:

- A conception of writing as the creative and intuitive ability to apply a wide range of knowledge and skill in ways that by definition transcend that knowledge and skill.
- Arguments that beyond the sentence level, writing is "domain-specific," the writing of a particular form of discourse in a particular social context, and that the only way to learn to write in each separate domain is by immersion, the acquisition of abilities tacitly, through experience.

- Empirical evidence that people learn to write particular genres by immersing themselves in the "culture" of the discipline, workplace, or social context in which that genre is written, an experience without formal instruction in how to write.

On the other side of the spectrum are a significantly larger number of scholars and researchers who do not oppose immersion so much as they argue in favor of the efficacy of explicit instruction. They insist that there are broad principles of learning and general strategies of writing that apply to most situations in which people write. As a result, these theorists tend to support certain kinds of writing instruction in classrooms, in which students learn particular skills or broad rhetorical strategies and receive practice in using these skills or in applying these strategies in a variety of, albeit hypothetical, rhetorical situations. Their arguments are as follows:

- Teaching-by-immersion theorists very carefully define writing as that aspect of composing that cannot be taught. However, these theorists cannot deny that writing in any social situation depends on a great deal of explicit knowledge—everything from a knowledge of spelling, punctuation, and paragraphing conventions to the discourse conventions of a particular discipline or work place and the particular forms of reasoning and kinds of evidence acceptable in each situation. Of course, these forms of knowledge need to be *applied* in each new situation, but by defining writing only as the manifestation of a passing theory or the application of what a writer knows in a particular situation, writing-as-immersion theorists are merely asserting that *by definition* writing cannot be taught. This is playing with semantics.
- The ability of writers to apply what they know effectively in particular situations may very well be acquired over time through immersion, but there is a great deal of evidence that acquiring general writing strategies—sensitivity to audience, flexibility in applying particular conventions and discourse formats—can be promoted in ways that will help beginning writers learn more quickly and with less trial-and-error.
- There is a huge body of empirical evidence—indeed, more evidence than for the effectiveness of immersion—that teaching the rules and formats of particular genres and the strategies necessary to apply them improves the writing of those genres. There is also some evidence that the ability to use these rules, formats, and strategies can be generalized across genres and disciplines, if—and the *if* is crucial—novice writers are taught to see the similarities in contexts that might require those rules, formats, and strategies.

Now it may seem as if the sides for or against teaching by immersion have joined in a real argument with clearly opposing points of view. But it strikes me that these apparently opposing points of view are no such thing, that the issues involved are more complicated than the two sides allow and that the "truth," to the extent that we know it—indeed, to the extent that we *can* know it—involves a dialectic between the two sides. And to return to my major theme: given our current concepts, paradigms, and models of writing, there seems to be no way to transcend this dialectic. That is, there seems to be no clear way to decide exactly how writing should be taught beyond the very broad principles and strategies I have already articulated.

Despite their acknowledged theoretical differences, there is a remarkable amount of agreement among those who promote acquiring writing ability through immersion and those who promote explicit teaching. Both sides agree that writing is largely contextual, but that in some sense writing must involve kinds of knowledge and broad strategies that writers must possess before they confront a new rhetorical exigency, that writers must know things and be able to do things that apply in a variety of contexts. Both sides also agree that the primary role of writing teachers is to help their students actually write. What is at issue is the nature and the degree of the support that teachers should provide. According to Freedman, a proponent of immersion, the primary role of a teacher is not to explicitly specify the formal features of the various genres or to articulate the underlying rules and conventions that forms of discourse may share with each other. Rather, teachers should "stage-manage exposure to a wide range of expository genres" in conjunction with "an occasion and a need to mean: some kind of rhetorical exigency which will elicit performance," "opportunities for meaningful use of [the students'] linguistic resources with their output being shaped by the assignments set and by feedback offered in response to these assignments" ("Show" 238–39). In providing opportunities for meaningful writing, teachers should engage in "collaborative performance by the expert and novice, a kind of co-operative interaction over the work-in-progress, with the teacher probing and responding tactfully where necessary, and giving more and more responsibility to the learner as the learning progresses" ("Show" 239–40).

Despite her warnings against explicitly teaching genre features and underlying rules, however, Freedman does concede that explicit teaching can be useful and effective in teaching certain things, such as "overall features of format or organization, for example, and a limited set of rules regarding usage and punctuation." Such a concession seems to contradict her major point against teaching the formal features of genres, or at least suggests that the difference between genre features and "overall features of format or organization" is exceedingly fine. In any case, Freedman also acknowledges that teachers should explicitly teach "heuristic or invention strategies as well as revising techniques such as cutting and pasting, or their word-processing counterparts" and "techniques for analyzing audience and context"

("Show" 237). She notes especially the rhetorical problem-solving strate-gies of Linda Flower ("Rhetorical") and the metaheuristics of Richard Coe.

It seems then that even in immersion pedagogies, novice writers may need some form of explicit instruction in such areas as background knowl-edge and context; they may need explicit information in order to write cer-tain kinds of discourse in the first place. Such information and instruction might include strategies for thinking and heuristics for sorting through this knowledge in certain kinds of situations. It might include aspects of the writing process, such as strategies for overcoming writer's block and strat-egies for composing different kinds of discourse for particular audiences using particular genre conventions.

The problem, however, is when and how to make this explicit instruc-tion explicit. The proponents of immersion would argue that we do not have adequate diagnostic measures for determining what our students re-ally need ahead of time, and in any case, "practice" in school genres does not give students sufficient practice in dealing with all of the contextual facts they must consider when applying explicit knowledge and broad strategies in new contexts.

In addition, proponents of immersion would argue that the problem of context does not go away if we require writing based on hypothetical rhe-torical situations, what are otherwise called case-study or scenario assign-ments. The major question for such a pedagogy is whether practice in writ-ing for such hypothetical situations can provide novice writers with enough of a sense of the situation that they can respond in a way that even approxi-mates the way an experienced writer would respond in a "real" situation.

Charles Hill and Lauren Resnick put the case against case study or sce-nario writing assignments in it strongest form. They invite us to imagine a writing assignment such as this one: "As the Director of Library Resources, write a memo to the president of the university, explaining why you should be given the necessary funds to keep the library open 24 hours a day" (147). Suppose in addition that the instructor who gives this assignment helps the students to think about what they want to accomplish with their writing and how to marshal whatever arguments and evidence they might need to convince the university president to keep the library open around the clock. Such help might lead the students in the class to see that the best way to argue in favor of increased hours for the library would be to survey the students at the university in order to determine if they would use the library during the hours it is now closed. And the need for this kind of evidence might lead in turn to a lesson on how to conduct survey research effectively.

Now we might think that this assignment encourages students to prac-tice thinking through the implications of a rhetorical situation and to use arguments and evidence targeted for a specific audience in a specific con-text. However, Hill and Resnick object that the assignment does no such thing. They argue, on the contrary, that hypothetical assignments such as this one are incapable of conveying enough of the context of a "real" rhetorical situation, so that students will not have enough information to respond appropriately. A true library director would know a great deal more about the context surrounding the issue—for example, the financial situation of the university: "Are many departments fighting over a steadily decreasing pool of funds? Did the library recently receive a large sum of money from the university for capital improvements? Did the president recently gain control of a large endowment that has not yet been spent" (147–48). In addition, memos like those called for in the library assignment are usually a part of a larger negotiating process, and as such, the purpose for writing the memo may not be the ostensible one of asking for money for a particular program. Rather a library director might write such a memo to give the president bargaining power with the Board of Regents or to negotiate a position for a protracted period of bargaining with the president over what percentage of the university budget the library is entitled to. Because hypothetical assignments present such "an impoverished concept of the nature of rhetorical situations," Hill and Resnick argue, they cannot give students effective practice in setting goals for writing or in dealing with the wealth of contextual factors a writer faces outside of the classroom (148).

In addition, Petraglia ("Spinning") points out, confronted with hypothetical rhetorical situations, students must necessarily role play their responses and imagine or invent many of the constraints they will face outside of the classroom. But in rhetorical situations outside the classroom, students cannot take such imaginative liberties, and as a result, at best, case study or scenario assignments are misleading: they suggest that writers are free to ignore actual constraints and create their own reality. And because they are hypothetical, such assignments are not emotionally engaging and require no commitments, just information.

Finally, Petraglia ("Spinning") notes that case study and scenario assignments have a dual audience, a hypothetical audience and the instructor, so that students may be confused about their ultimate goals: no matter how much the instructor may insist that they write for the hypothetical audiences, students will always know that they are writing for the teacher.

Indeed, there is a great deal of evidence that what students write in college does not sufficiently prepare them for writing in the workplace or in other nonacademic settings. For example, Chris Anson and L. Lee Forsberg followed six interns in a "writing apprenticeship" through a series of journals and logs. Overwhelmingly, the interns found that they had a difficult time adapting what they knew about business writing from school to the actual writing they had to do on the job. What is interesting is that they did not blame their lack of skills on their school; on the contrary, they found writing in the workplace frustrating because it took so long to learn the ins and outs of the organizations they were working for. They had to use trial-and-error to learn about all of the personal and social factors they needed to be aware of when they wrote. Anson and Forsberg put it this way:

> While certain surface-level writing skills are "portable" across diverse contexts, such skills are less important to making a successful transition as a writer than coping with the unfamiliar epistemological, social, and organizational characteristics of a new context. (201)

Note that the difficulties apprentices face cannot be mitigated in advance; apprentices simply have to work their way through the constraints of writing in social contexts their writing classes have not prepared them for (see also Freedman, Adam, and Smart). And in a sense, this problem does not go away in immersion pedagogies because being able to write in one social context does not necessarily prepare a person to write well in another social context. Immersion can prepare novices to write only a limited number of similar genres in similar social contexts.

To such arguments, the proponents of explicit teaching reply that there is an overwhelming body of research indicating that certain kinds of formal instruction can help students improve their writing. Most of this research has been summarized and analyzed by George Hillocks in *Research on Written Composition*. Hillocks found that the most effective pedagogies were what he called the environmental mode and focus on inquiry. Pedagogies in the environmental mode are characterized by:

> (1) clear and specific objectives, e.g., to increase the use of specific detail and figurative language; (2) materials and problems selected to engage students with each other in specifiable processes important to some particular aspect of writing; and (3) activities, such as small-group problem-centered discussions conducive to high levels of peer interaction concerning specific tasks. (122)

Pedagogies focused on inquiry are similar to those in the environmental mode. In focusing on inquiry, teachers offer students a selection of topics to write about rather than give students free rein to write about whatever they want. Teachers "focus on immediate and concrete data of some kind during instruction and practice" rather than allow students to write about more distant experience. And teachers promote specific strategies for dealing with the data rather than allow students to "use whatever strategies they have available" (180–81).

In other words, both the environmental mode and the focus on inquiry provide explicit instruction in certain specifiable aspects of writing that novices might need to know or be able to do *before* they try to write a particular genre in a particular context. However, both of these forms of instruction assume that novices are active learners who need practice in using and internalizing those aspects of writing the teacher has identified as important. The teacher does not just announce that specific details are important in writing narratives and give examples for the students to follow. The teacher arranges for the students to use specific detail to distinguish among objects so that they can see the effects of different levels of abstraction in writing. The teacher does not just announce that in making an argument students should use certain kinds of reasons. The teacher arranges for the students to confront a hypothetical situation and to determine the various ways in which it might be interpreted. In doing so, the students list the kinds of reasons various people might invoke in support of their interpretation.

The evidence of the success of explicit pedagogies similar to or modeled on the environmental mode and the focus on inquiry is overwhelming. The difficulty is that the primary way these pedagogies have been evaluated is through post-tests, in which students write certain kinds of school genres immediately at the end of the courses that used these pedagogies. Thus, we have no way to know if what the students learned in these courses has any long-term effect or whether they are helpful in writing genres outside the classroom. Theoretically, of course, if the objectives of explicit instruction are carefully chosen, explicit instruction ought to be helpful in the long run and outside of the classroom. It is noteworthy that Freedman, a major proponent of immersion, grants the effectiveness of the environmental mode of instruction ("Situating" 279).

However, the problem that will not go away, whether in classrooms or in externship, internship, or apprenticeship programs, is in determining what aspects of a particular genre ought to be made explicit and when and how to make those aspects explicit. There is not enough time in the sixteen years of formal schooling to teach all of the features of the major genres, all of the strategies writers bring to bear on particular writing tasks, all of the contextual factors writers must consider when they write. How then do we determine what is important enough to teach?

The Problem of Instructional Focus

What aspects of writing should be taught? In the tutorial or expert-novice model the question again never comes up. Because they are in the process of joining a particular discourse community and are in fact already involved in it, novices jump right in, using the genres they need in order to accomplish whatever they need to get done in the group. When they run into problems or if their writing is inadequate, they receive tips from the experts, who freely share their expertise as it is needed.

However, in classrooms, instructors have to somehow "stage manage" what their students might need to know in order to accomplish their assigned tasks. This might mean teaching such disparate things as invention strategies, sentence combining, domain-specific knowledge, plans for arguing or solving problems, proofreading techniques, or heuristics for questioning the role of a particular discourse in the larger culture.

It is difficult to determine what a large number of students with a wide variety of experience in literacy need to know, especially if they must write a genre for which there are no real contextual constraints except those arbitrarily imposed by the instructor. Such a situation might be analogous to government-controlled economies, which must determine the number and quality of certain goods to produce without the constraints of the market. How many shoes should a factory produce, in what style, or at what price? There are no answers to these questions outside the constraints of the market. Factories should produce sufficient shoes for people to buy in styles that they will in fact buy at a price they will pay. Businesses that make shoes know they are successful in only one way: when people buy their shoes, and especially when people buy their shoes rather than someone else's. If people do not buy their shoes, the shoe business must determine the reason. It may be that people will not buy their shoes because the price is too high, or the shoes are not in a popular style, or they simply do not last long enough. If any of these reasons is the case, then the only way for the shoe business to make people buy their shoes is to lower the price, make the shoes in styles that people prefer, or increase their quality. Likewise, in many ways, the only way to determine whether novice writers write adequately is to see if their writing accomplishes their purposes outside the classroom in the larger "marketplace."

Now obviously, not all writing must accomplish real effects in the world analogous to a company selling a product. I realize how potentially misleading my analogy is. However, my point here is this: without the constraints of that larger marketplace, how do instructors go about determining what students need to know in order to become better writers? Without anything but the crudest of diagnostic instruments—usually an impromptu in-class essay, in which the student can at best write a brief version of the five-paragraph theme—and with over twenty students per class, often with well over sixty students each semester, the maximum number recommended by CCCC, each student with a different background and experience and with different goals and aspirations as a writer, how does an instructor go about determining what to teach? Here I think my analogy with the shoe business does apply: Outside the constraints of the market, the world outside of the classroom; that is, without any sense of what the student can do, what that student has already done, in a variety of genres and contexts—in other words, without any sense of the student's current level of expertise—and without any sense of the student's goals and aspirations, of what this student might want to use writing for, there is no answer to the question of what to teach in a writing class. The instructor is free to teach anything the teacher wants because anything in general or nothing in particular will do.

And as far as I can tell, this is in fact the case in most writing classes in most colleges and universities. Writing classes may have some sort of unity within a particular institution or writing program. For example, the intro-ductory courses at College A may be devoted to writing about literature, while the first-year courses at University X may be focused on academic essays with some attention to grammar and editing. Except, perhaps, for the general characterization that students need to write whole discourse and practice broad rhetorical principles that include message, audience, and stance or voice, if possible for audiences other than the teacher (and many programs, even those promoted by some of the biggest names in composi-tion studies ignore this last feature), there is little consensus in the field about what the focus of instruction in introductory courses ought to be.

There may, however, be some consensus, albeit unarticulated, about the general skills that novices ought to learn in introductory courses. Although most of the published reports on the makeup of introductory courses usu-ally focus on subject matter, such as literature or argumentation, or on a school genre, such as the academic essay, there is occasional talk about more specific knowledge or skills that introductory writing courses are supposed to teach and statements about just what those involved in these courses hope their students will know or be able to do as a result of taking these courses. However, these statements are often so general as to give little indication of what an introductory writing course might actually be like in practice. For example, the Writing Program Administration Outcomes Statement for First-Year Composition focuses on a broad range of skills at a very high level of generality and does not confront the issues I have been raising. The state-ment suggests, for instance, that at the end of introductory courses, novice writers should be able to demonstrate what I have called "rhetorical matu-rity"; they should be able to "use writing and reading for inquiry, learning, thinking, and communicating"; they should be able to use certain writing processes, such as multiple drafts and "strategies for generating, revising, editing, and proof-reading texts"; and they should be able to use a variety of genre conventions appropriately. The WPA statement seems to assume that novice writers can demonstrate these competencies with any kind of subject matter or discourse in any kind of context in response to any sort of pedagogy. In other words, the WPA statement is of little help in decid-ing just what the content of a writing course should be.

Still, a number of theorists insist that it is perfectly possible to predict what sort of difficulties a wide range of novice writers will face when they are required to write certain genres or if they want to improve certain as-pects of their writing, such as their style or their ability to analyze a cer-tain problem. Therefore, these theorists argue, it is perfectly possible to set meaningful goals for instruction, give students practice in meeting those goals, and then invite them to apply what they have learned in whole discourse or classroom genres. In designing goals for instruction, teachers must analyze the genres they wish to teach and break these genres down into various kinds of knowledge and skill that writers must know in order to be successful in that genre. The most effective pedagogies in Hillocks's analysis are of this kind.

There is also a major theoretical reason why such teaching may be so successful. As Joseph Williams and Gregory Colomb point out, there is considerable evidence that we tend to think in "prototypical categories" (261). Although particular examples of a concept may not share many features and be related only by what Ludwig Wittgenstein calls "family resemblances," we tend to think of certain examples of a concept as being more typical, as "better" examples of the concept, than others. These conceptual prototypes may be socially conditioned, but that is beside the point. Williams and Colomb suggest, then, that we also conceive of aspects of discourse in terms of prototypes, and therefore there are good reasons for teaching prototypical examples of paragraphs or genres, "to focus younger students on the prototypical features of genres and to teach those features, not as rule-bound necessities, but as 'default' instances among a range of choices" (261).

However, such strategies may not always be as effective as they might because they must assume a certain degree of common experience and a certain degree of motivation for learning what the teacher has decided are the prototypical text conventions or composing strategies for the course. Such teaching discounts individual differences among students and assumes that they have similar backgrounds and a similar willingness to learn the kinds of writing offered in the course. Often for required first-year writing courses this is not the case.

The Problem of Teaching Transfer

To recall my analysis in chapter 6, novices probably best learn how to apply various strategies of thinking, composing, even editing, by "mindful attention" to how those strategies may apply from one genre to the next or one context to the next. Often novices are incapable of seeing how broad strategies may apply in new situations. Novices need to learn to look for similarities between genres and contexts and build up a repertoire of experience about what principles and strategies apply in what circumstances. In the words of Perkins and Salomon, the search for similarities among genres and contexts must be "cued, primed, and guided" ("Are" 19).

The difficulty here is obvious. In most colleges and universities, the content of writing courses is determined by individual instructors who are not aware of how writing is being taught in other courses across the curriculum. As a result, these instructors have no knowledge of the particular writing experiences their students have already had at their institutions, and so they do not have enough information to cue, prime, and guide their students through the difficulty of discovering how their students' previous knowledge and skill might apply in new situations. Indeed, under the guise of academic freedom, many writing teachers might be averse to learning how writing is taught outside their own classrooms, since learning this information takes time and attention and may distract them from their primary interest and obligation to their own disciplines and particular specialties.

We have little evidence that any particular form of instruction has any long-term effects. Longitudinal studies will always confound the effects of instruction with maturation and environmental influences. Over time, we simply cannot control all the factors that might influence the development of writing ability in any way. So our wisest and best guesses about writing instruction must be inferred from what we know from more controlled studies and from our larger models of language learning and development.

Future research may give us some local, historicized, and contingent information about how certain genres, certain kinds of instruction, certain contexts, certain methods of transfer may help certain kinds of students in certain contexts—in the short term.

As a group, the problems of genre, context, instructional focus, and transfer are part of the larger problem of how we understand literacy in the first place. If overall writing ability is tied in some way to the ability to write particular genres in particular contexts, then it may be that the kind or number of genres students learn to master is less important than their ability to master a few. Thus, at a certain point in their development—certainly by the time they are in college, if not before—novices may need to be immersed in the discourses they need or want to learn as part of their own goals and ambitions. They may need to have extensive practice in reading and writing the genres of these communities over time in order to develop real fluency. They may need to be introduced to the critical frameworks necessary to understanding how their groups function, so that they can develop a metacognitive sense of how writing functions in the group. They cannot get this practice, they cannot develop this fluency, they cannot develop this metacognitive ability in generic writing courses.

Can one learn this knowledge [of how to express feelings]? Yes, some can. Not, however, by taking a course in it, but through *'experience'.*—Can someone else be a man's teacher in this? Certainly. From time to time he gives him the right *tip.*—This is what 'learning' and 'teaching' are like here.

—Wittgenstein, *Philosophical Investigations*

8 *What Does It Mean to Be a Writing Teacher?*

IN 1998, ROBIN WILSON REPORTED in the *Chronicle of Higher Education* that a major shift was underway in who taught introductory writing courses at our major universities. Until the late 1990s, these courses were staffed overwhelmingly by graduate teaching assistants and adjunct instructors in English. However, because of steep increases in the number of entering first-year students, universities have increasingly gone outside English departments to find people to teach introductory writing. These instructors may come from such diverse disciplines as anthropology, law, history, music, political science, kinesiology, and women's studies. This situation has prompted a great deal of soul-searching in the profession about who teaches introductory writing courses and what constitutes sufficient training to qualify a person to be a writing teacher.

On the one hand, Wilson notes, there is no reason why the teaching of writing ought necessarily to be limited to people specializing in English as a discipline. He cites Paul Prior, the director of the rhetoric division at the University of Illinois at Urbana-Champaign, who asserts, "There are good writers and good writing distributed throughout the university. There is no reason to privilege English as the site of good writing" (qtd. in Wilson). Indeed, Wilson adds, "Some institutions long ago severed freshman writing from their English departments. . . . Meanwhile, institutions that teach 'writing across the curriculum' have for years used instructors outside of English."

On the other hand, if people from any academic discipline can teach writing, we might wonder just what qualifies a person to do so. The University of Illinois at Urbana-Champaign requires that potential writing instructors submit a writing sample and three letters of recommendation. They must also attend a week-long orientation and participate in a semester-long training seminar. However, it is not clear what the rhetoric division at Illinois is looking for when it studies the writing samples and letters of recommendation of potential writing teachers. Neither is it clear just what Illinois is training its instructors to do in its orientation and seminar. The writing courses at Illinois "have no common syllabus, and there are no precise requirements about the number and kind of papers freshmen must complete" (Wilson).

But of course, the problem of what a writing teacher should know and be able to do is not a new one. In 1952, the third year of the existence of the Conference on College Composition and Communication, Harold Allen, the chair of the organization, published an article entitled, "Preparing the Teacher of Composition and Communication." Allen had just recently toured the country, visiting forty-seven colleges and universities, twenty-nine of them with graduate programs in English, in order to see how these institutions prepared their instructors to teach writing. Allen found that for all intents and purposes, graduate programs in English did not explicitly prepare their graduates to teach anything, literature or writing. The ruling assumption of the period was that "a person who successfully completes the doctoral program in English literature is, *ipso facto*, a teacher of English literature ... and a teacher of composition" (4). However, a few graduate programs, the most noteworthy being the one at the University of Michigan, did offer "a regular course, with credit, in the teaching of composition in college" (7). In addition, a number of universities did offer experiences other than coursework to help beginning instructors teach writing. Those experiences included informal seminars, staff meetings with the regular faculty, and faculty mentoring programs.

Allen also talked to graduate students and beginning instructors wherever he went, and he found that they were often bitter about their lack of preparation to teach. What they wanted in their preparation was some knowledge of "current issues and trends in the field of higher education," some knowledge of "how people learn skills and information—call it the psychology of learning, if you will," especially how people learn language; rhetorical theory, and classroom management techniques (10–11). Allen concluded on a note of hope: that in the future, students in introductory courses in both writing and literature would be taught by "a person who is professionally prepared by teachers of English to do that particular job" (13).

"Professionally prepared." What I find interesting about the discussion of how to prepare writing teachers is that the issue has almost exclusively been framed in terms of credentials: how should a professional body go about certifying that its members are sufficiently knowledgeable about their subject matter and capable of fulfilling their professional responsibilities. But other than listing very broad subjects such as learning theory, rhetorical theory, or teaching methods, there is little discussion of just what the subject matter of courses to prepare writing teachers should contain and what a writing teacher should know or be able to do. The arguments, no matter which side the participants are on, are entirely about *coursework* in some form, either formal coursework for credit or informal coursework such as workshops, practicums, or other types of training sessions. Usually, the discussion is about whether writing teachers should be certified by the kind or number of graduate courses they have taken in rhetorical and composition theory or whether writing teachers need only be certified by participation in a series of meetings that cover certain topics, such as cognitive learning theory, rhetoric, and various teaching methods.

Once again, I think we need to get back to the basics, and here the basic question is this: What does it mean to be a writing teacher? What does a writing teacher need to know or be able to do? And once again, we need to confront the difficulty of what writing is, for if there is no such thing as generic writing beyond a certain fluency with syntax and a certain maturity in adapting particular genres to the demands of specific audiences and contexts, if writing is always the writing of something to someone in a specific context for a specific reason, then there may be no such thing as a generic writing teacher, someone who knows about all genres in all contexts.

Consider the following thought experiment: At a university-wide meeting several weeks ago, a faculty member, happened to be introduced to the president of the university, for the first time. Their conversation gradually came around to the subject of writing. The faculty member expressed some views on the subject, including an opinion that a major change was needed in the writing program at the institution. Throwing caution to the winds, the faculty member bemoaned the fact that the department did not seem to have the money to help further develop these new ideas, and a number of the faculty member's grant proposals had not been funded. Even though this faculty member might have behaved in a manner less than politic, the president seemed very interested, even excited. Throughout the conversation, the president addressed the faculty member personally and warmly. Now, totally unexpectedly, this faculty member has received a letter from the president offering $5,000 out of a special discretionary fund under the control of the president's office, for the faculty member's continuing research. The letter is strictly formal, although the president's first name only has been signed above the traditional full name in the typed signature. The faculty member is faced with writing a personal thank-you letter expressing gratitude for the president's generosity.

This task turns out not be as easy as the faculty member first thought it might be. The president is known for being a prickly sort of person who easily takes umbrage at behavior that does not follow traditional forms and procedures, although at their first meeting, the president was perfectly pleasant with the faculty member. The president's reputation, then, calls into question going outside of traditional channels in granting the faculty member the $5,000. In addition, this faculty member has little sense of the president's motivation for this action—the president has expressed only the desire to help scholars do interesting work that may benefit the university in the long term—and upon reflection the faculty member wonders just where the money is coming from. In short, the faculty member suspects that there might be a hidden agenda in the president's action.

This faculty member sits down to write the president a thank-you letter and, immediately, is blocked. The faculty member can't decide on an appropriate tone, can't decide whether to explain how the money will be used or to simply express gratitude and stop. The faculty member just simply doesn't know what to say or how to say it.

Here is my question. To whom would the faculty member go for help? Would the faculty member go to a writing teacher? And if so, on what basis? What would the faculty member expect the writing teacher to know that other people would not? I suspect that the faculty member would not expect a writing teacher to have any special expertise in writing thank-you letters. Thank-you letters as a genre are not studied by composition specialists, nor are thank-you letters generally taught in writing classes. In fact, most of us learn to write thank-you letters without instruction, although we have had some help when we were very young and wrote our first thank-you letters. Indeed, the problem is not that the faculty member, who's been writing thank-you letters since childhood, does not know how to write thank-you letters. The problem is that the faculty member does not know how to write *this* thank-you letter.

In addition, I suspect that this faculty member would not go to a writing teacher because the writing teacher has special expertise in helping novice writers improve their syntactic fluency and their sensitivity to rhetorical situations, or even their ability to overcome writing blocks. This faculty member feels perfectly fluent in the use of written language and generally knows enough to pay attention to audience and situation. Generally, this faculty member does not find writing difficult. Once again, the problem does not seem to be a lack of what we usually call writing ability. The problem is that this faculty member does not know the university president very well and does not know enough about why the president has given the money or what might be expected in return.

Finally, I take it that the faculty member would not go to a writing teacher for help thinking through the relevant issues of tone and content: how formal or informal to be, and whether to discuss what will be done with the money. The faculty member knows how to consider these issues, what the options are. The faculty member simply can't decide which options to take.

As a result, I suspect that in this particular situation, the faculty member would not go to a writing teacher for help at all. Instead, the faculty member would go to someone who knows the university president or someone who has insight into university politics, or someone who has written thank-you letters to the president in the past. After all, what seems to be the problem is that the faculty member lacks sufficient information about the president's character and motives or what might be the obligations in this unusual situation. That is, in some sense, the problem is that the faculty member doesn't have enough information about the context of the task and can't expect a writing teacher to know more about that context than the faculty member already does.

Now, it might be argued that this example is entirely beside the point. Thank-you letters are hardly a representative genre of writing, and writing thank-you letters to university presidents is not a common activity. Moreover, I have assumed that the faculty member is already a mature writer, generally in command of syntax and sensitive to a wide range of rhetorical situations. Writing teachers, it might be said, introduce novice writers to genres they might not otherwise encounter or learn on their own.

But I would counter that that is exactly my point. People don't generally receive explicit instruction from experts in how to write thank-you notes. If people write thank-you notes well, it is probably because they grew up in a household in which it was expected they would write invitations and thank-you notes to the friends they invited to birthday parties. In these situations, their parents may have given them some help in what to say. Or perhaps some people did not write thank-you notes at home but learned about thank-you notes in school when the teacher suggested that the class as a whole write a thank-you note to a guest speaker. In this situation, the teacher provided the students with a sense of what to say and how to say it. In these examples, neither their parents nor their teachers were credentialed "experts" on thank-you notes. They simply taught the children the way they themselves had been taught.

The problem posed by this thought experiment is that *most* genres are not studied by writing specialists. So when we claim to be writing teachers, just what sort of expertise are we claiming? What genres *are* writing teachers trained to write? Or better yet, in what particular genres in what particular social contexts do writing teachers have sufficient knowledge and experience so as to be called experts? As far as I can tell from my own experience, most writing teachers are not trained to write any genres, except research papers, critical analysis, and scholarly articles. As a graduate student teaching rhetoric at the University of Iowa in the 1960s and later in the 1980s, as a public school teacher in the 1970s, and as a composition specialist at Kansas State University in the 1980s and 1990s, no one has ever bothered to ascertain whether I really know how to write any of the genres I teach or whether I am capable of writing them very well. The institutions that hired me simply assumed that I could write any genre I would have to teach because I have an advanced degree in English and presumably—not that this was ever checked on either—I have been writing literary analyses and research papers in my English courses. And other than a semester review of my comments on a few sample papers from my students when I was a graduate student, no one has ever investigated whether anything I tell my students about their writing is particularly helpful, or even *appropriate*. I assume that in order to be hired for my first full-time job in the profession, my experience as a graduate student was less important than the fact that I had published an article of literary analysis. The fact that I could publish such an article was taken as evidence that I knew how to write and that I knew how to talk to others about any genres I wanted to teach. I wonder now if this is a reasonable assumption.

I realize that many college and university students lack syntactic fluency and rhetorical maturity. I do not mean to suggest that to some degree novice writers do not need practice in developing their ability to write a varied prose style for a variety of rhetorical purposes using the conventions of standard edited English. But once again, in my own case, no one ever bothered to ascertain whether I could write a varied prose style myself, whether I could teach that style to someone else, or even whether I knew the conventions of standard edited English. In which case, the question will not go away: what sort of genres and contexts, what sort of content knowledge, should a writing teacher be a master of?

In practice, of course, the answer to that question seems to be the one I noted in the previous chapter: the syntax and rhetorical considerations of school genres—personal essays; critical analyses unrelated to any rhetorical considerations outside the classroom; research reports that James Britton calls pseudo-informative and pseudo-persuasive, entirely hypothetical genres that do not really convey any information to anyone who needs the information, nor really try to persuade anyone of any particular viewpoint. For school genres, writing teachers do not have to be experts in anything but their own taste, since students write only to demonstrate that they can do the sorts of things the teacher wants them to do. However, I take it that no one *wants* to learn school genres; they are after all just practice, although students may want to learn how to write personal essays for their own private meditation.

The large issue I am raising here is whether there is something we might call *disciplinary knowledge,* which all writing teachers ought to share by the very fact that they are writing teachers. Of course, this is the argument of those theorists who promote the professionalization of composition studies (Phelps; Zebroski, "Toward"; Dobrin). These theorists, each in their own way, argue that writing is a global and unified phenomenon. As a result, they believe that writing can be a legitimate object of study for a profession or discipline. For example, James Zebroski argues that what unifies composition studies—or what *ought* to unify it—is a set of practices: writing practices, teaching practices, curricular practices, disciplinary practices, professional practices, and theorizing practices. The question is what that underlying unity is and how it is manifested in the many ways writing is practiced, learned, and taught.

Obviously, the entire point of my analysis from the very first chapter is that writing may not be global and unified phenomenon, that beyond a minimum degree of syntactic fluency and the ability to adapt the conventions of a genre to the demands of particular audiences and contexts, what we call writing ability may be very context-specific, a matter of knowing what we need to know or be able to do in whatever situations we find ourselves.

Given the model of instruction that I developed in the last chapter, we might think of writing teachers this way:

- Writing teachers participate in a particular field, profession, discipline, workplace, or other discourse community. They know about the workings of that discourse community and how writing *works* in that community. They are capable of analyzing and critiquing the practices and discourses of the community from a variety of points of view.
- Writing teachers know how to write the kind of discourse required in their discourse community. They are self-conscious about the craft of the discourse and are aware of how the traditional genre conventions in their community must be adapted in particular circumstances. They are also aware of the "alternative genres" people adopt when they write about the community from a variety of theoretical and critical points of view.
- Writing teachers are sensitive to the needs of those people whose writing they want to improve. They are encouraging and helpful. They give novice writers tips relevant to what they are trying to accomplish in a particular situation. These tips can be about any aspect of what these novice writers are trying to accomplish: their purpose, the information they need to accomplish that purpose or where they might find what they need, background knowledge, discourse formats or genres, ways of thinking about audience, editing. Writing teachers also encourage novice writers to analyze and critique the discourse community they wish to join, so that they can participate in that community more fully aware of what they are doing.

The model here is of teacher-practitioners, who know how to write particular kinds of discourse themselves, are self-consciously reflective and insightful about their own writing and how that writing participates in the workings of the larger discourse community, and are capable of sharing their knowledge and insight with others. In a way, this is the model used by those who run and staff creative writing programs: it is assumed in the field of creative writing that the best credentials for teaching fiction or poetry or drama is the ability to write the genre in the first place. However, most creative writers are not trained to study how the community of creative writers functions in the university or in society at large or to critique the practices of that community.

In the 1982 Position Statement on the Preparation and Professional Development of Teachers of Writing, the CCCC Task Force on the Preparation of Teachers of Writing stated unequivocally that "to provide effective instruction in writing . . . teachers need, first of all, experience in writing" (446). Of the taskforce's eight recommendations for preparing writing teachers, three focus directly on giving writing teachers sufficient background and experience in writing:

> Programs for the preparation and continuing education of teachers of English and language arts, at all levels, should included opportunities for prospective and active teachers:
>
> 1. *to write,*
>   (a) as a means of
>   (1) developing, shaping, representing, and communicating our perceptions of our world, our experiences, our beliefs, and our identity,
>   (2) finding sensory and aesthetic pleasure in working with and playing with language,
>   (3) developing our various intellectual skills;
>   (b) in a variety of forms, e.g.,
>   (1) prose that attempts to express what we think, feel, and imagine,
>   (2) poems representing experience and the fruits of imagination,
>   (3) narratives: autobiographical, fictional, historical,
>   (4) scripts for performance in class, on television, in film and radio,
>   (5) informative records and reports;
>   (c) in response to a variety of authentic rhetorical situations in which our work will be read and responded to by others, including teachers, classmates, family,and friends; readers of school and community publications; audiences at public readings of our work.

3. *to become perceptive readers of our own writing,* so that we can ask questions about, clarify, and reshape what we are trying to express.

. . . .

5. *to experience writing as a way of learning* which engages us in intellectual operations that enable or require us

   (a) to interpret what we experience and discover in light of what we already know, making connections, seeing relationships;

   (b) to re-shape impersonal data into knowledge that is meaningful to us personally;

   (c) to perform essential activities of mind such as analyzing, synthesizing, evaluating, testing, asserting;

   (d) to use what we already know in searching for what we don't know, making hypotheses, imagining new patterns. (447–48)

Clearly, a major assumption of the CCCC task force was that writing teachers should first and foremost be writers themselves, with sufficient insight into their own writing and with sufficient practice in thinking about their own writing that they could share their own writing experience with their students. Indeed, the major way that the task force recommends that writing teachers "*study and teach writing as a process*" is by "reflecting on [their] own writing" and by "studying authors' journals and notebooks for indications of their composing processes, and by comparing successive drafts of their work" (447).

Clearly, also, the task force thought that "some theoretical knowledge to guide classroom practice" was a secondary consideration. Of the other five recommendations, three focus on giving writing teachers practice in pedagogical skills—"*to read and respond to the writings of students, classmates, and colleagues,*" "*to study and teach writing as a process,*" and "*to learn to assess the progress of individual writers by responding to complete pieces of their writing and studying changes in their writing*"—and only two focus on giving writing teachers a background in scholarly research and theory—"*to study research and other scholarly work in the humanistic discipline of the teaching of writing*" and "*to study writing in relation to other disciplines*" (447–48).

I do not mean to suggest that the CCCC task force was an early proponent of the point I am making here, that writing teachers should have practice in the kind of writing they teach and practice analyzing the discourse communities in which they write. I think it is obvious from their first major point about giving teachers practice in writing that the task force conceives of writing as a global skill that can be acquired by practicing a wide variety of genres in a wide variety of contexts, and I have been systematically questioning this conception. In addition, the task force recommends that writing teachers study the writing of "professionals in other disciplines" in order to "learn what is asked" of them, not in order to become members of that discipline. In other words, the task force is not recommending that writing teachers be members of a discipline so that they can write from the "inside" of the discipline, as it were, or so that they can advise novice writers from personal experience about how writing functions in that discipline. Still, the task force does promote the notion that the major qualification of writing teachers ought to be the ability to write in a wide variety of genres and contexts and that writing teachers should have substantial experience reflecting on their own writing, not only in "authentic rhetorical situations" but in writing as learning.

How ironic then that all the evidence is that despite the increased professionalization of composition studies, the field has never confronted the issue of how to determine whether writing teachers write adequately themselves or whether they are sufficiently insightful about their own writing or the writing of others to be helpful to novice writers. All the evidence is that MA and PhD programs in composition and rhetoric and the programs designed to prepare graduate teaching assistants to teach introductory writing courses *assume* that their students are adequate writers, primarily because they write graduate papers in English. These programs assume, in the words of Tori Haring-Smith, that "the kind of writing done in [advanced writing seminars for graduate students] is close enough in subject, rhetorical situation, and purpose to freshman writing so that the two experiences can feed on one another. This simply is not so" (34–35).

In her survey of thirty-six academic institutions with GTA training programs, Catherine Latterell found that such training programs—apprenticeships, practicums, methods courses, or theory seminars—emphasize either pedagogical skills or "theory," broadly defined. That is, as in the apprenticeship program at the University of Massachusetts at Amherst, they emphasize "conducting peer-response sessions and student conferences, presenting the 'documented essay,' setting appropriate goals, and evaluating student writing" (11), or as in the teaching practicum at Syracuse, they provide occasions for GTAs to "talk about what to do in the classroom, develop course plans, share ideas with other first-year and experienced teachers, and work out whatever problems or questions [they] might have on a weekly basis" (qtd. in Latterell 13). The theory seminars "typically ask GTAs to consider the following: (1) the ways in which writing teachers inflect their instruction with philosophical/theoretical biases; and (2) what consequences such biases have on the nature of learning in the classroom" (17). Only the GTA course materials from Texas A&M appear to imply that GTAs should be adequate writers themselves. That university has as one of the goals of its practicum that GTAs become better writers themselves (14). None of the other institutions appears to concern itself at all with whether its writing teachers are adequate writers, or whether they have had any experience writing the genres they will be teaching, or whether they are particularly insightful in reading the kinds of genres they will be teaching.

Likewise, Stuart Brown, Paul Meyer, and Theresa Enos's survey of doctoral programs in rhetoric and composition reveals that of seventy-two programs, only thirteen have any requirement, or even an option among requirements, that students take a writing course. Overwhelmingly, the courses that are required or are an option among requirements seem to be in literary nonfiction and the essay or in writing for business, the professions, or the workplace. The same is true for graduate programs in literature (Sullivan).

Now, I realize that the model of the writing teacher as a practitioner has its difficulties. The main difficulty is to confront our felt sense that writing teachers must know *something* above and beyond how to write a particular genre in a particular context, how to analyze the writing practices of that context, and how to offer tips to novices trying to write in that social context. After all, there must be *something* we call *disciplinary knowledge,* the knowledge undergirding what Zebroski calls the teaching and curricular practices of the profession, knowledge that has traditionally been discussed in the field in terms of coursework: syntax and semantics, composition theory, rhetorical theory, teaching methods, and the like.

In addition, besides disciplinary knowledge, surely there must be *something* that Stephen North calls teaching "lore" and L. S. Shulman calls "pedagogical content knowledge," something that teachers know as teachers above and beyond their subject matter, something more substantial than the knowledge of a genre and context and the ability of offer "tips." The difficulty in both of these cases, however, is to characterize what that knowledge is and how to go about determining whether writing teachers possess that knowledge.

Disciplinary Knowledge

I see two major difficulties in trying to conceptualize what a writing teacher might need to know or be able to do *as* a writing teacher. First and foremost is the difficulty of conceptualizing what it is that expert writers know that novices do not. In a sense, this is an extension of the difficulty of conceptualizing writing ability, which I explored in chapter 1. Expert writers of particular genres in particular contexts are not necessarily very aware of how they write, nor are they necessarily very aware of how writing functions in the contexts in which they are expert. As a result, these writers may not be well prepared to teach others how to do what they can do. If people learn to write tacitly, with much less explicit training than the profession normally acknowledges, we should not find this lack of awareness surprising. Cheryl Geisler argues that the main difference between expert and novice writers in academic disciplines is the extent to which what experts know is "rhetorically constructed" while what novices know is the accepted "wisdom" of textbooks. That is, experts understand how their knowledge has been "constructed" by the evaluation of claims and evidence, while novices simply know the received wisdom of the field. Thus, experts write in their disciplines in ways that take into account not just what others have said, but who those "others" are and how their positions fit into a broader argument about what it known in the field. Geisler demonstrates how tacit this "rhetorical construction of knowledge" really is and how difficult it is to bridge the gap between writing that is based on "rhetorical knowing" and writing that is based on received wisdom (see especially 81–92, 210–31).

I suspect that something like Geisler's distinction accounts for the differences between most expert writers and novices, even in discourse communities outside of the academy. That is, expert writers have learned tacitly through immersion in a particular community how that community works rhetorically, how that community's discourse practices determine genre conventions, types of evidences, and patterns of reasoning.

Because what experts know is so tacit and assumed, it is difficult for them to do a good job of giving novices a sense of how writing is really done even in their own communities and areas of expertise. We in English are no exception. Look at introductory texts in how to write literary analyses or arguments, for example, or standard texts used to introduce graduate students to advanced study in English. Most introductions to writing about literature simply offer undergraduate students ways of talking about certain formal aspects of literature (see for example McMahan, Day, and Funk), although recently texts have begun to appear introducing undergraduates to theory (Bressler; Lynn). However, even in the more theoretical texts, students are primarily told how to follow certain broad rules for writing papers. The authors of these texts convey little or no sense that interpretations and theoretical discussions of literature are intensely contested and that outside of classrooms, such writing is always situated in the context of particular histories and particular controversies, that in short such writing is *situated*.

Introductions to graduate study in English are little better. Most introductions to graduate study assume that advanced students in the various subfields of English have already learned how to write, and they too ignore the rhetorical and contextual basis of scholarship, offering instead general overviews of the profession and its various subdivisions and prescriptions and generalizations about textual conventions (Gibaldi, *Introduction* and *MLA*). If Patricia Sullivan is correct, the limitations of these textbooks are reproduced in the classroom. The same is true in other disciplines (Prior; Berkenkotter and Huckin).

So the first major problem in conceptualizing the nature of disciplinary knowledge in composition studies is the difficulty in conceptualizing what expert writers know or are able to do. A second but closely related difficulty is in determining the degree to which various aspects of that expertise is specific to particular genres or contexts or to a more general knowledge and ability shared by all expert writers and the degree to which the more general kinds of knowledge and ability should be explicitly taught. Is there any broad kind of knowledge other than that of particular genres and contexts writing teachers might need to know? To put it another way, is there some kind of disciplinary knowledge that all writing teachers ought to have in common, no matter what genres and contexts they teach, knowledge of such things as learning theory, or grammar and syntax, or the principles of rhetoric, theories of invention or creativity, discourse analysis, or critical theory? Or perhaps a metacognitive sense of organizational patterns and style, principles of argumentation, or at least a sense of the difficult issues involved in these concepts?

Well, we might agree that all writing teacher should know *at least to some extent* about the nature of language, composing processes, error analysis, the basics of rhetorical theory and analysis, evaluation and assessment, and various theoretical frameworks for analyzing and critiquing social structures. But as Gerald Graff notes, academic disciplines seem to expand by accretion, and the standard way for English departments to deal with controversies in the curriculum is simply to add courses. Programs in composition and rhetoric are no exceptions to this phenomenon. The question is whether writing teachers need to take coursework in every area in which they should be expected to know or be able to do something, and if not, how else might a program go about guaranteeing writing teachers have been well prepared?

We might distinguish between what any teacher should absolutely have to know and what it might be helpful but not necessary to know, although drawing the line between useful background information and what is absolutely essential for all teachers to know in particular contexts is difficult to determine.

I can think of only one broad kind of knowledge besides being able to write various genres well themselves that writing teachers might need in order to be competent. I have no label for this kind of knowledge; I can only describe it. It is the knowledge that results from practice, investigation, and reflection on composing certain genres in certain social contexts. It is the knowledge that results from having extensive practice and experience in a certain kind of writing; the knowledge that results from talking to and observing other writers who work with similar genres in similar contexts; the knowledge that comes from studying the genres, the discourse practices, the social conditions in which the writer works; the knowledge that comes from self-consciously theorizing about the nature and value of those genres, discourse practices, and social conditions.

Robert Parker would call what I have just described two kinds of "theory": one in lowercase letters and one in uppercase. To Parker, "theory" in the lowercase is the personal exploration of how texts "as they are *explicitly* and *systematically* developed . . . already exist 'in' the participants as the personal viewpoints they have constructed from their experience of writing and teaching writing" (413). Lowercase "theory" is the introspective investigation of what writers tacitly know from actually being writers. It is, Parker says, "personal, concrete, context-bound, psychological" (413). THEORY in the uppercase is composed of "those more formal and abstract hypotheses about how large segments of the world work, or why they work as they do" (414). THEORY is "impersonal, abstract, context-free, logical" (413). THEORY is the systematic investigation of genres, discourse practices, and social conditions from a variety of theoretical frameworks and points of view. Parker's larger point is that writing teachers need to practice both kinds of "theory": they need to have their own experience and the experience of fellow writers confirmed by "theory," and they need to have their sense of the nature and value of their writing practices and their discourse communities examined and questioned by THEORY. In less abstract terms, Parker argues that teachers need to have enough experience in writing to give them some basis for working with THEORY; in fact, the only way THEORY will make any real sense to teachers is if it is grounded in practice, confirmed by experience. I would put the case even more directly: unless teachers themselves have faced particular difficulties in writing, from problems in editing to problems in theoretical critique, their ways of teaching and their advice to novices will always be suspect—the abstract, uncontextualized textbook knowledge of people who don't really know what they are talking about.

So we need to be more specific about the kinds of things we might expect writing teachers to teach, and we need to think about how we would prepare them in these areas:

- Writing-to-learn: If the effects of writing-to-learn are as narrow and context-dependent as I noted in chapter 5, then clearly, teachers who want to use the techniques of writing-to-learn need to be trained in the literature and research in writing-to-learn and in how to use specific kinds of writing to achieve specific kinds of knowledge. Once again, the rule is "You get what you teach for."
- Writing-to-think: If teachers get what they teach for, those who want to teach reflective practice, critical consciousness, or some forms of meta-awareness need to recognize that the relevance of their frameworks for analysis and critique may very well be limited to the subject matter, genres, and discourse communities with which they introduce these frameworks. This might mean training writing teachers in how to apply particular frameworks for reflection or theoretical critique to particular discourse practices and communities.
- School genres: As I noted in some detail in chapter 7, the primary rationale for school genres is that they train students to think and

write in certain generic ways; however, the generic prescriptions of school genres may have a very limited applicability. If this is so, then teachers may need to be trained to analyze how particular school genres prepare students for writing various genres in various contexts outside the classroom.

- Public genres that require a knowledge of common experience or knowledge in which people can become conversant by following the issues of the day in newspapers and on television, or by simply participating in the larger civic culture: Here I have in mind such genres as the personal narrative, memoir, or biographical fragment; the movie review; the Sunday supplement arts-and-leisure profile of an artist or creative enterprise; the newspaper editorial; and various kinds of informational and persuasive reports written by various constituencies that advocate positions on public issues. Once again, for these genres, it would seem as if writing teachers need to have experience and training not only in these genres but in the social contexts in which they occur.
- Genres of specific disciplines, professions, and workplaces, such as biology, architecture, or the software industry.

It strikes me that everything else we traditionally think of as "knowledge" in composition studies is really background for dealing with questions of how writing functions in particular contexts, or the degree to which classroom genres provide practice in certain kinds of discourse used outside the classroom. It strikes me that teachers need to know about grammar and syntax, composing processes, principles of rhetoric and other broad kinds of knowledge generally associated with writing instruction only to the extent that they help illuminate these other questions. Of course, all knowledge can be helpful; mastery of these topics might be very helpful. But like writing knowledge and skills in general, they might be best taught in context. That is, writing teachers might need to know not just grammar and syntax in general but the grammar and syntax of particular genres; not just about composing processes in particular but how people in particular communities compose given their particular purposes and tasks. Writing teachers need to know not just about theory and critique in the abstract but how theory and critique might actually be applied in specific social contexts in response to particular social concerns. Indeed, it might even be possible to make a case that teachers need to know about generic modes of organization or patterns of reasoning or argumentation or school genres such as the topic/subpoints essay or the five-paragraph literary analysis, but it seems to me that for each of these kinds of knowledge, the point is whether anyone can demonstrate what knowing or being able to use these generic modes, patterns or genres actually accomplishes.

I return to my thought experiment: what disciplinary knowledge would a writing teacher have to know in order to help a fellow faculty member write a thank-you letter to the president of the university? I suspect the answer to that question would be this: the writing teacher would of course need to know the conventions of formal thank-you letters and in general be sensitive to tone. But in this specific case, what the writing teacher would really need is experience in writing memos and letters to the members of this particular academic administration. This is not the kind of knowledge that can be taught in generic courses using generic textbooks.

The Writing Teacher and Pedagogical Content Knowledge

However, even if we could organize writing instruction in our colleges and universities as an integral part of initiating students into particular discourse communities, and if writing teachers were trained in how to present novice writers with useful information about particular genres in particular contexts, the model does not confront the reality of the way writing is usually taught at these institutions. In these institutions, writing is usually taught to groups of twenty to twenty-five novice writers with a wide variety of background and experience in writing, so that providing either practice and tips to individual writers is very difficult. It would seem that writing teachers need to know some techniques for instructing not individuals but groups of writers.

How do writing teachers influence the active learning of twenty novices, each with different backgrounds and experiences? How do writing teachers meet such a diverse group of students where they are; how do they consider what their students already know and can do and arrange for them to get the practice they need to build on their natural competence and invaluable previous experience? How do writing teachers know how to be helpful to students in ways that are meaningful to the students *themselves,* not simply in ways that uphold the "standards" of the discourse community in which the teacher is an expert? And the question is how to do all this with so many students and without adequate diagnostic techniques.

In addition, how do writing teachers deal with differences in power, gender, and class? The expert-novice relationship is one-on-one, and the differences in power are inherent in the discourse community. The expert is the person the novice wants to be; novices model themselves after the expert. Presumably, the discourse community itself provides the norm for issues of gender or class. But in most first-year writing programs, it is difficult for the instructors to have a one-on-one relationship with so many students, and the students do not necessarily look upon the instructors as a model. In fact, students may consider writing instructors, especially if they are graduate teaching assistants or part-time instructors, as the opposite of a model: they may consider writing instructors people in *training* to be experts, people who have not yet acquired the credentials necessary for giving appropriate advice. Worse, they may consider writing instructors merely as gatekeepers, protectors of standards, people they have to work their way past in order to further their own personal goals. And since many, if not most, university classrooms embody the diversity of the country, there are no norms for issues of gender and class, of how students ought to relate to each other and to the instructor. And so pedagogical content knowledge may involve a knowledge of how to teach groups and especially how to organize or conduct classes in ways that deal with issues of gender, power, and class, although as far as I can determine there is no consensus in the profession about how to do so.

As I have indicated earlier, proposals about how to teach writing have been many and varied, some with odd-sounding names: the environmental mode and focus on inquiry, procedural facilitation, distributed cognition, and scaffolding, to name a few. All of them are problematic. However, as I noted in chapter 7, the concept of "scaffolding" may be the most promising. In order to be proficient in the teaching methods implicit in scaffolding, teachers would be able to teach writing in the areas of their special expertise; they would be able to immerse students in the discourse practices and issues of the communities in which they themselves use their expertise; they would be able to focus their attention on ways to make their own expertise explicit, through modeling, through a shared analysis of the genre conventions and practices in that community, and if necessary, through various kinds of "drill," which students might need in order to help them internalize particular aspects of these practices. Moreover, in an ideal curriculum, the students would choose the writing courses and communities they wish to join, and therefore there would be less tension between the goals and methods of the teacher and the needs and desires of the students.

In providing scaffolding, teachers might do the following,

- Take into account the background and experience of the students, their linguistic and cultural differences, especially their differing experiences with texts and writing, and find ways to use those differences as a resource. This might mean affirming the students' own language and culture and finding ways to help students investigate the differences between their language and culture and the language and practices of a discourse community they wish to join (see for example the programs at the universities of Wisconsin, reported in Weese, Fox, and Greene, and Massachusetts-Boston, reported in Kutz, Groden, and Zamel).
- Think of ways to provide access, to make explicit the nature and values of the discourse community the teacher represents; to provide frameworks to analyze and critique that community; and to make explicit the discourse practices the teacher has mastered. This might mean something as simple as teachers sharing with students how they themselves write or how they deal with certain problem in writing certain genres. It might mean something as difficult as ana-

lyzing the discourse practices of the community, conceptualizing those practices as useful discrete units of knowledge or skill, and providing practice or help in mastering those kinds of knowledge or skill. As I pointed out earlier, useful analyses of discourse practices are hard to find, even in the discipline of English.

- Find ways especially to bridge the gap between school genres with their limited contexts and constraints and those genres written outside of the classroom (see also Cope and Kalantzis). Russell suggests that bridging the gap may take more than one course. He distinguishes among discipline-specific genres at three levels: for General Liberal Education, Beginning Professional Education, and Advanced Professional Education. Russell's example is of biology. Most students in introductory biology courses will not go on in the field, and therefore they need only a general sense of how knowledge is constructed in biology and how writing functions in that process. As a result in introductory courses that are not writing intensive, perhaps students need only the broadest grasp of the discourse of biology, a sense of the accumulated knowledge in the field, which they can learn from textbooks, and a sense of how writing may be done in biological research, which they can learn from writing lab reports or other school genres. However, at the next level, students might begin to think of themselves as biology majors, so that in more advanced courses, the writing should be more closely related to the actual practice of biologists and the genres they write, although such writing will be limited because it must focus on the content of the course rather than the particular specialties the course might be preparing students for, such as medicine, science journalism, or science education. Finally, at the most advanced levels in Russell's curriculum, students would write genres almost indistinguishable from those outside the academy. The question at each level, of course, is how to introduce students to the level of expertise they need at that level. Using activity theory, Russell explains in detail the conflicts involved in trying to integrate writing into courses designed to accommodate a large number of interlocking interests, those of the university, those of particular professions, and those of the students who must decide at every level the degree to which they want to participate in these interests ("Rethinking" 525–45). Deciding how to structure a course to accommodate these competing interests involves pedagogical content knowledge.

Finally, there is a great deal of evidence that good teachers have attitudes conducive to learning. Good teachers expect students to do well, they are empathetic, and they believe that they can make a difference (McLeod, *Notes* 106–21). Good teachers are accessible to students outside of class and provide occasions for this contact (Pascarella and Terenzini 97–102). Good teachers seem to be "student-oriented" (Astin 228).

Of course, my personal vision of scaffolding does not necessarily solve any of the problems of large group instruction or of gender, race, and class, and I certainly do not mean to downplay the importance of these issues. There is a large literature, both explications of theory and personal narratives of success and failure in the classroom, dealing with these problems and no obvious or easy answers (on the subject of race in teaching writing, see for example Delpit, "Silenced," "Skills"; Prendergast; on the subject of class, see Cushman; Hourigan; Schroeder). Still, it seems to me in reading this literature that many of the difficulties associated with both of these problems can be attributed to teachers who do not want to deal with students as they are or to students who do not want what their teachers are offering them. I am referring not only to "traditional" teachers who may find it difficult to deal with their students' lack of expertise in textual conventions but also to more "critically conscious" teachers who may find it difficult to deal with their students' lack of interest in being critical or reflective about various social issues. I am referring not only to students who blow off writing classes because these classes are too boring or irrelevant but also to students who underperform because they are ashamed of their abilities or who are resentful because their writing classes do not address their particular needs more directly. Scaffolding is not a panacea. However, in my vision, scaffolding does assume that writing classes should be organized according to the specific kinds of expertise teachers possess by virtue of their being members of a discourse community and their desire to open that community to new members; it also assumes their desire to offer membership in that community without sentimentality by offering students the chance to analyze and critique that community. It assumes that students should participate in these classes primarily because they want to join these communities. If we could find some way to implement the principles behind scaffolding, such a curriculum might go a long way toward dealing with problems of large group instruction and the problems of gender, race, and class.

Problems with Certifying Writer-Practitioners

So to determine whether candidates for writing teacher positions would be good writing teachers, we would need to determine how well they wrote the discourses they were supposed to teach and how well they could analyze the genres and contexts they would be introducing their students to. We would need to know how well they could organize instruction to make their students aware of how various aspects of those genres functioned in particular contexts and how well they provided appropriate tips to students on how to improve their writing. We would have to find a way to evaluate the degree to which the candidates were insightful about their own writing practices, the degree to which they knew how writing functions in their discourse communities, and the degree to which they could analyze and critique the writing in that community from a variety of critical frameworks. How would we go about determining these things? If we wanted to do it through coursework, what sort of coursework would we require and what would the content of the coursework be?

If the notion of a writing-practitioner makes any kind of sense, it would seem that the best way to prepare writing teachers would be to train them to write the genres they would be expected to teach, and to train them in the rhetorical, social, and critical analysis of those genres in the contexts in which they are used. The best way to organize a curriculum to prepare writing teachers then would be according to the genres and contexts in which these teachers would be expected to be experts: writing-to-learn, writing-to-think, or thinking-to-write in various disciplines, professions, workplaces, and public arenas. In this vision of teacher training, potential teachers would take coursework in the rhetoric and discourse of particular genres—say, the personal essay—and the analysis and critique of how those genres are used in particular public forums, disciplines, professions, or workplaces. Such a course on the personal essay, for example, would be devoted to teaching potential writing teachers how to write personal essays in all their various manifestations, whether for personal reflection or for the many venues outside the classroom in which essays are published, how to analyze the style and rhetoric of essays, and how to analyze the social circumstances under which essays are written. Recall one of the main points in chapter 2: that the way to achieve fluency in a genre just as with a language is to be familiar with that genre in as many of its manifestations in as many contexts as possible. Courses organized by genre and context might be called the Rhetoric of the Essay, the Rhetoric of writing-to-learn, the Rhetoric of Engineering, or the Rhetoric of Corporate Culture. Of course, because the concept of a discourse community has fuzzy borders, the precise nature of the discourse communities represented by these courses will always be problematic.

The way for prospective writing teachers to demonstrate their expertise in a variety of genres would be for them to produce a portfolio of writing containing examples of those genres they had written.

And the way for prospective writing teachers to demonstrate their ability to teach in certain ways would be through a portfolio containing samples of the genres they are competent to write, samples of writing they had assigned and responded to, and videotapes of their teaching.

The point here is to get away from coursework as the major credential for teaching writing and to focus on what potential writing teachers can actually do: in their own writing, in response to the writing of others, and in designing ways to help novices understand the intricacies of the discourse practices of particular communities. Most of my suggestions are only tentative solutions to the central hermeneutic problem of how to generalize from specifics: To what degree can we infer that a person is an adequate writer from these samples? To what degree can we infer that a person is an adequate teacher from these responses to papers or from these sample lessons? The evidence of competence in teaching will always be problematic. However, I think the field of composition studies needs to take these questions much more seriously than simply requiring of potential writing teachers a certain amount of coursework.

That is, Discourses are not mastered by overt instruction ..., but by enculturation ('apprenticeship') into social practices through scaffolded and supported interaction with people who have already mastered the Discourse.... If you have no access to the social practice, you don't get in the Discourse, you don't have it.
—James Paul Gee, *Social Linguistics and Literacies*

9 A R/Evolutionary Program

AS STEPHEN NORTH AND a number of other theorists have convincingly demonstrated, composition studies is not a coherent field of inquiry. Rather, it is a set of related subfields, each with its own social practices, its own set of assumptions, its own research methods, and especially its own pedagogical strategies. No major questions dominate the field. Obviously, by analyzing various conceptual problems in our knowledge of how people acquire and learn how to write, I have assumed that the field *should* be dominated by a number of questions, the questions I have been dealing with all along: What is writing? How is writing learned? How then should writing be taught, promoted, or nurtured? And I have suggested that the basic concepts, models, paradigms, and frameworks the field has developed to answer these questions are widely known and accepted in principle, although what they *mean* or how they are to be applied is problematic, at best. I suspect that further research on these questions will not substantially alter the broad outline, the substantial picture, of what we already know; it will not resolve the ambiguities and indeterminacies inherent in what we know. The problem facing composition studies as a field is how to respond to the substantial picture of what we know, given the ambiguity and indeterminacy inherent in that picture.

What we know is that writing may not be a simple, single ability but a complex web of related knowledge and skills that writers acquire over time by being immersed in literate environments. Those environments must, of course—at least at first—include a great deal of explicit instruction, usually through formal schooling, but there is ample evidence that after learning what we might call the technology of writing—the meaning of the alphabet, the physical ability to get words on paper; a certain level of expertise in using certain fundamental text conventions, such as spelling, punctuation, and usage; and a certain amount of syntactic fluency and rhetorical maturity, novice writers increase their knowledge and skill primarily by immersing themselves in the various tasks and contexts that require writing. They increase their knowledge and skill by using writing in a wide variety of contexts, to achieve a wide variety of goals, and by tacitly acquiring a sense of how writing as a "tool" can be used in different ways for different reasons. Because the knowledge and skill involved in writing vary so much from situation to situation, it might be better to conceptualize writing not as a list of discrete kinds of information or ability but as the ability to accomplish certain tasks. Writers develop particular expertise in various writing tasks because they already are or because they wish to become a part of discourse communities that use writing to accomplish those tasks. Expert writers and mentors can help in this process of socialization or acculturation by providing occasions for novice writers to work on particular tasks, by providing feedback and support, by providing analysis and critique, a meta-awareness, of the writing practices and social context in which the novice is writing. But ultimately, it is the novice writers themselves who must acquire the knowledge and skill they need in order to write; it is the novice writers themselves who must want to write in particular ways, who must need to write in particular ways. All that experts and mentors can do is offer support and the opportunity.

The overwhelming problem facing composition studies, then, is how to design a writing program, a writing curriculum, which in effect institutionalizes a process of socialization in many different discourse communities for masses of students, who are all at different stages of development in their writing and who all write at different levels of expertise from one community to the other. The problem is not helped by the fact that the concept of a discourse community itself is fundamentally indeterminate, and thus there will always be disagreement about the nature of the communities novice writers might want to join and what constitutes expertise in the discourse practices of those groups.

However, this much *is* clear: no one ever learned to write primarily by completing a two-course sequence in writing at a college or university. This is not to say that introductory writing classes may not do some good. Indeed, they may be very helpful in giving students the opportunity to practice a certain number of skills; they may give students important feedback about certain aspects of their writing or thinking; they may introduce students to genres or ways of thinking they may have never used before. But literacy as most people usually understand the term, as the mastery of an undetermined number of genres or as the ability to use written language effectively in an undetermined number of contexts, involves too much knowledge and skill and too many different kinds of knowledge and skill for most students to do anything more than refine their ability to do a few things in the nine months they participate in a two-course introductory writing sequence.

The problem of promoting writing in higher education, then, is not going to be solved by abolishing required writing courses, as certain major theorists in the profession are beginning to advocate (see, for example, Crowley "Personal"; Connors "New"). Making writing courses elective does not confront any of the issues I noted in chapter 7: it does not solve the problems of genre, context, focus, and transfer. On the contrary, my analysis suggests that if we want to improve literacy in colleges and universities, we are going to have to give our students more practice and more feedback in a broader range of writing; we are going to have to introduce them to the discourse practices of a wider range of communities than can be offered in a two-course sequence; in a sense we are going to have to make writing instruction the responsibility of more than composition specialists and writing programs.

How might we begin to confront the problem of designing a post-secondary writing program to account for the notion of writing as the process of socialization into many different discourse communities? There are no easy or obvious answers to this question. However, in this chapter, I am going to propose a program that fulfills the requirements I have outlined. Obviously, many teachers and scholars in composition studies may find this program ambitious, to say the least; perhaps even revolutionary. However, in the next chapter, I will argue that my program may not be as revolutionary as it sounds; that it may indeed be fundamentally evolutionary because over the past twenty years, individual institutions have been gradually implementing programs that go in the direction I recommend. In fact, I will argue that so many institutions are headed in the direction I recommend, the basic structures for implementing my program are already in place, and I will argue that current debates over the nature of English studies more generally provide an appropriate forum for discussing my program and offering ways to put it into effect.

My program involves significant r/evolutionary change in four major areas: the undergraduate writing curriculum, graduate training in composition studies, institutional policies for promoting and rewarding faculty, and the personal goals of writing teachers.

The Undergraduate Writing Curriculum

Because writing is conceived of as a unitary ability for which students simply need some sort of unspecified generic practice, writing courses are usually offered with much less structure than other courses in the university. Generally, the movement is from introductory "skills" courses to more advanced courses, some of which may introduce students to the formats and conventions of writing in particular disciplines, such as Business Writing, or Written Communication for Engineers; others may simply be courses in the generic writing of the introductory courses but at a more "advanced" level, whatever that may mean. Sometimes these more advanced courses are concerned with style. Often, if they are writing-intensive, they require the writing of personal essays about the particular subject matter of the course.

Given all that I have argued to this point, however, I think a writing curriculum justified by current research would look like this:

Organizing the Curriculum

If learning to write beyond the sentence level is learning to master the knowledge and genre conventions of a wide variety of discourse communities, it follows that there is no one standard of literacy by which we can measure our students' ability to write and no common writing curriculum to which we can hold all students accountable. The best we can offer our students is practice in writing for a variety of purposes, what I have called writing-to-learn, writing-to-think, and thinking-to-write, and especially practice in thinking-to-write a range of genres used in public arenas, disciplines, professions, and workplaces. It is the range of experience in writing that will make students generally literate.

In addition, if learning to write is, at least in part, a matter of internalizing a broad but weak set of strategies for achieving syntactic fluency and rhetorical maturity, and a matter of developing a number of reflective or metacognitive strategies for thinking about writing as a social practice, then in order to be more effective, the writing curriculum as a whole will have to in effect "institutionalize" pedagogical procedures for helping students to notice the differences in the purposes and genres and contexts of writing, and give them the theoretical frameworks necessary for thinking critically about the way writing functions in various discourse communities.

Moreover, the precise nature and value of those practices and those communities will always be in dispute. Certain scholars in the humanities will always dispute the value of learning to write for business, the sciences, and the professions. Certain scholars in business, the sciences, and the professions will always dispute the value of learning to write imaginative literature, self-reflective essays, and theoretical critique. Scholars in composition studies will always dispute the relative merits of expressive writing as opposed to academic writing; reflective writing as opposed to informative writing; imaginative writing as opposed to critical and theoretical writing. The reason for the contentiousness of these disputes over the nature and value of various kinds of writing is that the disputes are not just about writing. The disputes are about the nature and value of the discourse communities the writing represents. They are about the purposes to which writing is being put, and the practices for which writing is only one of many tools. In a sense, disputes over the nature and value of various kinds of writing are disputes over ultimate values: the value of various kinds of education, the value of various ways of relating to other human beings, the value of various ways of "being" in the world.

What the undergraduate curriculum should offer then is a range of writing experiences—writing-to-learn, writing-to-think, and thinking-to-write—in a variety of courses and contexts across the curriculum. In addition, these courses should provide more advanced writing in the genres students want or need in order to further their own objectives and goals. Eventually, students should receive some sort of practice in writing as it is actually done outside of classrooms in a variety of disciplines, professions, workplaces, and public arenas.

This means that colleges and universities should not require students to take just one or two narrowly conceived "introductory" writing classes but to get as much practice as possible writing for a variety of purposes and in a variety of genres in a variety of disciplines and social contexts both inside and outside the academy. However, we must also recognize that many beginning writers come to the university with limited background and experience in writing per se and with limited experience in the social contexts for which they hope the university will train them. These writers need a graduated entry into the writing of various genres; they need appropriate "scaffolding."

An appropriate curriculum might proceed in three stages, although I recognize the problems in labeling any progression of courses by "stages" or "levels." The point is not that the sequence of courses would be developmental or even that they would necessarily build on one another in terms of what we usually call "skills." I noted in chapter 2 that writing is too complex to expect novices to be fluent in all of the text conventions of particular genres, even if they can write those genres with a certain amount of sophistication. The point is that my proposed sequence of courses *would* require an increasing level of domain-specific knowledge.

A first introductory course, then, might give students practice in sentence fluency and editing and introduce them to the analysis and critique of writing practices in one or more social contexts (see Carter 284; Lloyd-Jones and Lunsford 27–28; Russell, "Activity" 69–74). Such a course might be called Introduction to Writing as a Social Practice. A few such courses have already been proposed.

A course recommended by the English Coalition Conference emphasizes not just writing but all language in the context of the students' own social environment and a more specific discourse community. The conference recommends that introductory writing courses be redesigned around "three basic principles: investigation or critical inquiry, collaboration, and conscious theorizing" (Lloyd-Jones and Lunsford 28). To put these pedagogical principles into practice, the coalition recommends a "yearlong, entry-level course that will use current theory and research to focus on the uses of language; the value-laden nature of all such uses; and the ways we and our students use writing, reading, speaking, listening, and critical thinking to construct ourselves as individuals and as members of academic and other communities" (Lloyd-Jones and Lunsford 27). As a concrete example, the coalition proposes a course with two focuses: one on personal identity and how students can shape their identity and how their identities are in turn shaped through language in particular social circumstances; the other on the language of a particular discourse community. For the first focus, the coalition recommends that students "investigate the construct of self" by reading autobiographies, writing journals and narratives about their own experiences, that they "collect and analyze samples of their own ideolects," and that they share these findings with others in the class. Later the course would shift to a study of the language of particular workplaces, social groups, or academic disciplines. For this study of particular genres, students might take field notes based on observations of these discourse communities in action and read texts written for and about these communities, all of which might lead to a formal or critical analysis, either written or oral, of how language works in the community under study (Lloyd-Jones and Lunsford 27–28; for a similar "ethnographic" emphasis in first-year writing see Kutz, Groden, and Zamel; Soliday; Weese, Fox, and Greene). My own inclination would be to limit the coalition's proposed introductory course to one semester and to shift the primary responsibility for studying and writing the genres of particular discourse communities to departments and disciplines across the university.

David Russell has also put forward a proposal for an introductory course similar to that of the English Coalition Conference. Russell proposes that introductory writing courses not have as their object "teaching students to write or improving their writing per se, any more than an introductory psychology course claims to make students better adjusted or a course in music appreciation claims to make its students better singers. . . . Rather its object would be to teach students what has been learned about writing in those activity systems that make the role of writing in society the object of their study" ("Activity" 73). In other words, such a course would be structured to help students learn what research in writing from a variety of frameworks—rhetoric, cultural studies, critical theory, and ethnography, to name just a few—have shown about how writing functions in a range of discourse communities, and to give them practice using the genres of composition studies to in effect write about writing. Students would write "discourse analyses, rhetorical analyses, ethnographic accounts, cultural criticism, and so on" ("Activity" 73). Such a course would at least have the advantage of allowing teachers with graduate training in English to teach to their strength. Presumably the kind of writing trained writing instructors in English know how to do best and what they have had specific practice in doing is the writing of their MA and PhD theses using the genres Russell mentions.

To these two suggestions I would add a third possibility, an extension of the course proposed by the English Coalition Conference: an introductory course in the analysis and critique of the discourse practices of a particular discourse community, one the instructor is a participant in, and the writing of the genre or group of related genres of that community. The precise nature of the discourse community does not matter. It might be the community of academic fiction writers; it might be the community of cultural studies theorists; it might be the community of biologists studying DNA; it might be the community of scholars studying small business management. Or it might be the community of those who actively participate in a particular social issue, such as abortion, in particular social contexts, such as through the writing of various activist pro-life or pro-choice organizations: letters to the editor, brochures, and public position statements designed to sway public opinion during elections. Whatever the discourse community, however we conceive of a discourse community, the point would be to immerse novice writers into a variety of related genres in order to give them the background they need to understand the writing practices of the community, to analyze and critique those practices, and to help them internalize the wide range of genre conventions of the various discourses. In other words, the introductory course would help novices practice sentence fluency and editing in a particular context.

I recognize that in proposing a course entitled Introduction to Writing as a Social Practice I am avoiding the problem of what to do with students who come to the university with little experience in the kinds of literate practices we associate with academic disciplines, the workplace, or even various public forums, such as letters to the editors in newspapers or informative reports to various cultural and civic groups. In keeping with the terminology of many people in composition studies, I call such students "basic writers." A great deal of research has indicated that most basic writers are not cognitively or culturally deficient, whatever those terms may mean. Rather, most basic writers *are* literate in the particular genres used in their homes and the social groups they belong to outside of the university. These genres may include letters; thank-you notes; notes as substitutes for oral messages, such as records of phone calls or notes written to school officials; memory aids, such as grocery lists and lists of things to do; financial writing, such as for budgets; reports for or to church and civic organizations; personal creative writing; autobiographical writing; and of course school writing before college: creative writing, personal essays, literary analyses, and research papers (see Taylor and Dorsey-Gaines 123–90 for charts of the various kinds of writing common to children and adults across socio-economic groups).

So the problem is how to introduce students with very limited background and experience in the concepts, ways of thinking, and kinds of discourse practices that are the heart and soul of college and university life; the problem is how to integrate these new concepts, ways of thinking, and kinds of discourse practices into those that basic writing students already know. And my response to this problem is that there is no recipe for doing so; there are no panaceas. There is no such thing as instant literacy in any discourse community. As with anyone introduced to new concepts, new ways of thinking, and new ways of using writing, introducing basic writers to all of the concepts, ways of thinking, and text conventions they might need in order to participate in a variety of discourse communities in college and universities takes patience and time. It certainly takes longer than one or two courses offered as "remedial" or "developmental" or "basic" before students are required to take the usual two-semester introductory writing sequence.

And so part of the solution to the problem of "basic writing" must be telling the truth about how people learn to write—they master the many different aspects of writing with varying degrees of accomplishment and at different paces—and holding all those who teach writing at all levels across the curriculum responsible for providing the scaffolding that basic writers need to master the various aspects of writing, depending on their level of accomplishment. This means that instructors in "upper-level courses" must not just expect all of their students to have mastered the conventions they do not want to teach. They must know the literature on error analysis and revision and be prepared to help students not only with the major concepts and genre conventions of their particular discourse communities but also with spelling, punctuation, syntax, and usage. They must be part of a broad university-wide program that introduces all novice writers "slowly but steadily and systematically" to new genres and social contexts, a program that encourages students to develop their "structural, rhetorical, stylistic facility" over time (Rose 112).

The second stage of my proposed curriculum would promote advanced practice in particular knowledge domains, disciplines, professions, or discourse communities organized around social issues after students have taken the Introduction to Writing as a Social Practice and after they have been introduced to academic life. This would place responsibility for teaching the knowledge, skills, and genre conventions, as well as the social critique of the discourse practices of various discourse communities squarely on those who participate in those discourse communities. Each major academic unit of the university would then be responsible for introducing

novices in that academic discipline—majors and minors and other interested students—into the writing practices of the discipline or into ways of
learning or thinking with writing about some aspect of that discipline or
some subject associated with that discipline. This might result in writing-
to-learn and writing-to-think courses, in which students would use writing
to study and reflect on various disciplinary subjects. Joseph Harris's course
on writing reflectively about film and Kurt Spellmeyer's course *(Common)*
on the personal essay would come under this category. Or this second stage
might result in thinking-to-write courses such as Writing in Political Science, Writing in Horticulture, and Writing in Architecture, which would introduce students to the kinds of genres actually written in those disciplines.
In any case, departments of English would be responsible only for teaching the knowledge, skills, genre conventions, and social critique of writing
in English or in subjects related to English as a discipline, or in those interdisciplinary specialties in which members of English departments might
have a particular expertise.

   In many ways, the second-level courses I envision are similar to those
advocated by John Trimbur, who has proposed courses across the curriculum focused on some aspect of writing, such as the Rhetoric of Technology, or on particular genres devoted to particular subject matter, such as
"a science writing course on disease and public health (for pre-meds, biology and biotechnology majors, science studies and history of science students, and writing majors)" (25). However, Trimbur is suspicious of limiting writing courses to "the transmission of expertise from the faculty in a
discipline to the students entering it" because such courses would "simply
reproduce the traditional departmental model" of English departments, in
which students do not learn to analyze and critique writing practices from
other perspectives (24).

   I realize that disciplines across the university may not be prepared to study,
critique, and promote their own discourse practices because their knowledge of the subject is largely tacit. This is where academic disciplines might
need help from those with training in composition studies. Later, I will propose a major shift in graduate education in composition studies in order
to foster more study and critique of various disciplinary writing practices.

   More problematic is giving students advanced practice in writing genres
outside the realms of particular academic specialties, what I have called
public discourse: editorials, position statements, informative and persuasive reports for particular public forums or societal and governmental constituencies. Here the relevant courses might also be similar to those proposed by Trimbur: the interdisciplinary study and critique of the discourse
practices involved in particular issues relative to particular institutions and
communities. Such courses might be offered under a general rubric, such as
Writing about Social Issues, and individual courses might explore the dis-

course practices of those individuals, groups, and institutions that write about abortion, discrimination, and evolution and creationism. These courses would emphasize not only the students' personal exploration of these issues but the analysis and critique of the particular writing practices used in the various social contexts in which those writing practices are used.

The goal of these courses would be to initiate novices into the discourse communities of those arguing these issues and to make them sufficiently competent to actively participate in the community. This might mean something as simple as helping students to write letters to the editors of those publications dealing with these issues. It might mean something as advanced as helping them write scholarly reports and recommendations to the relevant public forums or to those institutions that are in a position to advocate one side or the other on these issues.

At the second level of my proposed curriculum, there should also be opportunities for students to receive advanced practice in the tradition of belles lettres or in literary nonfiction. Such courses could be offered through English departments. However, the courses I envision would differ from more traditional courses in writing essays and other literary nonfiction genres in that they would focus on the analysis and critique of the conventions of writing these genres—who writes these kinds of discourse, for whom do they write, what social roles does such writing play—and they would promote the writing of literary genres for particular journals and audiences—or to use the more appropriate term, markets. (For an account of one "second level" writing-intensive program, see Brannon.)

Finally, the third stage of my proposed curriculum would initiate novice writers into some aspect of writing outside the classroom, by providing an experience in a mentor/apprenticeship program in an academic discipline or a profession or workplace outside of the academy. This experience would differ from advanced courses in that it would be writing "on the job," as it were, but it would not necessarily be restricted to the workplace. It might be for an academic unit or for a service organization, some discourse community outside the classroom for which, in the formulation of Patrick Dias and his colleagues, students would write for a social purpose rather than as an epistemic exercise to demonstrate knowledge and be evaluated (185–200).

I realize that such opportunities to write "outside the classroom" in an academic discipline might be difficult to distinguish in some cases from second-level courses. However, the key distinction is this: in second-level disciplinary courses, students would be initiated into the writing practices of the discipline through analysis and critique: they would still be, in effect, outsiders looking on from a distance, studying, analyzing, critiquing, trying to understand the discipline as a *subject*, although they would also begin to write in some introductory way the genres of the discipline. At the third level, students would actually participate in the discipline. They might be assigned to a professor's research team or to do individual research of their own with the aid of a faculty mentor: they would be involved in the discipline as a *participant*.

Of course, the point of my proposed curriculum would not be to limit the requirements to just three courses, but to encourage institutions to offer and require as much writing as possible. Once again, the principle is what matters: students should get a variety of reflective guided practice over time, and this practice should become more and more connected to writing as it is actually done outside the classroom.

Indeed, I would carry the principle of offering as much writing as possible one step further. Because no particular genre of writing is privileged and we all become literate in a wide variety of genres and knowledge domains, and because general literacy can be achieved only through exposure to a wide variety of genres and contexts, no single example of which is necessary and sufficient for being literate, I see no reason to limit the kinds of writing students should be able to study and practice or to limit the discourse communities they might wish to join. This means that the university should offer as much variety as possible so that students may in effect choose the ways in which they wish to become literate—a wide range of writing across the curriculum for a wide range of purposes: writing-to-learn, writing-to-think, and thinking-to-write. For each writing course beyond the required introductory one, teachers should specify in their course descriptions, syllabi, and lesson plans how their courses and lessons attempt to contribute to the writing of particular kinds of discourse for particular purposes and for particular discourse communities or activity systems. Students would then be allowed to choose the kinds of genres they wish to be proficient in and the kinds of discourse communities they wish to join. In learning to write in the popular sense—in learning to write competently in a variety of situations, it is not the practice in a particular kind of writing that is important; it is the range of practice in a variety of genres and a variety of contexts over time that matters.

There is another reason for giving students as many options in writing courses as possible, and that reason is ethical. In a diverse culture with few behavioral or ethical norms, and with many scholars in composition studies arguing that all instruction is political, choice is one way of honoring the unique subjectivities of our students. In discourse communities outside of school, the communities themselves are the norm, with their own particular ways of negotiating differences. In university classes, the goals for the course and, in a sense, the norms of behavior for the course are determined by the instructor, and no amount of theorizing by scholars of critical pedagogy and cultural studies can resolve the problem of differences in power between teacher and students, of how teachers should treat students, who are also "subjects" with the same rights to personhood and respect as any other, of how to teach those with radically different points of view from our own. How do we preserve the rights of individuals to be as different from us as they choose, even when we consider their points of view wrong or immoral, racist or sexist, paranoid or chauvinistic?

I find Jeff Smith's argument persuasive. To Smith, universities are "intentional communities" of adults, who attend universities as a means to an end, not necessarily as an end in itself, and students are active ethical agents, in charge of their own lives with all that that entails: students are responsible for their own choices, their own goals, their own values, and we are bound to respect those choices, those goals and values. Indeed, broadly speaking, as the participants of the intentional community who teach others, we as teachers are primarily obligated to help our students achieve their own ends, not ours. We may legitimately help our students think through their own positions; we may present them with alternative views, give them strategies or frameworks for critique. But ultimately, our job is not to convert them. Our job is, in Smith's wonderful phrase, to take our students seriously. We may help them to clarify what they believe and why they choose to act as they do, but we must also honor the choices they make, and even defer to those choices "if at all possible. To do otherwise is undemocratic at best, if not infantilizing and frankly oppressive. It is to treat others instrumentally as means to *our* ends, rather than as ends in themselves" (317). And Smith's rule for taking his students seriously is this: we cannot set ourselves up as experts in ends, in what students might choose to do with their lives. We can only offer our judgment of means: we can only offer our opinion of "the best way to learn this thing that you and I have agreed should be taught" (317). One way we can honor our students as agents of their own ends is to give them as much help as possible in choosing the ends they wish to pursue.

In order to help students decide which courses to take, course descriptions in the university catalogue should specify the purpose of the writing required in the course, the theoretical or ideological framework of the course, and the discourse community to which the course is designed to introduce students. Sample course descriptions for second- and third-level courses in writing-to-think might look like this:

> BIO 150. Principles of Biology. An introduction to plants, animals, and microbes, with special emphasis on biological molecules, cells, and genetics. Studio format incorporates lecture and lab. Lecture requires written micro-themes; lab requires written reports.

> ARCH 350. History of Architecture. Survey of the history of architecture worldwide from prehistory to the present. Requires the written analysis and critique of buildings from a number of aesthetic and utilitarian points of view.

And sample course descriptions for second- and third-level courses in thinking-to-write might look like this:

ENGL 200. Writing about Film. Study of film reviews and articles about film in popular magazines and semi-professional journals from a social perspective. Intensive practice in writing these genres.

ECON 600. Writing Economics. Study of the discourse practices of professional economists in both academia and the workplace, using Foucauldian analysis. Intensive practice in writing the research article and the corporate report.

The Teaching of Transfer

Clearly, what I have been calling "transfer" is essential to how people learn in the first place. However, we cannot predict with any certainty how students will take what they have learned in one context and apply it in another context. This means that *even if* writing is generalizable and transferable, we have few ways of influencing how writers generalize and transfer what they learn and few ways of assessing what they know, except to ask them to write in new contexts. The constraints of context will always qualify how much we can generalize about a person's writing ability from limited samples.

As a result, one major way to improve instruction in writing is to *teach to the transfer.* Currently, writing is taught in individual classrooms in ways that are generally decided upon by individual instructors. Just what aspects of writing students learn in these classrooms and what they can and do transfer to later contexts in which they are called upon to write is left entirely up to chance, or to what the students generalize and transfer on their own, according to their own background and experience. To insure that students do generalize certain aspects of writing, colleges and universities will have to make writing in different courses more related and systematic, so that instructors can build on what students have learned previously. They will have to implement what Arthur Applebee calls an integrated curriculum made up of "independent but interacting experiences" that offer students the opportunity to "revisit earlier material in the light of new understanding," to continually note similarities and differences (77). However, such "interacting experiences" require close cooperation among all teachers across the curriculum and disciplines, not just writing teachers, so that students get a common sense of how writing can vary from context to context, discipline to discipline. Somehow we have to break down the barriers between writing classes and the barriers between the instructors of those classes; we have to get over the notion that instructors are mini-dictators of their own private domains. We have to accept that to teach writing more effectively than we do now, instructors must self-consciously build on the previous experience of their students. In order to do that, instructors need to know what those experiences are.

Obviously the most effective way to accomplish this sort of cooperation has already been modeled by writing-across-the-curriculum and writing-across-the-disciplines programs. It involves getting faculty together on a regular basis to learn what specific writing and thinking strategies and what specific genre conventions students have learned in other contexts, which can be applied in new contexts. It involves getting faculty together to discuss how the discursive practices of their communities reflect the group's values, patterns of reasoning, and uses of evidence, and how those practices might differ from academic community to academic community, so that faculty will have a better sense of how to fit their instruction into what their students are learning across the university. Such discussions should also raise those critical and theoretical questions that make for a healthy disciplinary community: What *are* the values reflected in our discourse practices? Should they be our values? How do we go about initiating novices into those values and practices?

One way to encourage this kind of discussion across the curriculum is to require some sort of capstone course or portfolio evaluation, in which faculty from a variety of disciplines must read and respond to student writing gathered over the course of the students' college career or produced near the end of their career. Peter Elbow ("Writing") has proposed a three-credit introductory writing course he calls "heterogeneous"; that is, composed of both mainstream students and basic writers. The only requirement for the course would be that students produce a portfolio acceptable to the program. The criteria for the portfolios would be determined by each individual institution. What is revolutionary about Elbow's idea—he calls it utopian—is that students could proceed at their own pace and when their portfolios were acceptable, they could leave the course. I would expand on Elbow's idea and suggest that students be given more time to develop their expertise in a wider range of genres and discourse communities than can be offered in an introductory course. I would suggest that universities require portfolios with a broad range of writing from a variety of disciplines, professions, and workplaces as the student nears graduation. Of course, this would necessarily engage the faculty in an intense discussion about the requirements for the portfolio and would provide the opportunity to think about and perhaps organize the curriculum in ways that would allow instructors in a variety of disciplines to learn about the discourse practices of other communities.

Graduate Training in Composition Studies

If students learn to write best by being immersed in a discourse they need or want to master, and if students become truly literate by becoming acquainted with a wide range of literate practices, then universities ought to offer courses in a variety of genres and social contexts so that writing courses can more accurately reflect students' needs and desires. If other disciplines are less devoted to this enterprise than composition studies, then perhaps composition studies has an obligation to supply the expertise needed to help students write in a wide variety of disciplines other than English and in a variety of professions, workplaces, and other public forums. Graduate programs in composition studies, then, would need to make the nature of writing and writing pedagogy both in and outside of the academy the central focus of the graduate curriculum.

Currently, master's and doctoral programs in composition and rhetoric tend to require coursework in only five major areas: composition theory, rhetorical theory, the history of rhetoric, research methods, and pedagogy. The overwhelming majority of courses in these areas are relatively generic and cover such topics as "process of composing" or "audience issues." Only a few graduate programs offer coursework in the writing of specific disciplines or discourse communities. In fact, in a survey of doctoral programs in composition and rhetoric conducted by Stuart Brown, Paul Meyer, and Theresa Enos, of seventy-two reporting colleges and universities, only thirteen programs, by my count, required or offered as an option any course in the writing or analysis of discourse-specific writing. Of those thirteen, all were either in essay writing, literature, or literary nonfiction.

Many institutions *do* offer graduate writing courses outside of composition and rhetoric programs. However, these courses are designed to teach writing academic discourse in special fields, such as "Public Administration, Law, Business, Technical Communications, Physics, Chemistry, Entomology, Urban Studies, Computer Science, Sociology, Anthropology, English" (Golding and Mascaro 171; for an example of such a course taught in an English department, see Gaillet). They are not designed to train students to analyze and critique the discourse practices of their respective fields or to teach others about those discourse practices.

Contrary then to current practice, I would propose that graduate programs in composition studies be organized in order to promote the training of compositionists as writers of particular kinds of discourse, as scholars of particular discourse communities, and as specialists in pedagogy.

First, writing instructors ought to be trained as writers, and not just as generic writers. In fact, I think it would be helpful if we abolished the expression "writing instructor" and replaced it with a title that includes the kind of discourse the instructor teaches: newspaper editorial instructor, for example; or biology lab report instructor. Writing instructors ought to be trained as writers in specific kinds of discourse for specific social contexts or for specific disciplines. If colleges and universities continue to offer general skills writing instruction, there is no reason that the school genres in these courses should be only simplified versions of the discourse practices of English departments. They could just as well be simplified versions of the discourse practices of any discipline in the academy.

For certain kinds of public discourse, this training might occur entirely within English departments, but for training in how to write in various disciplines, professions, workplaces, and public forums, graduate programs in composition studies might have to forge dual-degree programs with other academic units. As a result, they might offer graduate degrees in the teaching of business writing, for example, or in the teaching of writing in biology, degrees in which instructors become insiders in the fields, disciplines, and professions in which they teach writing and practice the genres they will be teaching in these fields.

Of course, designing programs of study around discourse communities is problematic because of the difficulties of designating just what a discourse community is in any given case (see chapter 4). In addition, for many kinds of public genres, there is no specific content. Think of what a writer needs to master in order to write newspaper editorials, for example, or informative or persuasive reports to government agencies. However, difficulties with the concept of a discourse community are never going to go away. I propose to deal with these difficulties, at least provisionally, as I have already indicated: by conceiving of discourse communities not just as generally recognized disciplines, professions, and workplaces but as groups that use certain genres or public forums in order to focus on certain issues. I would like to see scholars in composition studies becoming experts not only in the writing of sociology, the law, and Microsoft, but also in the writing of those who advocate various positions on social issues through a variety of public forums.

Secondly, because there is a certain amount of evidence that practitioners writing in particular discourse communities are not consciously aware of what they do or why they do it, writing teachers need to be trained in the analysis and critique of the genres and discourse communities they specialize in, from a variety of perspectives: stylistic, rhetorical, and cultural critique. In this vision, graduate programs might offer advanced courses in the Linguistic and Rhetorical Analysis of Business Culture or the Sociology of Communication in Biology. One model for such courses in the interdisciplinary study of discourse practices might be the apprenticeship program described by Patrick Dias and his colleagues. In that model, groups of students are assigned to work on specific rhetorical problems for communities outside the university; they could also be assigned to disciplines and professions other than English at the university. In either case, students would be assigned to disciplines and professions, workplaces, or public forums in which they have had some previous coursework or experience. The students would interview people in these communities and study the texts they write from a variety of social and rhetorical perspectives, such as cultural studies or activity theory. Then they would use their analysis as the background for writing the kinds of texts produced by the community. The instructor and the rest of the class would provide the support and feedback students would need to write the genres of their new community, but eventually the students would submit their writing to the community itself for its response. Thus, class members would be introduced to the analysis and critique of a discourse community they wished to specialize in, and they would also receive practice in writing for the community. They would experience both the support of the classroom and all the difficulties faced by new members to any discourse community. Courses such as these would try to help potential writing specialists to be both *members* of particular communities and critical *observers* of those communities, and they would try to help students negotiate the transition from classroom writing to writing outside the classroom.

And finally, writing teachers need to be trained in pedagogical practices, immersed in the conversation about writing pedagogy, the pros and cons of what works and what does not work, from a variety of theoretical perspectives and points of view, recognizing all the while that the ultimate goal of all writing pedagogy is to help novice writers become more mature in their use of genre conventions, their analysis of audience and context, and their sense of the nature and value of the communication practices of the communities they wish to write in.

Graduate programs in composition studies also need to confront the fact that overwhelmingly, writing is not taught in postsecondary institutions by tenure-track faculty holding the PhD. Writing is taught in postsecondary institutions by graduate teaching assistants (GTAs); instructors, both full- and part-time, many with either a master's degree or a PhD; and by adjuncts with MAs and PhDs. Indeed, as many critics of the profession have argued, composition studies and the discipline of English more generally have promoted this two-tier system in order to preserve certain privileges for tenure-track faculty. Most of these privileges allow tenure-track faculty, even tenure-track faculty in composition studies, to avoid teaching writing: the privilege of having time to do research rather than teach and the privilege of being allowed to choose to teach courses that the profession sees as most closely connected to doctoral training—specialized upper-level courses related to faculty members' dissertation topic or the focus of their exams. For faculty in composition studies, this might mean teaching courses in composition or rhetorical theory, in the history of rhetoric, or in one of the increasing number of upper-level courses devoted to specialized topics in the field. In addition, many faculty in composition studies administer writing programs and supervise other writing teachers rather than teach the courses themselves.

In short, the profession has tacitly conceded that a doctoral degree is not necessary for the teaching of writing. As a result, I would propose that the master's degree, or even a graduate certificate of some kind, be the accepted terminal degree for the great majority of writing teachers. Individual institutions could decide for themselves just what mix of coursework in writing, the analysis and critique of discourse practices, and pedagogy, combined with internship programs, would be necessary to certify that a student was a capable writer in a particular discourse community, an astute critic of that community, and an effective teacher capable of initiating students into the discourse practices of that community.

I would reserve the PhD, then, as a specialized degree dedicated primarily to research in the discourse practices of particular communities and to research in the training of writing teachers for those communities. Doctoral programs would be distinguished from master's and certificate programs by their additional course work in research methods and the training not just of writers and writing teachers for particular discourse communities but the training also of those to teach writing teachers in those communities. Ideal dissertations in the field would then be ethnographic case studies of particular discourse communities and their practices; studies of those practices from a variety of stylistic, rhetorical, and critical points of view; and studies of the impact of various pedagogical practices in improving literacy in these communities. I think the work of Carol Berkenkotter and Thomas Huckin, Aviva Freedman, Cheryl Geisler, and Paul Prior would be excellent models on which to base further work. All of them study the discourse of particular academic disciplines and how novices are socialized into the practices of the group; Freedman and her colleagues study the discourse of various workplaces. I know of little serious work analyzing and critiquing the nature and rhetoric of discourse communities and demonstrating how such analyses and critique can be used to change those communities for the better. There is a lot of work to be done.

All of this is not to say that doctoral programs should not continue to offer courses in composition theory, the history of rhetoric, feminist rhetoric, or cultural studies. It is to argue that these courses be viewed primarily as a necessary background for cutting-edge investigations into the way discourse works in specific contexts, how analysis and critique can be used to initiate novices into discourse communities more effectively, and how such analysis and critique can be used to make these discourse communities better places.

Institutional Policies for Promoting and Rewarding Faculty

If the ultimate goal of composition studies is to promote literacy not only in departments of English and university writing programs but also in the culture at large, then teachers, scholars, and researchers of writing are going to have to try to extend their influence beyond the narrow bounds of the profession. They will have to find ways to promote writing in the public schools and in the culture at large both inside and outside of the university. Of course, if colleges and universities insist that the rewards of faculty work depend entirely on the publication of articles written primarily for "peers" in the profession both nationally and internationally, then compositionists and those who promote writing in their own discourse communities will have little time to devote to the development of literacy. University faculty will have time and energy to devote to promoting literacy only if that activity is rewarded by the system.

Colleges and universities, then, will need to reconceptualize research and scholarship in composition studies as it is commonly understood and begin to think of the promotion of literacy as one aspect of that research and scholarship. As long as service continues to be the weakest and least valued part of a university faculty's mission, faculty in composition studies will never be rewarded for those aspects of what they do that may have the most impact on the teaching of writing: spreading the word about research and scholarship in writing outside the bounds of the field. This might involve, for example, counting as the equivalent of research, scholarship, or creative endeavor such activities as organizing or participating in writers-in-the-schools programs; organizing and participating in workshops and in-service training for elementary, middle school, high school, and college teachers; and participating in state English organizations. It might involve counting as the equivalent of research, scholarship, or creative endeavor serving on university committees that oversee cross-curricular writing programs or groups of faculty who evaluate portfolios.

Personal Goals for Writing Teachers

Perhaps the hardest of all to implement: composition studies will be effective only if those in the profession think of themselves as teachers of writing and begin to prefer teaching writing to teaching other courses, such as composition and rhetorical theory, the history of rhetoric or writing instruction, the sociology of the profession, and research methods. We will really have conducted a revolution in the academy when the tenure-track composition and rhetoric faculty insist that they want to be known as *writers* in particular disciplines, professions, workplaces, and public forums, that they want to study and do research in the style, rhetoric, and critique of the discourse practices of these groups, and that they have an overwhelming desire to share their expertise not just in analysis and critique but in *writing* with undergraduate students, master's students, instructors, and graduate teaching assistants.

As I have already indicated, my entire proposal may be considered entirely too far-fetched, perhaps even beyond the realm of the possible. However, in my next and final chapter, I want to argue that it may not be as far-fetched as it sounds. Indeed, I want to argue that in the current context of intense debate about the nature and future of English studies more generally, now is the time to get my program on the table. Now is the time to note that for the past twenty years, institutions have been gradually implementing programs that go in the direction I recommend, and now is the time to suggest that these programs go several steps further in order to become models of how writing ought to be taught in colleges and universities.

At present, the profession [of English Studies] does not have much of a public rationale for itself.... [W]e need to find a rhetoric of justification....
—Michael Bérubé, *The Employment of English*

[I]ntellectuals, administrators, and students are no different from anyone else who works in a large bureaucratic system: they need to be *persuaded* that change is necessary, they would prefer to exercise some control over how change is implemented and assessed, and they want to be certain that the proposed changes will not make their own work obsolete or more difficult.
—Richard E. Miller, *As If Learning Mattered*

All politics is local.
—Tip O'Neill

10 Furthering the R/Evolution

IT IS NOT JUST COMPOSITION STUDIES that is in turmoil. The entire discipline of English, or English studies, as some now call it, is in crisis. The primary reasons are two. The first is the shift in the discipline away from the formal study of a limited number of literary texts towards a more comprehensive notion of textuality viewed from a wide range of social, historical, and theoretical perspectives. This shift has resulted in such a fragmented and arbitrary curriculum in English studies at both the undergraduate and graduate levels that many scholars and critics now argue that it is difficult to say just what an education in English studies *means* anymore (Stewart; Huber; North et al.). Fierce debates now rage in English studies over the focus of research in the field and the nature of the curriculum.

The second reason for the crisis is the job market for those who graduate with doctoral degrees in the field. New PhDs have less than a 50 percent chance of getting a full-time job in a tenure-track line at a college or university, which calls into question the size and relevance of current graduate programs to the actual work available ("Final" 28). The debates about these issues are well documented elsewhere, and I bring them up now only to provide a context in which any realistic discussion of the nature of writing instruction must take place.

Both issues in the current debate in English studies are relevant to a discussion of how writing should be taught at the post-secondary level. The first issue involves the relationship between English studies as a whole and one area of specialization in that discipline: composition studies. Although over seventy academic institutions now offer doctoral programs in composition studies, those programs have been highly influenced by the nature of doctoral study in English more generally and by the curricular issues brought on by the rise of high theory and cultural studies. Because of its connection with English, either as a track, an area of specialization, or an independent academic unit with a previous affiliation with English, composition studies has generally assumed that it is the representative of a particular area of knowledge and expertise and is thus entitled to recognition in the academy as a distinct field. Like specialists in nineteenth-century American literature or contemporary feminist theory, compositionists assume that "writing," broadly conceived, is their unique province. As masters of a particular disciplinary expertise, then, they are entitled to the benefits and responsibilities that accompany such professionalization and the attendant obligation to meet academic standards for teaching, research, and service; to produce knowledge the specialty certifies as worthwhile; and to pass this knowledge-making capability on to new generations of specialists.

But the crisis in English studies as a whole provides the opportunity to rethink the entire role and nature of composition studies and its relationship not only to English studies, but to the university as a whole. If all writing at some level, even literature traditionally understood, is always the writing of particular genres in particular contexts, if writing always involves particular discipline-, domain-, and context-specific knowledge, if writing teachers have to know not just about writing in general but about how to write particular genres in particular contexts, then it is not at all clear in what sense or in what degree composition studies can be a field with a form of expertise separate or distinct from the expertise inherent in being a member of particular discourse communities with their own unique forms of knowledge and their own distinctive discourse practices.

Neither is it clear how this conception of writing would fit into the traditional organizational structure of English departments with its typical distinctions between literature, creative writing, and expository writing; between courses that emphasize the reading of texts and courses that emphasize the writing of texts; and with reading courses organized by historical period and the writing courses organized by genre.

One aspect of the current discussion of the nature of English studies, then, might involve a discussion about the role and nature of composition studies and whether as a profession, it should face the fact that to a certain extent it cannot claim a unique form of expertise, that it must share much of its expertise with those disciplines, professions, workplaces, and public forums outside of English studies that have particular kinds of knowledge and skill and particular genre and discourse practices. And part of this discussion might be devoted to the issue of whether composition studies ought to continue to model itself after departments of English or whether it ought to actively seek ways to make itself more interdisciplinary, whether it might work to integrate itself into other disciplines and fields across the campus and to greatly reduce its role as the main source of writing instruction on campus.

The second issue involves the fact that most PhDs in English studies, indeed most PhDs in composition studies, provide only a very small part of the writing instruction in colleges and universities: a 1996–97 MLA committee found that even in English departments that conferred just the BA, only 50 percent of all first-year writing courses were staffed by regular full-time tenure-track faculty. Among MA-granting departments, the average was 36 percent; among PhD-granting departments, the figure was an astonishing four percent ("Final" 28). As many critics of the profession have noted, one reason for the decline of the job market for PhDs is that the profession has promoted this two-tier system, in which PhDs do research and teach anything but writing, while the great majority of courses offered by English departments, introductory writing courses, are taught by graduate students, adjuncts, and instructors, many of whom are part-time. As a result, PhDs do not do the major work of the profession, which involves the teaching of writing, and those who *do* teach writing are marginalized and not adequately compensated (Schell; Schell and Stock). Whatever influence composition studies has on the teaching of writing may be primarily through the work of directors of writing programs at larger institutions, many of whom now have PhDs in composition studies.

Because of the size of introductory writing programs, it is not financially feasible for most writing courses to be taught by those with doctoral training. There are simply too many students in post-secondary education who need help in writing too many genres in too many contexts for those with doctoral degrees in composition studies to do the job (Gappa and Leslie 112; Murphy 21). If we continue with the current system, writing will continue to be taught at major universities by graduate teaching assistants in English with little interest and little or no training in teaching writing. At best, these GTAs receive an orientation in how to teach generic school genres that lasts a week, or even a semester. And writing will continue to be taught at two- and four-year colleges by instructors with, at best, general master's degrees in English and a course or two in composition or rhetoric or by PhDs in literature, also with little interest or training in the teaching of writing. And most of these instructors will be part-time and adjunct faculty, who receive low pay and few, if any, benefits. Any improvement in the teaching of writing will have to involve specialized training of those who do not have doctoral degrees and those who actually do the teaching of writing, and it will have to involve ways to integrate writing teachers more fully into colleges and universities, with all of the compensation and benefits that entails. As a result, the doctoral degree may have to be reconsidered as a degree conferred only on those who do research and who can apply that research to train others to teach specific kinds of writing in specific contexts.

Because of the dual crises over the curriculum and jobs, English studies is groping for what Michael Bérubé in *The Employment of English* calls a "rhetoric of justification." Such a rhetoric of justification is necessary because of the failure of previous reform movements in both public schools and at the post-secondary level. Many studies have documented why these reform movements have failed (see Mary Kennedy; Hillocks, *Ways*; Cuban; Russell, *Writing*; Tyack and Tobin). What these studies and others indicate is that teachers and the educational institutions that support them, indeed the culture that supports them, have no vested interest in improving writing. Most teachers across the curriculum think that integrating writing into traditional courses takes too much time and energy and that it detracts from the content of their courses. Moreover, tenure-track faculty are not rewarded for teaching writing; in fact, teaching writing may actually detract from the ability of tenure-track faculty to achieve professional success and recognition, to say nothing of financial rewards. To the extent that teaching writing requires these faculty members to reconceptualize and reorganize the way they teach, it may be time consuming and detract from those activities that do in fact earn them recognition and rewards: doing research and publishing in peer journals.

In addition, reformers have not "cultivate[d] the kind of broader social movement that might nourish educational and social change"; rather, reformers have concentrated on convincing their peers of the value of reform (Tyack and Tobin 477). Traditionally, there have been few major constituencies outside of the academy demanding educational and social change. There are few now. In general, the culture at large likes things the way they are. As a result, except for a fairly low-level and constant media drone about a "literacy crisis," a minor irritant in the consciousness of the larger culture, there is no demand for significant change in the way writing is taught.

In the context of these current arguments about the nature of English studies, it seems to me that the time is ripe to consider the fundamental issues I have been raising and to ponder their implications for the ongoing debate about the nature and structure of English studies. I propose then to offer a "rhetoric of justification" for my program, which provides a number of rationales for restructuring composition studies and the way writing is taught in post-secondary education. Unlike the rhetoric of Bérubé and other participants in this discussion, the rhetoric I offer is designed, in the words of Richard Miller, to *persuade* faculty at all levels across colleges and universities that change is necessary, that they can exercise some control over how change is implemented and assessed, and that they can be reassured that the proposed changes will benefit their students, their departments, and their own careers. Moreover, the rhetoric I offer is designed to persuade stakeholders and constituencies outside the university that a major restructuring of the way writing is done is necessary in order to achieve larger social goods. The rhetoric I offer is based in the following claims:

1. Writing instruction involves real intellectual work, the work of rhetorical and stylistic analysis; the work of critiquing disciplinary, pro-

fessional, and public discourse practices; and the work of integrating this scholarship into the teaching practices of the various disciplinary, professional, and public discourse communities at the post-secondary level.

2. This intellectual work will be beneficial to those academic units that participate in writing instruction. It will aid those academic units in recruiting students, initiating and integrating them into their particular disciplines, professions, and public forums.

3. My proposal will aid university administrations as a whole because it provides a way to spread the cost of writing instruction across all academic units and may help administrators deal more effectively with the problem of part-time and adjunct faculty.

4. In addition, my program will strengthen the role of the doctoral degree in composition studies by making the degree relevant to every disciplinary and programmatic unit in the university. Although traditional English departments will lose some funding for the teaching of introductory writing courses, which will be taught across the curriculum, English departments will continue to be the natural home for tenure-track faculty in composition studies, who will have dual-degrees in both composition studies and other disciplines on campus. Of course, the hiring practices of local institutions would determine where holders of the doctorate in composition studies would reside.

5. A program of analyzing, critiquing, and teaching the discourse practices of particular communities will also be beneficial to society as a whole, not only by increasing literacy but by making a wider variety of discourse communities more open and inclusive.

I also argue that my proposals are not as revolutionary as they may sound. Many existing programs already provide a basis for putting my proposals into effect: undergraduate programs with multi-track specialties other than literature, undergraduate programs in writing-across-the-curriculum and cultural studies, and undergraduate programs that include internships, apprenticeships, and service learning; as well as graduate programs that emphasize cultural critique and the extension of writing instruction beyond the classroom. All of these programs are well on their way to achieving the kind of instruction that puts into practice what we know about the way people learn to write.

Writing Instruction as Intellectual Work

In trying to justify English studies as a way of promoting both cultural critique and social and economic utility, Bérubé frames the issue as a dichotomy: a choice between critique and service. Bérubé finds this dichotomy problematic for cultural studies, but not for writing instruction, which he calls "politically *reversible*": writing instruction "can be used to justify English as a discipline that fosters critical thinking at the same time it can be used to justify English as a discipline that fosters employability, business competence, and maybe even long-term financial security" (32–33). Bérubé recognizes the long tradition in English studies that assumes the teaching of writing is the kind of low-level work that can be adequately taught by people with little or no training in any particular kind of writing. But interestingly, Bérubé does not see that writing instruction could incorporate cultural critique or that it might involve particular kinds of expertise. In this he is not alone. Composition studies as a profession has accepted the general societal consensus that writing can be taught by people who do not have to demonstrate any specific knowledge or abilities. Clearly, then, the lack of an adequate rhetoric of justification for writing instruction is the real fault of the profession: it has not made the case that teaching writing involves real intellectual work.

A rhetoric of justification for writing instruction might start then by asserting what we know about how people learn to write and how instruction can help them learn to write: the main tenets I have argued in this book. People learn to write by being immersed in various discourse communities, and they learn the discourses practices of those communities by a process of assimilation, which can be aided by appropriate scaffolding, forms of overt instruction that make them self-consciously aware of the genre conventions used in the discourse of the community and the social practices those conventions embody and codify. The intellectual work of writing instruction involves the intense study and critique of the social and discourse practices of various discourse communities, the knowledge and ability to actually write the genres of the community, and the knowledge and ability to help novices in the community understand how the community functions, to critique that community and its discourse from a variety of points of view, and to use the discourse conventions of the community to further their own goals, whether they be to fit into the community or to change it.

In other words, we can adequately justify writing instruction in the academy only if we can argue that it involves real expertise, expertise that disciplines, professions, workplaces, and public forums can get nowhere else. In making this case, we must argue against the common perception that anyone can teach writing because, after all, they speak the language and have a bachelor's degree, or even a master's degree in English. This perception seems to assume that any native speaker of a language with a certain amount of education can intuit how any kind of writing is done and can show others how to do it, an assumption that is patently false. Worse yet, the perception that anyone with college coursework in English can teach writing may also assume that writing is nothing more than a collection of artificial rules and formulas we have inherited from the nineteenth century, rules about theses and topic sentences, introductions and conclusions, not using personal pronouns and contractions, avoiding fragments and run-ons, rules and formulas that get repeated over and over from elementary school through college, until even educated people think they are true. If writing instruction involves only such rules and formulas, which are often taught as early as middle school, is it any wonder that most people think *any* generally educated person can teach writing?

But of course, if we argue that writing instruction involves real intellectual work and special expertise, we have to be prepared to offer evidence that our conception of how people learn to write is the most accurate and most convincing among competing conceptions and that our notion of writing instruction is the most theoretically sound among competing notions, that it *makes sense* that writing teachers should be both members of a discourse community and masters of the discourse of and about that community. I hope I have presented this evidence adequately in earlier chapters, especially chapters two and eight.

The Benefits of Writing Instruction to Higher Education

Bérubé's argument that there is an inherent split between the intellectual value and the social or even economic benefits of cultural critique has been a point of discussion in composition studies for some time. Many critics have pointed out that those who promote critical pedagogy and cultural critique in writing classes teach a very narrow range of writing, what I have called writing-to-learn and writing-to-think: writing as an aid to reflection and analysis, using very narrow theoretical models. It is writing designed to help students learn various theoretical frameworks and forms of analysis; it is writing designed to promote strategies for thinking "metacognitively" about such matters as race, class, gender, and power; it is writing designed to help students ponder and reflect on their own positions on these issues. These are perfectly legitimate goals for a writing pedagogy, but they are very generic and generally do not give students sufficient context to truly ponder the implications of their positions.

What most cultural studies and critical pedagogies seem to ignore is the role of writing beyond analysis and reflection, the role of writing to actually help accomplish the political goals identified by analysis and reflection, what I have called thinking-to-write. Very few of the published accounts of these pedagogies focus on the rhetorical and political discourses outside the writing class that writers would need to master in order to work for change in the public arena. Very few of these pedagogies offer novice writers heuristics and strategies for actually writing the public discourses necessary to accomplish social change. As Susan Miller has argued, "By teaching texts rather than their making, by teaching awareness rather than rhetoric, and by teaching the power of meanings rather than the making of statements, we inadvertently reproduce a politics that is aware but passive." Miller goes on:

> I worry, consequently, about composition courses that frame student writing in imperatives to *reflect*. The content of such courses is not writing—is not persuasion to assume the positions of those whose acts of writing are interventions. Nor is it systematic demonstrations of *how* to write—not "well," but powerfully, to subvert more and less conventional subject positions. Writing taught as reading, that is, accomplishes political stasis. ("Technologies" 499; see also Drew)

To which I would add: theorists of critical consciousness have not adequately conceptualized how radical discourse participates in various discourse communities. That is, could we promote change more effectively if we considered radical critics to be members of a particular discourse community trying to change that community from within, or if we considered radical critics to be outsiders, the modern equivalent of Old Testament prophets, belonging to their own separate group of critics and theorists, calling for change in other communities from a higher, more authoritative, more theoretically informed point of view?

The same sorts of questions apply to genres and the kinds of reasoning and evidence that critical pedagogy requires. In teaching students to be critics and promoters of change, should we be teaching them common genres used in public forums (editorials, handouts, newsletters) and generally accepted methods of persuasion and argumentation, or should we be teaching them the genres, patterns of reasoning, and kinds of evidence used by particular discourse communities, so that they can work for change in particular social contexts? I suspect that my answer to these questions should be obvious by now: institutional change can be best accomplished on the inside, and it can best be done by members of the communities involved. But members of various communities can promote change in their communities only if they have the necessary tools.

In overlooking the connection between cultural studies and writing instruction, Bérubé has missed a major opportunity to promote both cultural studies and writing instruction. Appropriately understood, cultural critique, which includes the stylistic, rhetorical, and cultural analysis of particular discourse communities and which incorporates this knowledge into the training of new members of these communities, is not and cannot be separated from its social and economic utility. In other words, we should justify writing instruction entirely on the grounds of its social and economic utility—that it prepares students to write for particular discourse communities and therefore increases their chances of being employed; it gives them the tools to better understand how these discourse communities function, both in and of themselves and in the culture as a whole; and it gives them the tools to work for positive change within their communities. We should be teaching lower-level undergraduate majors the genres, patterns of reasoning, and kinds of evidence used by particular discourse communities as a way to initiate them into the community, and we should be teaching upper-level undergraduate majors and graduate students advanced courses in the discourse practices of their disciplines and the public forums associated with them. We should be teaching both undergraduate majors and graduate students how their discourse communities function, how they determine membership in the community, how they include and exclude people, how the practices of the community have evolved over time, how those practices reward some and punish others, and how those practices can be changed if the group determines that such change is worthwhile.

The Benefits to Academic Programs and Departments

Currently, the most common conception of academic culture is that it is a collection of elite groups whose primary job is to maintain disciplinary standards; to act as gatekeepers, as it were, in order to insure that only the most appropriately socialized and trained novices enter the discipline. Such a conception of academic disciplines is inherently exclusionary and may account for the difficulty these disciplines have in recruiting and retaining new members, especially those from diverse backgrounds: women, minorities, people of color. It may also account for the constant complaint among member of these disciplines that those who seek to join the discipline, both undergraduate majors and graduate students, cannot write well. Of course, what the members of the discipline often mean by "writing well" is the knowledge and ability to write the way they want novices to write, often without instruction.

Against this conception of academic disciplines, we must offer a model of the disciplines as open and evolving, continually renewed by new scholarship and research, continually reformulating their discursive practices. In David Russell's words, we need to promote a model of academic disciplines that questions "the convenient notion that disciplines are static repositories of knowledge" and that considers "a model of disciplines as communities that are continually being reformed through their discursive practices, including those of students" (*Writing* 302). Such a model would naturally question how novices are initiated into and become members of the community and would actively investigate ways to make that initiation more self-conscious, especially in the ways that novices learn to write the discourses of the community. Russell goes on:

> consciously translating the discipline's rhetorical universe into language that students at lower levels could understand may be seen as trivializing or watering down the very knowledge the discipline is charged with upholding. Ini-

tiating greater numbers into its ranks may thus pose a threat to the status of the discipline. Attempts at creating well-articulated secondary and undergraduate curricula incorporating writing have been largely unsuccessful in part because they were perceived as lowering standards. A discipline might improve its work by becoming conscious of its sociorhetorical structures, if only because it could more effectively train neophytes—or train more of them. (*Writing* 29–30)

So we must argue that integrating the teaching of writing into academic units for both undergraduates and graduate students will better "socialize" them to the discourse practices of the discipline and thus make them more "literate" in the practices of the discipline. This will in turn make it easier for departments and disciplines to recruit and retain majors.

Such is the avowed purpose of a variety of courses for both undergraduate majors and graduate students labeled the way they are in my department: "Introduction to Literary Study" and "Introduction to Graduate Study." However, as I noted in chapter 8, what these courses lack is any sense of how the departments and disciplines offering them are actually constructed, how they function both in the university and in society at large, and how the discourse practices of these groups have evolved a host of conventions to guide their thinking, their research, and the way they communicate with others in the group and those outside it. Learning how to write, learning how to be literate, assumes a knowledge of all these things in a wide variety of academic disciplines.

In making this case, we must also argue that this conception of writing instruction *works*. Here we must cite the work of Aviva Freedman on immersion and the literature on transfer I summarized in chapter 6. At the graduate level, we can also cite the work of Cheryl Geisler, Carol Berkenkotter and Thomas Huckin, and Paul Prior on how graduate students are socialized into their disciplines.

In addition, we should argue that integrating writing into coursework across the disciplines and in communities outside the university is a way to strengthen faculty research. Faculty across the disciplines who specialize in the study of the discourse of their disciplines and related workplaces and public forums can expect to teach classes directly related to their research interests and can integrate students into their research as a way of initiating the students into their discipline. This is not a new idea. The Boyer Commission on Educating Undergraduates in the Research University has for years advocated learning "based on discovery guided by mentoring rather than on the transmission of information," that every course should be an opportunity for students to learn through research and discovery-based methods:

In the sciences and social sciences, undergraduates can become junior members of the research teams that now engage professors and graduate students.

211 Furthering the R/Evolution

In the humanities, undergraduates should have the opportunity to work in primary materials, perhaps linked to their professors' research projects.

Such immersion in the ongoing research of the university should culminate, according to the Boyer Report, in internships that allow the student "concrete contexts in which to apply research principles." If such internships were also supervised by writing faculty doing research in the discourse of their discipline and related areas, the internships would benefit not only the students but also the supervising faculty, who would have greater access to those discourse communities related to their disciplines and a way to study those communities.

Benefits to Colleges and Universities as a Whole

My proposal offers two major arguments for institutions of higher learning to consider when they deal with the problem of how to include writing in the curriculum and how to pay for this instruction. First, my proposal provides a convincing rationale for writing instruction as a form of intellectual work in specific academic units, a form of intellectual work with many benefits to the unit. The expertise of writing instructors would be unique to the unit, providing stylistic, rhetorical, and critical analysis unavailable from other faculty. Thus, the case could be made that they deserve adequate compensation because of the benefits to the unit and the unique nature of their expertise.

My proposal would also offer a way to spread the cost of writing instruction across the university, so that it would be born by all academic units, not just departments of English and colleges of arts and sciences. Of course, there is no way to deny that writing instruction is expensive, and ideally the compensation of individual instructors would increase to reflect their expertise, but institutions might find some savings by integrating instructors into the curriculum at more advanced levels; that is, by integrating writing instruction into courses currently taught by tenure-track faculty anyway, courses introducing both undergraduates and graduates to the major, courses in social issues related to the major, courses in the history and nature of the major. Here is how such an arrangement might work at a large university.

My proposed first-year Introduction to Writing as a Social Practice would be a single course that could be offered across the curriculum. Of course, in the best of all possible worlds, all sections of the course would be coordinated in such a way that they had a common format or syllabus, which included at least three units: the construction of the self in writing, an analysis of the genre of a particular discourse community so that students could then write an example of that genre themselves, and a critique of the discourse and social practices of the community and a proposal for change. Since the subject matter of the course would vary substantially, the primary requirement for hiring instructors would be that they have experience writing in a certain context and be trained to think about how that writing is done.

Until graduate programs in composition studies begin producing such instructors, individual institutions would have to train new instructors in this kind of pedagogy, much as they train new graduate teaching assistants and instructors now. Although the administrative costs to the college or university as a whole would remain roughly the same as they are now, the costs would be spread across all the larger units of the institution: colleges, schools, divisions, and departments. And some institutions might find some savings in requiring only one introductory writing course instead of two.

My proposed second- and third-stage courses would also be offered by units across the curriculum and staffed much like current programs in writing-across-the-curriculum or those that offer writing-intensive courses. Here some institutions may achieve some financial relief because these upper-level courses could be offered as alternatives to traditional courses already in the catalog, such as introductions to the major or introductions to graduate study, or they could be offered as writing-intensive courses in a particular subject matter of the discipline.

The Campus Writing Program at the University of Missouri-Columbia, for example, requires students to take three courses: a common introductory course, and then two more upper-level writing-intensive courses. Every semester, the university offers over one hundred writing-intensive courses from across the curriculum, such diverse courses as Introduction of Ecological Economics, Basic Microbiology, Contemporary Europe, and Women and Music. The goal of these courses is primarily writing-to-learn; they "require students to express, reformulate, or apply the concepts of an academic discipline," and the primary means of accomplishing this goal is through small classes, multiple writing assignments throughout the semester, and required revision ("Guidelines"). To help regular faculty teach these courses, the Campus Writing Board funds graduate teaching assistants for courses larger than twenty, a quarter-time GTA for every twenty students.

I am not suggesting that the program at Missouri-Columbia is an ideal model. I would argue that the range of writing it offers is much too narrow, and it has no mechanism for disciplinary analysis and critique. The curriculum generally does not encourage students to think about the nature of disciplinary communities or to socialize students into these communities, although the program does offer a number of capstone courses, internships, and service-learning experiences. Neither can I hold up Missouri-Columbia as a model for dealing with the problem of adjuncts and part-timers. The director of the Campus Writing Program, Martha Townsend, suspects that requiring regular faculty across the curriculum to participate in the program has not lessened the need for adjuncts and part-timers; it has merely shifted the work of adjuncts and part-timers from writing courses to other kinds of courses. I *am* suggesting, however, that Missouri-Columbia *does* have a curricular structure that would accommodate my program and spread the responsibility for teaching writing across the curriculum, where it belongs.

The Benefits to Doctoral Programs in Composition Studies
and English Departments Generally

Obviously, I am proposing a radical restructuring of doctoral programs in composition studies. But in another sense, I am simply taking seriously a recommendation of the MLA Committee on Professional Employment. That committee stated in no uncertain terms that in response to the downturn in opportunities for PhDs in English studies, English and foreign language departments generally would "have to change their thinking about the nature of the work we do, its purpose and its structures" ("Final" 39). More specifically, the committee recommended

- that doctoral programs offer students courses in pedagogy that will prepare them for a range of teaching situations.
- that programs offer PhD students experiences designed to familiarize them with the complete system of postsecondary and secondary education in this country (comprising four-year liberal arts colleges, community colleges, universities, and private as well as public high schools) and the full range of job opportunities available in that system.
- that such introductions to pedagogy and to the varieties of academic work involve not only colloquia, seminars, and conferences but also, for instance, mentored internships, residencies, and exchanges among institutions along with experiences outside teaching, such as involvement in institutional, administrative, governance, and editorial tasks. ("Final" 41; see also "Preparing.)"

Of course, the MLA committee studiously avoids here any engagement with the issue of *how* to train graduate students in the teaching of writing, but its three-point recommendation provides a framework for discussing my proposals. According to the committee, graduate programs need to prepare students to teach writing in a variety of circumstances and to use other means than coursework, such as "mentored internships, residencies, and exchanges among institutions" to further this goal. One argument in favor of my proposals is that they do just that.

Moreover, my proposals would result in a much broader market for PhDs in English with specialties in composition studies: indeed the market would be as broad as the number of disciplines and programs in the curriculum of higher education. This would contrast with the current market, which follows the model of English departments generally: faculty have to cover prescribed areas in the curriculum: medieval literature, feminist criticism, children's literature, critical theory, and composition and rhetoric, to name just a few. In many programs, the few faculty in composition studies are there as token members of an academic area that has to be covered, or they were hired to administer the writing program. The suspicion is that when every department has its token specialist in composition and rhetoric, the market will dry up. But the market for specialists in composition studies should not be limited to English departments. The market for writing instructors should be as wide as the number of discourse communities that need to be studied; it should be as wide as the number of discourse communities that need and want to initiate new members into their practices. My proposal accounts for this need.

However, within English departments, composition faculty with specializations in the discourse of English studies would be the most obvious faculty to cover courses such as Writing about Literature or Introduction to Graduate Study, courses in Writing Studies, or indeed any courses about the many discourses of English studies or related workplaces and public forums. With the advent of cultural studies, these workplaces and public forums are wide indeed. They range from large corporations to small service-learning agencies, from special interest lobbying groups to our major intellectual magazines and journals.

I am also proposing that the doctoral degree be reserved primarily for research specialists in the discourse practices of particular discourse communities, although, of course, the field will continue to need scholarly attention to its traditional subject matter: learning theory, the history and theory of rhetoric, language and linguistics, and pedagogy. But by channeling new doctoral candidates into ethnographic studies of particular discourse communities, my proposal promotes those scholarly areas where the most work needs to be done.

The Benefits of Writing Instruction to Society as a Whole

We must argue to the culture at large that focusing our instruction on scaffolding and situated practice, overt instruction, critical framing, and transformed practice in particular contexts is our best hope for making people more literate. We must argue that discourse communities can make people more literate only by being more open and inclusive, by analyzing and critiquing how the discourse practices of various communities actually function, and by developing methods of incorporating novices into those communities. Such work must of necessity be *political* in the most fundamental and straightforward sense of that term. It must be designed to promote massive social change in the way people think about writing and the way people think writing ought to be taught.

This means that composition studies, through such representative bodies as the National Council of Teachers of English, the Conference on College Composition and Communication, the Modern Language Association, and other organizations, must lobby for a new "picture" of writing in society as a whole, a "picture" of writing not as a unified and generic skill but as a tool that has to be adapted to the discourse practices of particular groups, a "picture" of writing in which novices are not taught primarily by formula and rote learning but by immersion in the practices of the groups they wish to join. We must also argue that teaching writing well *means* being open and inclusive, trying to incorporate novices more effectively into the group; it *means* accommodating a wide variety of points of view about the nature of the group and being open to change. In short, we must argue that teaching writing well will not only make people more literate; it will also make them better citizens, and it will make our country as a whole more open and accommodating, more fair and equal, a better place to live.

Undergraduate Evolutions

A host of undergraduate programs across the country have already taken steps toward accomplishing the program I envision. We might classify these evolutionary steps into four groups.

Multi-Track Majors in English

Multi-track or multi-specialization curricula are already in place in many college and university English departments across the country. On the basis of a study conducted in 1987, Donald Stewart reported that of 197 English departments, 74 offered a "block of courses" or track other than literature, either in creative writing or "practical or applied composition." Fifty-three additional departments offered individual courses in "practical or applied composition," such courses as "professional and technical writing," "writing and editing," or "career writing" (190–91). In other words, about 40 percent of the reporting departments now offer undergraduate students the opportunity to specialize in writing for a major in English, and another 25 percent offer coursework in expository writing. These courses are opportunities to put into practice the kind of pedagogy I have been advocating, which is the writing of particular genres for particular discourse communities.

In addition, many college and university departments are adding capstone courses in order to promote the synthesis and application of what the students have learned in the major. Carnegie-Mellon University, for example, offers a capstone course in the "cultural and rhetorical interpretations" of a "network of texts" ("Bachelor"). My proposals would encourage as many academic units as possible to have such capstone courses.

Programs in Cultural Studies

A number of English departments are already organized around concepts from cultural studies and are geared toward critique of social institutions. All of them are heading in the direction I have indicated. The program at the University of Pittsburgh emphasizes "problem-posing" in both reading and writing, a phrase borrowed from Paulo Freire. At Pitt, students in literature classes study how texts are "culturally and historically situated" and investigate issues of interpretation. Students of "General Writing" work through a series of related writing assignments designed to allow them "to take a position, revise it, look at a new example, hear what someone else has to say, revise it again, and see what conclusions [they] can draw about [their] subject" (Paul Smith 57). Another program, the one at Carnegie-Mellon University, engages students in issues of positionality and representation, all the while reinforcing traditional skills in argument, such as summarizing sources, synthesizing points of view, and analyzing various positions. Ultimately, students craft their own arguments in an ongoing conversation they wish to join (Alan Kennedy 37–41). Both of these programs are primarily based on writing-to-think. They would be more effective, it seems to me, if they engaged students in analyzing not only the contexts for literature but the contexts in which students themselves are or would be expected to write, and if they engaged students in a broader range of writing, especially thinking-to-write.

A cultural studies curriculum that comes close to fitting all of the requirements of my program is the one at Syracuse University. Syracuse's curriculum is organized into a series of four writing studios, each with a "'topic of inquiry,' in which student and teacher co-investigate and write from a variety of perspectives on a single issue" (Zebroski, "Syracuse" 88). The more advanced studios focus on "developing expertise in rhetorical practices, rhetorical awareness, and intellectual abilities in specific discipline(s) of expertise," encouraging students to reflect on the writing they have done during the course of their university careers, and investigating "the rhetoric of writing in nonacademic settings" (89–90). In fact, the only reservation I have about the program at Syracuse is that the issues explored in the first three studios seem rather abstract and may be unrelated to writing in specific contexts outside of the studio. Once again, the challenge at Syracuse might be to relate analysis and critique to specific discourse communities and to promote a range of writing across disciplines, professions, workplaces, and public forums. And once again, I would argue that if these three institutions can begin to base their curricula on the four-step pedagogy of situated practice, overt instruction, critical framing, and transformed practice, other institutions can follow.

Writing-Across-the-Curriculum Programs

According to the Modern Language Association, more than a third of the 194 four-year colleges and universities responding to a survey have some form of writing instruction across the curriculum; that is, in these institutions, writing is taught in discipline-specific or particular content courses in addition to those courses designated as writing courses *(Survey)*. A later and more extensive survey by Susan McLeod and Susan Shirley confirmed these results: of 1,112 institutions, including two-year community colleges, 38 percent have some form of writing-across-the-curriculum (103).

The kind of writing being taught in these programs seems to be primarily writing-to-learn and writing-to-think. Most of the evaluations of WAC programs focus on how faculty have responded to the workshops they have attended introducing them to the WAC movement. And overwhelmingly, faculty state in these evaluations that what they value from the workshops and what they have put into practice in response are writing-to-learn techniques: journals, impromptu essays, micro-themes. For writing more extended genres, they usually require fairly traditional classroom genres, such as the research report. They credit WAC workshops with helping them make their instructions for these research reports more explicit and "user-friendly" (Walvoord et al.).

Then there is the evidence of WAC textbooks. The readings in writing-across-the-curriculum textbooks generally contain literary essays and popular articles on a range of subject matter; they do not contain genres unique to the various disciplines in the university (Thaiss, Rice). This seems to indicate that WAC programs emphasize traditional essay writing designed to help students reflect on certain issues in the disciplines, what I call writing-to-think.

What writing-across-the-curriculum programs do not seem to be doing in any systematic way is initiating novices into the discourse communities of academia and introducing them to the ways of thinking and writing that produce the genres actually used in the disciplines and professions of the academic community. Neither are WAC programs incorporating analysis and critique of discourse communities into writing instruction.

However, there are hopeful signs that some of WAC's most prominent proponents are starting to respond to criticism of WAC's narrow focus and recognize the value of critique in WAC pedagogy. Susan McLeod and Elaine Maimon cite the work of Donna LeCourt, Charles Bazerman, and David Russell as evidence that the WAC movement has been "influenced by the 'new thinking' that critiques the 'social turn' in composition studies" (578). Bazerman in particular provides evidence that rhetorical analyses of how discourse functions in disciplinary communities "does not necessarily indoctrinate [students] unreflectively into forms that will oppress them and others"; rather, using the field of sociology as an example, Bazerman demonstrates that recent critical work in ethnography has revealed how studying "who speaks, who owns the discourse, who receives, how the self becomes changed in the interaction between self and other, and for what ends the discourse is carried out" can change the way research is done in the field ("From Cultural" 64–65). LeCourt has followed Bazerman's lead by requiring first-year students "to investigate and perform a rhetorical analysis of the discourses of their chosen majors in collaborative groups using the techniques of cultural criticism they learned earlier in the course" (398). And as a WAC consultant and facilitator for her campus, LeCourt promotes similar rhetorical investigations among her colleagues in other disciplines and has met "little resistance to this idea since we already use rhetorical criticism in these workshops to help faculty gain metaknowledge about discursive norms" (399).

The work of Bazerman and LeCourt indicates that writing-across-the-curriculum programs could be extended to include instruction in the genres of the disciplines and related workplaces and public forums, and they could usefully incorporate stylistic and rhetorical analysis and cultural critique. All such programs are waiting for is the personnel to promote these changes.

Apprenticeship, Internship, and Service-Learning Programs

Many institutions have already begun programs that fulfill the third stage of my proposed curriculum: providing students with a transition out of the classroom and into a discipline, business, or community-based organization, where they can learn the practices of a particular group. Such experiences are common, for example, in the field of journalism, and they are becoming increasingly popular in writing programs. Carnegie-Mellon University, for instance, offers writing internships for its BA in professional writing. Stanford University and San Francisco State University have service learning programs.

However, the goals of these programs vary widely. Some programs place students in a workplace for an extended period of time and expect them to produce the sort of documents used in the workplace. Other programs study non-academic settings and focus on reflecting and writing *about* these settings rather than writing the genres actually used in these settings. Still other programs divide their time and energy between the classroom and other places where writing is done. Members of the class write the genres of the discipline, business, or community organization they visit for short periods, but they also reflect on and write about their experiences in these non-academic settings using school genres: journals, notebooks, personal essays, research reports.

As a result, apprenticeship, internship, and service-learning programs also differ widely on the degree to which they integrate students into non-academic settings and the degree to which they provide mentoring in order to help the process of acculturation into a new community. Potential mentors in disciplines, professions, and workplaces outside of the classroom often have little stake in helping to integrate novice writers into their discourse communities. In fact, in many discourse communities, the attitude of more experienced people is that novices should "learn on their own time."

As James Paradis and his colleagues have shown, in many workplaces, novice writers are expected to pick up how to write by their participation in ongoing tasks. The primary way novices receive feedback is not by direct responses but by "document cycling," the practice of having documents read and commented on by many people and then returned to the original writer for her to incorporate what everyone else has said (see also Smart 131; Dias et al. 195–96). Most reports of service-learning programs indicate that students receive more help from their academic writing teachers than they do from experts or mentors in non-academic communities (see, for example, Bacon; Cooper and Julier; Dorman and Dorman; Stock and Swenson).

Perhaps the best way to address the dual problems of integrating and mentoring students in discourse communities outside of the academy is offered by Patrick Dias and his colleagues. Their model for a successful internship/apprenticeship program, albeit one for very advanced students, is for students in systems analysis. Perhaps this kind of a program is as good as such programs *can* get, if it could be extended somewhat along the lines I have suggested. For this program, only selected students from an advanced course in systems analysis are allowed to work as intern/apprentices at various client organizations. Each student is assigned to a group of five. At least one member of each group must have a background in accounting, and at least one member must have a background in computing. Friends may not be in the same group, "so that students gain experience working with people that they are not already familiar with or even fond of" (207).

Each group is assigned to work on a specific problem for one of the client organizations. While working on this project, the group must produce three documents: a "problem definition document," based on a feasibility study; a "systems specification document," based on a systems analysis; and a "general design document." In order to accomplish these tasks, the groups interview a number of people who work for the client organizations. The instructor for the course accompanies the groups on their first visits and helps to insure that the students learn what they need to know in order to write the documents. Because the interns are working for additional course credit, they report back to the class as a whole and receive peer responses and intensive feedback from the instructor. Only when the instructor is satisfied is a written document presented to the client, sometimes accompanied by an oral presentation, if the client so desires (207).

What students gain from this program is experience in dealing with the kinds of difficulties writers face outside of the classroom: multiple audiences who expect results that fit in with the organization's larger goals, problems with no obvious right answers, and having to work with colleagues who are unfamiliar and perhaps irritating. However, in this program, students are also nurtured in a classroom environment and receive the kind of support and feedback that can be provided only in a controlled educational setting.

Such programs may be the best way to bridge the gap between classroom practice and writing in the world outside the classroom.

What programs such as this *lack* is any instruction and participation in critical framing and transformed practice, any critical analysis of the discourse practices of the workplace or public forum, and any attempt to transform those practices. Of course, it would be a delicate matter for students to critique the discourse communities they were working for and to suggest ways that it could be changed. But at a minimum, such analysis could be done in the relatively sheltered environment of the classroom, and the relevant issues could be raised in ways that confront the practical realities of change: given this particular critique in this particular social context, how might we go about changing things for the better? Such concrete discussions of social change would be potentially much more effective than generic critiques of society.

Graduate Evolutions

A number of graduate programs across the country have also begun to implement the kind of cross-disciplinary graduate training I am advocating, but of course none of them has implemented my proposals extensively. Still, the signs are positive, and an indication, I think, that the profession is starting to realize the limitations of traditional graduate education in composition studies.

First of all, many programs, primarily at the master's level, offer courses in Business, Technical, and/or Professional Communication, a tacit admission that the writing of particular discourse communities necessitates a particular form of expertise. In fact, the master of arts in professional communication at Clemson University offers students a wide range of cognate courses in disciplines for which a degree in professional communication might be appropriate. These cognate courses are in fields as various as consulting, human resources, and public relations ("Academic"). Graduate students at Clemson, then, take courses in two disciplines, and although it appears from the program's website that there is little integration of the two sets of coursework, I would consider the Clemson MA in professional communication as a first step on the road to a truly interdisciplinary graduate program in composition studies.

Other programs offer internships in particular workplaces, professions, and public forums, and courses in rhetorical and cultural critique. Unfortunately, these courses are not integrated. For example, the master of arts degree with an emphasis in technical and professional communication at New Mexico State University offers an internship that "involves at least 10–15 hours per week of paid or unpaid work, typically for a semester or longer. . . . During the internship students keep an activity log, submit a report on their internship experience, and give an oral presentation to an appropriate audience" ("Technical"). However, there is no evidence that these internships include cultural, rhetorical, and stylistic analysis and critique.

On the other hand, the master of science in rhetoric and technical communication at Michigan Technological University requires at least one course in the "Social/Cultural Contexts of Language and Representation": "These courses emphasize the ways in which texts and communication practices are shaped by and help shape social and cultural structures and values" ("Rhetoric"). The graduate program I envision would combine these courses in social and cultural context with the theoretical analysis and critique of particular discourse communities. Such courses might be modeled on the course in Discourse Analysis, which is part of the PhD program in rhetoric at Carnegie Mellon University. Discourse Analysis at Carnegie Mellon "explores how to move from a stretch of speech or writing or signing outward to the linguistics, cognitive, cultural, psychological, and rhetorical reasons for its form and function" ("Ph.D."). In my proposal, such courses would be offered in the particular kinds of discourse of a wide range of discourse communities.

And as I noted in chapter 8, according to one survey of seventy-two doctoral programs in rhetoric and composition, only thirteen have any requirement, or even an option among requirements, that students take a writing course, and most of these courses are in literary nonfiction and the essay or in writing for business, the professions, or the workplace (Brown, Meyer, and Enos). Nevertheless, this is a start. In my vision, all doctoral students should become writers and critics of at least one particular discourse community.

Of course, so far I have avoided the main issue, and the main issue is how to implement my proposal in college and university settings, in which I have already admitted there is little or no impetus for radical change in the curriculum. If indeed all academic politics, like governmental politics, is "local," there may be few generalizations to be made about how to go about furthering the r/evolution I am proposing. Nevertheless, the spread of the writing-across-the-curriculum movement is instructive. The most successful programs appear to have started from the bottom-up, by groups of interested faculty who worked together on common needs and concerns and freely shared their expertise in what Barbara Walvoord calls the "Faculty Dialogue Model" (14). In Walvoord's model, WAC programs are begun by an "initiator," who plans the first meetings, consults widely, and avoids setting forth "a rigid, preconceived outcome or agenda" (16). Eventually, a group of interested faculty put together a planning committee or conduct a workshop for core committed faculty to set an agenda, design programs, and find ways to further the goals set in the initial meetings. Indeed, communication theorists who study the spread of innovations have long known that institutional change involves the active participation of "change agents" and "innovation champions" who build a case for change, develop rapport with potential clients, diagnosis problems, and generally meet the clients' needs (Rogers 336–37, 398). In other words, my proposals can be put into effect only one institution at a time, if a local "initiator" or "change agent" finds the proposals persuasive and is willing to start a dialogue among faculty on implementing them. Eventually, these proposals will succeed only to the extent that they help to provide a way for a core group of faculty to think about the needs and concerns of their own institutions.

David Kaufer and Richard Young have demonstrated how faculty across disciplines can learn from each other through honest sharing, analyzing, and evaluating each other's mutual expertise. The difficulty for "change agents" is how to help groups of faculty "institutionalize" their expertise: to make it explicit and available to students through a curriculum (see also Judy Segal and her colleagues on the difficulties scholars of rhetoric face in trying to influence the communities they study).

The English department at the State University of New York–Albany provides one interesting model for how to revise a curriculum, in this case a graduate program. This model involves a strategy that Stephen North calls "fusion": "bringing disparate elements together under sufficient pressure and with sufficient energy to transform them into a single new entity, one quite distinct from any of the original components" (North et al. 73). Fusion requires three kinds of commitment: (1) Various unit representatives need to be "sequestered in the disciplinary and professional equivalent of a locked room for what amount to do-or-die negotiations." (2) All parties in the unit need to "be afforded a major role in the deliberations." SUNY-Albany included graduate students in its deliberations. Other programs might include part-time and adjunct faculty. (3) Regular faculty need to be "willing to renegotiate their disciplinary and professional status vis-à-vis" the other parties, such as graduate students and part-time and adjunct faculty (North et al. 73–75). Other strategies might work better in other contexts, but all strategies for change need to make the case that writing instruction needs to benefit all the parties involved, not just students, but also faculty, the institution of higher learning, and society at large.

The work to change the way writing is taught in higher education must of necessity be *political* in the most fundamental and straightforward sense of that term. It must be designed to promote massive social change in the way people think about writing and the way people think writing ought to be taught. It must involve all the relevant parties and stakeholders and be designed to persuade them that a new and different way of teaching writing will benefit them, the discourse communities they belong to, and society as a whole.

If it makes sense to reconstitute composition studies as the study of particular discourses in particular contexts, there is, in the words of Paul Kameen, "theoretically, no longer any need for such a 'discipline'"as composition:

> if the long-standing territorial boundaries between and among the constituent disciplines of the curriculum do in fact begin to blur, even break down; if the various disciplines do in fact create a common ground for mutual discourse about their discourses, share a common understanding that on the most fundamental level all of their "bodies of knowledge" are constituted of and by their various "rhetorics," there would be little need for exclusive programs in "composition." (185)

Such a dissolution of traditional disciplinary boundaries may then, paradoxically, capture a fundamental unity: that composition studies as a field can be "a common ground for mutual discourse about . . . discourse," an enterprise that can bring together the analysis and critique, the rhetoric of all other discourses. And as a common ground for the promotion and nurturing of many other "bodies of knowledge" with their various "rhetorics," composition studies can work to abolish the teaching of writing as writing and to foster the teaching of specific genres in specific contexts. Such an alternative would be an appropriate, and perhaps more helpful, end for composition studies.

Works Cited
Index

Works Cited

"Academic Requirements." *About the Master of Arts in Professional Communication.* Clemson University. <http:/www.clemson.edu/caah/mapc/academic.htm>. 29 Dec. 2001.

Ackerman, John. "The Promise of Writing to Learn." *Written Communication* 10 (1993): 334–70.

Adler-Kassner, Linda, Robert Crooks, and Ann Watters, eds. *Writing the Community: Concepts and Models for Service-Learning in Composition.* Washington, DC: AAHE, 1997.

Akinnaso, F. Niyi. "On the Differences Between Spoken and Written Language." *Language and Speech* 25 (1982): 97–125.

Alexander, Patricia A., Diane L. Shallert, and Victoria C. Hare. "Coming to Terms: How Researchers in Learning and Literacy Talk about Knowledge." *Review of Educational Research* 61 (1991): 315–43.

Allen, Harold B. "Preparing the Teacher of Composition and Communication—A Report." *CCC* 3 (1952): 3–13.

Anson, Chris M., and L. Lee Forsberg. "Moving Beyond the Academic Community: Transitional Stages in Professional Writing." *Written Communication* 7 (1990): 200–31.

Applebee, Arthur N. *Curriculum as Conversation: Transforming Traditions of Teaching and Learning.* Chicago: U of Chicago P, 1996.

Applebee, Arthur N., et al. *Learning to Write in Our Nation's Schools.* Princeton: ETS, 1990.

Astin, Alexander W. *What Matters in College: Four Critical Years Revisited.* San Francisco: Jossey, 1993.

"Bachelor of Arts in English." *English Department.* Carnegie Mellon University. <http://english.cmu.edu/programs/ba/English/>. 7 Sept. 2001.

Bacon, Nora. "Community Service Writing: Problems, Challenges, Questions." Adler-Kassner, Crooks, and Watters 39–55.

Bakhtin, M. and P. N. Medvedev. *The Formal Method in Literary Scholarship: A Critical Introduction to Sociological Poetics.* Cambridge: Harvard UP, 1985.

Bartholomae, David. "What Is Composition and (If You Know What It Is) Why Do We Teach It?" Bloom, Daiker, and White 11–28.

Bazerman, Charles. "Discursively Structured Activities." *Mind, Culture, and Activity* 4 (1997): 296–308.

———. "From Cultural Criticism to Disciplinary Participation: Living with Powerful Words." *Writing, Teaching, and Learning in the Disciplines.* Ed. Anne Harrington and Charles Moran. New York: MLA, 1992. 61–68.

Beach, Richard. "Differences in Autobiographical Narratives of English Teachers, College Freshmen, and Seventh Graders." *CCC* 38 (1987): 56–69.

Beaufort, Anne. "Operationalizing the Concept of Discourse Community: A Case Study of One Institutional Site of Composing." *Research in the Teaching of English* 31 (1997): 486–529.

Belenky, Mary Field, et al. *Women's Ways of Knowing: The Development of Self, Voice, and Mind.* New York: Basic, 1986.

Bereiter, Carl. "Development in Writing." *Cognitive Processes in Writing.* Ed. L. W. Gregg and E. R. Steinberg. Hillsdale: Erlbaum, 1980. 73–93.

———. "Toward a Solution of the Learning Paradox." *Review of Educational Research* 55 (1985): 201–26.

Bereiter, Carl, and Marlene Scardamalia. "Learning about Writing from Reading." *Written Communication* 1 (1984): 163–88.

———. *The Psychology of Written Composition.* Hillsdale: Erlbaum, 1987.

Berkenkotter, Carol, and Thomas N. Huckin. *Genre Knowledge in Disciplinary Communication: Cognition/Culture/Power.* Hillsdale: Erlbaum, 1995.

Berlin, James. "Contemporary Composition: The Major Pedagogical Theories." *College English* 44 (1982): 765–77.

———. "Poststructuralism, Semiotics, and Social-Epistemic Rhetoric: Converging Agendas." Enos and Brown 137–53.

———. "Rhetoric and Ideology in the Writing Class." *College English* 50 (1988): 477–94.

Berlin, James, and Michael J. Vivion, eds. *Cultural Studies in the English Classroom.* Portsmouth: Boynton, 1992.

Bérubé, Michael. *The Employment of English: Theory, Jobs, and the Future of Literary Studies.* New York: New York UP, 1998.

Beyer, Barry K. "Critical Thinking: What Is It?" *Social Education* 49 (1985): 270–76.

Birnbaum, June Cannell. "Reflective Thought: The Connection Between Reading and Writing." *Convergences: Transactions in Reading and Writing.* Ed. Bruce T. Petersen. Urbana: NCTE, 1986. 30–45.

Bizzell, Patricia. *Academic Discourse and Critical Consciousness.* Pittsburgh: U of Pittsburgh P, 1992.

———. "Composing Processes: An Overview." Petrosky and Bartholomae 49–70.

Bloom, Lynn Z., Donald A. Daiker, and Edward M. White, eds. *Composition in the Twenty-First Century: Crisis and Change.* Carbondale: Southern Illinois UP, 1996.

Booth, Wayne. "The Rhetorical Stance." *CCC* 14 (1963): 139–45.

Boyer Commission on Educating Undergraduates in the Research University. "Reinventing Undergraduate Education: A Blueprint for America's Research Universities." <www.notes.cc.sunysb.edu/Pres/boyer.nsf/webform/I>. 21 Sept. 1999.

Braddock, Richard. "The Frequency and Placement of Topic Sentences in Expository Prose." *Research in the Teaching of English* 8 (1974): 287–302.

Braddock, Richard, Richard Lloyd-Jones, and Lowell Schoer. *Research in Written Composition.* Champaign: NCTE, 1963.

Brandt, Deborah. *Literacy as Involvement: The Acts of Writers, Readers, and Texts.* Carbondale: Southern Illinois UP, 1990.

———. "Sponsors of Literacy." *CCC* 49 (1998): 165–85.

Brannon, Lil. "(Dis)Missing Compulsory First-Year Composition." Petraglia, *Reconceiving* 239–48.

Bressler, Charles E. *Literary Criticism: An Introduction to Theory and Practice.* 2d Ed. Upper Saddle River: Prentice, 1994.

Bridwell, Lillian S. "Revising Strategies in Twelfth Grade Students' Transactional Writing." *Research in the Teaching of English* 14 (1980): 197–222.

Britton, James. "The Composing Processes and the Functions of Writing." *Research on Composing: Points of Departure.* Ed. Charles R. Cooper and Lee Odell. Urbana: NCTE, 1978. 13–28.

———. *Language and Learning.* 2d ed. Portsmouth: Boynton, 1993.

Brodkey, Linda. "Writing Permitted in Designated Areas Only." *Higher Education under Fire: Politics, Economics, and the Crisis of the Humanities.* Ed. Michael Bérubé and Cary Nelson. New York: Routledge, 1995. 214–37.

Brown, Ann L., Doris Ash, Martha Rutherford, Kathryn Nakagawa, Ann Gordon, and Joseph C. Campione. "Distributed Expertise in the Classroom." *Distributed Cognitions: Psychological and Educational Considerations.* Ed. Gavriel Salomon. Cambridge: Cambridge UP, 1993. 188–228.

Brown, Stuart C., Paul R. Meyer, and Theresa Enos. "Doctoral Programs in Rhetoric and Composition." *Rhetoric Review* 12 (1994): 235–389.

Bruner, Jerome. *Actual Minds, Possible Worlds.* Cambridge: Harvard UP, 1986.

Campbell, Jay R., Kristen E. Voelki, and Patricia L. Donahue. *Report in Brief: NAEP 1996 Trends in Academic Progress.* Washington, DC: Nat. Ctr. for Ed. Stats., 1998.

Carter, Michael. "The Idea of Expertise: An Exploration of Cognitive and Social Dimensions of Writing." *CCC* 41 (1990): 265–86.

Caulfield, Peter J., "Talk, Thought, Writing and Politics." Fitts and France 295–96.

CCCC Task Force on the Preparation of Teachers of Writing. "Position Statement on the Preparation and Professional Development of Teachers of Writing." *CCC* 33 (1982): 446–49.

Chafe, Wallace L. "Integration and Involvement in Speaking, Writing, and Oral Literature." *Spoken and Written Language: Exploring Orality and Literacy.* Ed. Deborah Tannen. Norwood: Ablex, 1982. 35–53.

Chase, Geoffrey. "Accommodation, Resistance and the Politics of Student Writing in Composition." *CCC* 39 (1988): 13–22.

Chin, Elaine. "Redefining 'Context' in Research on Writing." *Written Communication* 11 (1994): 445–82.

Christensen, Francis. "A Generative Rhetoric of the Sentence." *CCC* 14 (1963): 155–61.

Clark, Eve V. "The Young Word Maker: A Case Study of Innovations in the Child's Lexicon." *Language Acquisition: The State of the Art.* Ed. Eric Wanner and Lila R. Gleitman. New York: Cambridge UP, 1982. 390–425.

Claxton, C. S., and W. F. Smith. *Learning Styles: Implications for Improving Educational Practices.* ASHE-ERIC Higher Education Report No. 1. Washington, DC: George Washington U, School of Ed. and Human Dev., 1984.

Coates, Jennifer. *Women, Men, and Language: A Sociolinguistic Account of Sex Differences in Language.* New York: Longman, 1986.

Coe, Richard. *Process, Form and Substance.* 2d Ed. Englewood Cliffs: Prentice, 1990.

Connors, Robert J. "Composition History and Disciplinarity." *History, Reflection, and Narrative: The Professionalization of Composition, 1963–1983.* Ed. Mary Rosner, Beth Boehm, and Debra Journet. Stamford: Ablex, 1999. 3–21.

———. *Composition-Rhetoric.* Pittsburgh: U of Pittsburgh P, 1997.

———. "The New Abolitionism: Toward a Historical Background." Petraglia, *Reconceiving* 3–26.

Connors, Robert J., and Cheryl Glenn. *The St. Martin's Guide to Teaching Writing.* 3d Ed. New York: St. Martin's, 1995.

Cooper, David D., and Laura Julier. "Democratic Conversations: Civic Literacy and Service-Learning in the American Grain." Adler-Kassner, Crooks, and Watters 79–94.

Cooper, Marilyn M., and Michael Holzman. *Writing as Social Action.* Portsmouth: Boynton, 1989.

Cope, Bill, and Mary Kalantzis, eds. *The Power of Literacy: A Genre Approach to Teaching Writing.* Pittsburgh: U of Pittsburgh P, 1993.

Corbett, Edward P. J. "The Usefulness of Classical Rhetoric." *CCC* 14 (1963): 162–64.

Crowhurst, Marion, and Gene L. Piché. "Audience and Mode of Discourse Effects on Syntactic Complexity at Two Grade Levels." *Research in the Teaching of English* 13 (1979): 101–9.

Crowley, Sharon. "Around 1971: Current-Traditional Rhetoric and Process Models of Composing." Bloom, Daiker, and White 64–74.

———. *Composition in the University.* Pittsburgh: U of Pittsburgh P, 1998.

———. "A Personal Essay on Freshman English." *Pre/Text* 12 (1991): 156–76. Rpt. in *Composition in the University.* Sharon Crowley. Pittsburgh: U of Pittsburgh P, 1998. 228–49.

Crystal, David. *The Cambridge Encyclopedia of Language.* New York: Cambridge UP, 1987.

Cuban, Larry. *How Teachers Taught: Constancy and Change in American Classrooms, 1880–1990.* 2d Ed. New York: Teachers College P, 1993.

Cushman, Ellen. *The Struggle and the Tools: Oral and Literate Strategies in an Inner City Community.* Albany: State U of New York P, 1998.

Damasio, Antonio R. *Descartes' Error: Emotion, Reason, and the Human Brain.* New York: Grosset, 1994.

Davis, Barbara Gross. *Tools for Teaching.* San Francisco: Jossey, 1993.

de Beaugrande, Robert. *Text Production: Toward a Science of Composition.* Norwood: Ablex, 1984.

Delpit, Lisa D. "The Silenced Dialogue: Power and Pedagogy in Educating Other People's Children." *Harvard Educational Review* 58 (1988): 280–98.

———. "Skills and Other Dilemmas of a Progressive Black Educator." *Harvard Educational Review* 56 (1986): 379–85.

Devitt, Amy J. "Genre, Genres, and the Teaching of Genres." *CCC* 47 (1996): 605–15.

Dias, Patrick, et al. *Worlds Apart: Acting and Writing in Academic and Workplace Contexts.* Mahwah: Erlbaum, 1999.

Dobrin, Sidney I. *Constructing Knowledges: The Politics of Theory-Building and Pedagogy in Composition.* Albany: State U of New York P, 1997.

Dorman, Wade, and Susan Fox Dorman. "Service-Learning: Bridging the Gap Between the Real World and the Composition Classroom." Adler-Kassner, Crooks, and Watters 119–32.

Drew, Julie. "(Teaching) Writing: Composition, Cultural Studies, Production." *JAC* 19 (1999): 411–29.

Dyson, Ann Haas. "Emerging Alphabetic Literacy in School Contexts." *Written Communication* 1 (1984): 5–55.

Eastman, Carol M. *Aspects of Language and Culture.* San Francisco: Chandler, 1975.

Elbow, Peter. "Reflections on Academic Discourse: How It Relates to Freshmen and Colleagues." *College English* 53 (1991): 135–55.

———. "Writing Assessment in the Twenty-First Century: A Utopian View." Bloom, Daiker, and White 83–100.

Emig, Janet. *The Composing Processes of Twelfth Graders.* Urbana: NCTE, 1971.

Engelhard, George, Belita Gordon, and Stephen Gabrielson. "The Influences of Mode of Discourse, Experiential Demand, and Gender on the Quality of Student Writing." *Research in the Teaching of English* 26 (1992): 315–36.

Enos, Theresa, and Stuart C. Brown, eds. *Defining the New Rhetorics.* Newbury Park: Sage, 1993.

Erneling, Christina E. *Understanding Language Acquisition: The Framework of Learning.* Albany: State U of New York P, 1993.

Faigley, Lester. "Competing Theories of Process: A Critique and a Proposal." *College English* 48 (1986): 527–42.

———. "Names in Search of a Concept: Maturity, Fluency, Complexity, and Growth in Written Syntax." *CCC* 31 (1980): 291–300.

———. "Nonacademic Writing: The Social Perspective." *Writing in Nonacademic Settings.* Ed. Lee Odell and Dixie Goswami. New York: Guilford, 1985. 231–80.

Faigley, Lester, et al. *Assessing Writers' Knowledge and Processes of Composing.* Norwood: Ablex, 1985.

"Final Report of the MLA Committee on Professional Employment." *ADE Bulletin* 119 (1998): 27–45.

Fitts, Karen, and Alan W. France, eds. *Left Margins: Cultural Studies and Composition Pedagogy.* Albany: State U of New York P, 1995.

Flavell, John H. "Metacognition and Cognitive Monitoring: A New Area of Cognitive-Developmental Inquiry." *American Psychologist* 34 (1979): 906–11.

Flower, Linda. "Cognition, Context, and Theory Building." *CCC* 40 (1989): 282–311.

———. "Rhetorical Problem Solving: Cognition and Professional Writing." *Writing in the Business Professions.* Ed. M. Kogen. Urbana: NCTE, 1989. 3–36.

Flower, Linda, and John R. Hayes. "The Cognition of Discovery: Defining a Rhetorical Problem." *CCC* 31 (1980): 21–32.

Flower, Linda, et al. "Detection, Diagnosis, and the Strategies of Revision." *CCC* 37 (1986): 16–55.

Flower, Linda, et al. *Reading-to-Write: Exploring a Cognitive and Social Process.* New York: Oxford UP, 1990.

Flynn, Elizabeth. "Composing as a Woman." *CCC* 39 (1988): 423–35.

Foertsch, Julie. "Where Cognitive Psychology Applies: How Theories of Memory and Transfer Can Influence Composition Pedagogy." *Written Communication* 12 (1995): 360–83.

Forster, E. M. *Aspects of the Novel.* New York: Harcourt, 1927.

Freed, Richard C., and Glenn J. Broadhead. "Discourse Communities, Sacred Texts, and Institutional Norms." *CCC* 38 (1987): 154–65.

Freedman, Aviva. "Genres of Argument and Arguments of Genre." *Perspectives on Written Argument.* Ed. Deborah P. Berrill. Creskill: Hampton, 1996. 91–120.

———. "Show and Tell? The Role of Explicit Teaching in the Learning of New Genres." *Research in the Teaching of English* 27 (1993): 222–51.

———. "Situating Genre: A Rejoinder." *Research in the Teaching of English* 27 (1993): 272–81.

Freedman, Aviva, Christine Adam, and Graham Smart. "Wearing Suits to Class: Simulating Genres and Simulations as Genres." *Written Communication* 11 (1994): 193–226.

Freedman, Aviva, and Ian Pringle. "Why Students Can't Write Arguments." *English in Education* 18 (1984): 73–84.

Fukuyama, Frances. *The End of History and the Last Man.* New York: Free, 1992.

Fulkerson, Richard. "Composition Theory in the Eighties: Axiological Consensus and Paradigmatic Diversity." *CCC* 41 (1990): 409–29.

Gaillet, Lynee Lewis. "Designing a Cross-Disciplinary Graduate Course in Academic Writing." *Issues in Writing* 9 (1998): 43–65.

Gappa, Judith M., and David Leslie. *The Invisible Faculty: Improving the Status of Part-Timers in Higher Education.* San Francisco: Jossey, 1993.

Gardner, Howard. *Artful Scribbles: The Significance of Children's Drawings.* New York: Basic, 1980.

Gee, James Paul. *Social Linguistics and Literacies: Ideology in Discourses.* New York: Falmer, 1990.

———. "Vygotsky and Current Debates in Education: Some Dilemmas as Afterthoughts to *Discourse, Learning, and Schooling.*" *Discourse, Learning, and Schooling.* Ed. Deborah Hicks. Cambridge: Cambridge UP, 1996. 269–82.

Geisler, Cheryl. *Academic Literacy and the Nature of Expertise.* Hillsdale: Erlbaum, 1994.

Gentry, J. Richard, and Jean Wallace Gillet. *Teaching Kids to Spell.* Portsmouth: Heinemann, 1993.

Gerber, John C. "The Conference on College Composition and Communication." *CCC* 1 (1950): 12.

———. "Three-Year History of the CCCC." *CCC* 3 (1952): 17–18.

Gere, Anne Ruggles. Introduction. *Into the Field: Sites of Composition Studies*. Ed. Anne Ruggles Gere. New York: MLA, 1993. 1–6.

Gibaldi, Joseph, ed. *Introduction to Scholarship in Modern Languages and Literatures*. 2d Ed. New York: MLA, 1992.

———. *MLA Handbook for Writers of Research Papers*. 4th ed. New York: MLA, 1995.

Gick, Mary L., and Keith J. Holyoak. "The Cognitive Basis of Knowledge Transfer." *Transfer of Learning: Contemporary Research and Applications*. Ed. Stephen M. Cormier and Joseph D. Hagman. New York: Academic, 1987. 9–46.

Gilligan, Carol. *In a Different Voice: Psychological Theory and Women's Development*. Cambridge: Harvard UP, 1982.

Giltrow, Janet. "Genre and the Pragmatic Concept of Background Knowledge." *Genre Knowledge and the New Rhetoric*. Ed. Aviva Freedman and Peter Medway. London: Taylor, 1994. 155–78.

Gleason, Jean Berko, ed. *The Development of Language*. 4th Ed. Boston: Allyn, 1997.

Golding, Alan, and John Mascaro. "A Survey of Graduate Writing Courses." *JAC* 6 (1985–86): 167–79.

Goody, Jack, ed. *Literacy in Traditional Societies*. New York: Cambridge UP, 1968.

Goody, Jack, and Ian Watt. "The Consequences of Literacy." Goody 27–68.

Grabe, William, and Robert B. Kaplan. *Theory and Practice of Writing: An Applied Linguistic Perspective*. New York: Longman, 1996.

Graff, Gerald. *Professing Literature*. Chicago: U of Chicago P, 1987.

Graff, Harvey J. *The Labyrinths of Literacy: Reflections on Literacy Past and Present*. New York: Falmer, 1987.

Graves, Donald. *A Case Study Observing the Development of Primary Children's Composing, Spelling, and Motor Behaviors During the Writing Process*. Washington, DC: Nat. Inst. of Ed., 1982.

———. "What Children Show Us about Revision." *Language Arts* 56 (1979): 312–19.

Greenfield, Patricia Marks. "A Theory of the Teacher in the Learning Activities of Everyday Life." *Everyday Cognition: Its Development in Social Context*. Ed. Barbara Rogoff and Jean Lave. Cambridge: Harvard UP, 1984. 117–38.

Grego, Rhonda, and Nancy Thompson. "Repositioning Remediation: Renegotiating Composition's Work in the Academy." *CCC* 47 (1996): 62–84.

"Guidelines for Writing Intensive Courses." *Campus Writing Program*. University of Missouri-Columbia. <http://cwp.missouri.edu/guidelines.html>. 8 Nov. 2001.

Gundlach, Robert A. "Children as Writers: The Beginnings of Learning to Write." *What Writers Know*. Ed. Martin Nystrand. New York: Academic, 1982. 129–47.

———. "On the Nature and Development of Children's Writing." *Writing: The Nature, Development, and Teaching of Written Communication*. Ed. C. H. Frederiksen and J. F. Dominic. Hillsdale: Erlbaum, 1981. 133–51.

Hacking, Ian. *The Social Construction of What?* Cambridge: Harvard UP, 1999.

Halliday, Michael A. K. *Explorations in the Functions of Language*. London: Arnold, 1973.

———. *Language as a Social Semiotic: The Social Interpretation of Language and Meaning*. Boston: Arnold, 1978.

Haring-Smith, Tori. "The Importance of Theory in the Training of Teaching Assistants." *ADE Bulletin* 82 (1985): 33–39.

Harmon, David. "Illiteracy: An Overview." *Harvard Educational Review* 40 (1970): 226–43.

Harré, Rom. *The Principles of Scientific Thinking.* Chicago: U of Chicago P, 1970.

Harris, Joseph. *A Teaching Subject: Composition since 1966.* Upper Saddle River: Prentice Hall, 1997.

Harris, Muriel. "Composing Behaviors of One- and Multi-Draft Writers." *College English* 51 (1989): 174–91.

Haswell, Richard H. *Gaining Ground in College Writing: Tales of Development and Interpretation.* Dallas: Southern Methodist UP, 1991.

Hawes, Kenneth. "Understanding Critical Thinking." *Varieties of Thinking.* Ed. V. A. Howard. New York: Routledge, 1990. 47–61.

Hayes, John R., and Linda Flower. "Identifying the Organization of Writing Processes." *Cognitive Processes in Writing.* Ed. L. Gregg and E. Steinberg. Hillsdale: Erlbaum, 1980. 3–30.

Heath, Shirley Brice. *Ways with Words: Language, Life and Work in Communities and Classrooms.* New York: Cambridge UP, 1983.

Higgins, Lorraine, Linda Flower, and Joseph Petraglia. "Planning Text Together: The Role of Critical Reflection in Student Collaboration." *Written Communication* 9 (1992): 48–84.

Hill, Charles A., and Lauren Resnick. "Creating Opportunities for Apprenticeship in Writing." Petraglia, *Reconceiving Writing* 145–58.

Hillocks, George, Jr. *Research on Written Composition.* Urbana: NCRE, 1986.

———. *Ways of Thinking, Ways of Teaching.* New York: Teachers College P, 1999.

Holladay, Sylvia A. "Order Out of Chaos: Voices from the Community College." Bloom, Daiker, and White 29–38.

Horgan, John. *The End of Science.* New York: Broadway, 1997.

Hourigan, Maureen M. *Literacy as Social Exchange: Intersections of Class, Gender, and Culture.* Albany: State U of New York P, 1994.

Huber, Bettina J. "A Report on the 1986 Survey of English Doctoral Programs in Writing and Literature." Appendix. *The Future of Doctoral Studies in English.* Ed. Andrea Lunsford, Helene Moglen, and James F. Slevin. New York: MLA, 1989. 121–75.

Humboldt, Wilhelm von. *Linguistic Variability and Intellectual Development.* Trans. George C. Buck and Frithjof A. Raven. Philadelphia: U of Pennsylvania P, 1971.

Hunt, Kellogg W. *Grammatical Structures Written at Three Grade Levels.* Research Report No. 3. Urbana: NCTE, 1965.

———. *Syntactic Maturity in Schoolchildren and Adults.* Monograph of the Society for Research in Child Development No. 134. Chicago: U of Chicago P, 1970.

Hunter, Carmen St. John, and David Harmon. *Adult Illiteracy in the United States: A Report to the Ford Foundation.* New York: McGraw, 1979.

Jacobs, Suzanne. "The Development of Children's Writing." *Written Communication* 2 (1985): 414–33.

Jarratt, Susan C. "Feminist Pedagogy." Tate, Rupiper, and Schick 113–31.

Johnson, Lois V. "Children's Writing in Three Forms of Composition." *Elementary English* 44 (1967): 265–69.

Judy, Stephen N., and Susan J. Judy. *An Introduction to the Teaching of Writing.* New York: Wiley, 1981.

Kamberelis, George. "Genre Development and Learning: Children Writing Stories, Science Reports, and Poems." *Research in the Teaching of English* 33 (1999): 403–60.

Kameen, Paul. "Coming of Age in College Composition." Petrosky and Bartholomae 170–87.

Karrfalt, David H. "The Generation of Paragraphs and Larger Units." *CCC* 19 (1978): 211–17.

Kaufer, David, and Richard Young. "Writing in the Content Areas: Some Theoretical Complexities." *Theory and Practice in the Teaching of Writing: Rethinking the Discipline.* Ed. Lee Odell. Carbondale: Southern Illinois UP, 1993. 71–104.

Kellogg, Ronald T. *The Psychology of Writing.* New York: Oxford UP, 1994.

Kennedy, Alan. "Committing the Curriculum and Other Misdemeanors." Berlin and Vivion 24–45.

Kennedy, Mary M. *Learning to Teach Writing: Does Teacher Education Make a Difference?* New York: Teachers College P, 1998.

Kent, Thomas. *Paralogic Rhetoric: A Theory of Communicative Interaction.* Lewisburg: Bucknell UP, 1993.

———, ed. *Post-Process Theory: Beyond the Writing Process Paradigm.* Carbondale: Southern Illinois UP, 1999.

Kitzhaber, Albert R. *Themes, Theories, and Therapy: The Teaching of Writing in College.* New York: McGraw, 1963.

Krupa, Gene. *Situational Writing.* Belmont: Wadsworth, 1982.

Kuhn, Thomas S. *The Structure of Scientific Revolutions.* 2d ed. Chicago: U of Chicago P, 1970.

Kurfiss, Joanne Gainen. "Helping Faculty Foster Students' Critical Thinking in the Disciplines." *The Department Chairperson's Role in Enhancing College Teaching.* New Directions for Teaching and Learning No. 37. Ed. A. F. Lucas. San Francisco: Jossey, 1989. 41–49.

Kutz, Eleanor. "Between Students' Language and Academic Discourse: Interlanguage as Middle Ground." *College English* 48 (1986): 385–96.

Kutz, Eleanor, Suzy Q. Groden, and Vivian Zamel. *The Discovery of Competence: Teaching and Learning with Diverse Student Writers.* Portsmouth: Boynton, 1993.

Langer, Judith A. "The Effects of Available Information on Responses to School Writing Tasks." *Research in the Teaching of English* 18 (1984): 27–44.

———. "Learning Through Writing: Study Skills in the Content Areas." *Journal of Reading* 29 (1986): 400–506.

Langer, Judith A., and Arthur N. Applebee. *How Writing Shapes Thinking.* Urbana: NCTE, 1987.

Latterell, Catherine G. "Training the Workforce: An Overview of GTA Education Curricula." *WPA* 19 (1996): 7–23.

LeCourt, Donna. "WAC as Critical Pedagogy: The Third Stage?" *JAC* 16 (1996): 389–405.

Lloyd-Jones, Richard, and Andrea A. Lunsford. *The English Coalition Conference: Democracy Through Language.* Urbana: NCTE, 1989.

Loban, Walter. *Language Development: Kindergarten Through Age Twelve.* Urbana: NCTE, 1976.

Lu, Min-Zhan. "Conflict and Struggle: The Enemies or Preconditions of Basic Writing?" *College English* 54 (1992): 887–913.

Lynn, Steven. *Texts and Contexts: Writing about Literature with Critical Theory.* 2d Ed. New York: Longman, 1998.

MacDonald, Susan Peck. "Problem Definition in Academic Writing." *College English* 49 (1987): 315–31.

———. "Voices of Research: Methodological Choices of a Disciplinary Community." *Under Construction.* Ed. Christine Farris and Chris M. Anson. Logan: Utah State UP, 1998. 111–23.

MacNealy, Mary Sue, Bruce W. Speck, and Barbara Simpson. "Fiddling Around with Text: Implications for Composition from a Study of a 'Non-Reviser.'" *Issues in Writing* 8 (1996): 27–53.

Maimon, Elaine P., Barbara F. Nodine, and Finbarr W. O'Connor, eds. *Thinking, Reasoning, and Writing.* New York: Longman, 1989.

Mansfield, Margaret A. "Real World Writing and the English Curriculum." *CCC* 44 (1993): 69–83.

Marzano, Robert, et al. *Dimensions of Thinking: A Framework for Curriculum and Instruction.* Alexandria: Assoc. for Supervision and Curriculum Dev., 1988.

McCarthy, Lucille Parkinson. "A Stranger in Strange Lands: A College Student Writing Across the Curriculum." *Research in the Teaching of English* 21 (1987): 233–65.

McKibben, Bill. *The End of Nature.* New York: Random, 1989.

McLeod, Susan H. *Notes on the Heart: Affective Issues in the Writing Classroom.* Carbondale: Southern Illinois UP, 1997.

———, ed. *Strengthening Programs for Writing Across the Curriculum: New Directions for Teaching and Learning* 36. San Francisco: Jossey, 1988.

McLeod, Susan, and Elaine Maimon. "Clearing the Air: WAC Myths and Realities." *College English* 62 (2000): 573–606.

McLeod, Susan, and Susan Shirley. "National Survey of Writing Across the Curriculum Programs." McLeod, *Strengthening* 103–30.

McLeod, Susan, and Margot Soven, eds. *Writing Across the Curriculum: A Guide to Developing Programs.* Newbury Park: Sage, 1992.

McMahan, Elizabeth, Susan X. Day, and Robert Funk. *Literature and the Writing Process.* 4th Ed. Upper Saddle River: Prentice, 1996.

McPeck, John E. "Critical Thinking and the 'Trivial Pursuit' Theory of Knowledge." Walters, *Re-Thinking* 101–17.

Meade, Richard, and W. Geiger Ellis. "Paragraph Development in the Modern Age of Rhetoric." *English Journal* 59 (1970): 219–26.

Mellon, John C. "Issues in the Theory and Practice of Sentence Combining: A Twenty-Year Perspective." *Sentence Combining and the Teaching of Writing.* Ed. Donald A. Daiker, Andrew Kerek, and Max Morenberg. Conway: L and S, 1979. 1–38.

Miller, Carolyn. "Genre as Social Action." *Quarterly Journal of Speech* 70 (1984): 151–67.

Miller, George A., and Patricia M. Gildea. "How Children Learn Words." *Scientific American* Sept. 1987: 94–99.

Miller, Richard. *As If Learning Mattered.* Ithaca: Cornell UP, 1998.

Miller, Susan. *Rescuing the Subject.* Carbondale: Southern Illinois UP, 1989.

———. "Rhetorical Maturity: Definition and Development." *Reinventing the Rhetorical Tradition.* Ed. Aviva Freedman and Ian Pringle. Conway: L and S, 1980. 119–27.

———. "Technologies of Self?-Formation." *JAC* 17 (1997): 497–500.

———. *Textual Carnivals: The Politics of Composition.* Carbondale: Southern Illinois UP, 1991.

Missimer, Connie. "Why Two Heads Are Better Than One: Philosophical and Pedagogical Implications of a Social View of Critical Thinking." Walters, *Re-Thinking* 119–33.

Murphy, Michael. "New Faculty for a New University: Toward a Full-Time Teaching-Intensive Faculty Track in Composition." *CCC* 52 (2000): 14–42.

Neel, Jasper. *Aristotle's Voice: Rhetoric, Theory, and Writing in America.* Carbondale: Southern Illinois UP, 1994.

Nelson, Jennie. "This Was an Easy Assignment: Examining How Students Interpret Academic Writing Tasks." *Research in the Teaching of English* 24 (1990): 362–96.

Newell, George E. "Learning from Writing in Two Content Areas: A Case Study/Protocol Analysis." *Research in the Teaching of English* 18 (1984): 265–87.

Newkirk, Thomas. "The Hedgehog or the Fox: The Dilemma of Writing Development." *Language Arts* 62 (1985): 593–603.

———. *More Than Stories: The Range of Children's Writing.* Portsmouth: Heinemann, 1989.

Newkirk, Thomas, and Nancy Atwell. "The Competence of Young Writers." *Perspectives on Research and Scholarship in Composition.* Ed. Ben W. McClellend and Timothy R. Donovan. New York: MLA, 1985. 185–202.

New London Group. "A Pedagogy of Multiliteracies: Designing Social Futures." *Multiliteracies: Literacy Learning and the Design of Social Futures.* Ed. Bill Cope and Mary Kalantzis. New York: Routledge, 2001. 9–37.

North, Stephen M. *The Making of Knowledge in Composition: Portrait of an Emerging Field.* Upper Montclair: Boynton, 1987.

North, Stephen M., et al. *Refiguring the Ph.D. in English Studies: Writing, Doctoral Education, and the Fusion-Based Curriculum.* Urbana: NCTE, 2000.

Nystrand, Martin. "A Social-Interactive Model of Writing." *Written Communication* 6 (1989): 66–85.

———. *The Structure of Written Communication.* New York: Academic, 1986.

Nystrand, Martin, Stuart Greene, and Jeffrey Wiemelt. "Where Did Composition Studies Come From: An Intellectual History." *Written Communication* 10 (1993): 267–333.

"Objectives and Organization of the Composition Course: The Report of Workshops No. 3 and No. 3A." *CCC* 1 (1950): 9–14.

Olson, David R. "From Utterance to Text: The Bias of Language in Speech and Writing." *Harvard Educational Review* 47 (1977): 257–81.

Olson, Gary, and Evelyn Ashton-Jones. "From Artifact to Utterance: Toward a Revised Conception of Critical Thinking in Advanced Composition." *Teaching Advanced Composition: Why and How.* Ed. Katherine H. Adams and John L. Adams. Portsmouth: Boynton, 1991. 195–210.

Ong, Walter. *Orality and Literacy: The Technologizing of the Word.* New York: Methuen, 1982.

Pan, Barbara Alexander, and Jean Berko Gleason. "Semantic Development: Learning the Meanings of Words." *The Development of Language.* Gleason 122–58.

Paradis, James, David Dobrin, and Richard Miller. "Writing at Exxon Ltd.: Notes on the Writing Environment of an R and D Organization." *Writing in Nonacademic Settings.* Ed. Lee Odell and Dixie Goswami. New York: Guilford, 1985. 281–308.

Parker, Robert P. "Writing Courses for Teachers: From Practice to Theory." *CCC* 33 (1982): 411–19.

Pascarella, Ernest T., and Patrick T. Terenzini. *How College Affects Students.* San Francisco: Jossey, 1991.

Paul, Richard W. "Teaching Critical Thinking in the Strong Sense: A Focus on Self-Deception, World Views, and a Dialectical Mode of Analysis." Walters, *Re-Thinking* 181–98.

Pemberton, Michael A. "Modeling Theory and Composing Process Models." *CCC* 44 (1993): 40–59.

Penrose, Ann M. *Strategic Differences in Composing; Consequences for Learning Through Writing.* Technical Report No. 31. Berkeley: Ctr. for the Study of Writing, 1989.

———. "Writing and Learning: Exploring the Consequences of Task Interpretation." *Hearing Ourselves Think: Cognitive Research in the College Writing Classroom.* Ed. Ann M. Penrose and Barbara M. Sitko. New York: Oxford UP, 1993. 52–69.

Perkins, David, and Gavriel Salomon. "Are Cognitive Skills Context-Bound?" *Educational Researcher* 18 (1989): 16–25.

———. "Teaching for Transfer." *Educational Leadership* 46 (1988): 22–32.

Perl, Sondra, and Arthur Egendorf. "The Process of Creative Discovery: Theory, Research, and Implications for Teaching." *Linguistics, Stylistics, and the Teaching of Composition.* Ed. Donald McQuade. Akron: Dept. of English, U of Akron, 1979. 118–42.

Petraglia, Joseph, ed. *Reconceiving Writing, Rethinking Writing Instruction.* Mahwah: Erlbaum, 1995.

———. "Spinning Like a Kite: A Closer Look at the Pseudotransactional Function of Writing." *JAC* 15 (1995): 19–33.

———. "Writing as an Unnatural Act." Petraglia, *Reconceiving* 79–100.

Petrosky, Anthony R., and David Bartholomae, eds. *The Teaching of Writing.* 85th Yearbook of the National Society for the Study of Education. Chicago: Natl. Soc. for the Study of Ed., 1986.

"Ph.D. in Rhetoric." *English Department.* Carnegie Mellon University. <http://english.cmu.edu/programs/phd/rhetoric/courses.html>. 7 Sept. 2001.

Phelps, Louise Wetherbee. *Composition as a Human Science.* New York: Oxford UP, 1988.

Pinker, Steven. *The Language Instinct: How the Mind Creates Language.* New York: Morrow, 1994.

Pitkin, William. "Discourse Blocs." *CCC* 20 (1969): 138–48.

Popken, Randall L. "A Study of Topic Sentence Use in Academic Writing." *Written Communication* 4 (1987): 209–28.

Porter, James E. *Audience and Rhetoric.* Englewood Cliffs: Prentice, 1992.

———. "Intertextuality and the Discourse Community." *Rhetoric Review* 5 (1986): 34–47.

Prendergast, Catherine. "Race: The Absent Presence in Composition Studies." *CCC* 50 (1998): 36–53.

Preparing Future Faculty Project Statement of Principles." NCTE. <http://www.ncte.org/college/ppf_principles.shtml>. 8 Nov. 2001.

Prior, Paul A. *Writing/Disciplinarity: A Sociohistoric Account of Literate Activity in the Academy.* Mahwah: Erlbaum, 1998.

Raforth, Bennett A. "The Concept of Discourse Community: Descriptive and Explanatory Adequacy." *A Sense of Audience in Written Communication.* Ed. Gesa Kirsch and Duane H. Roen. Newbury Park: Sage, 1990. 140–52.

Ramage, John, John Bean, and June Johnson. *Writing Arguments.* 5th Ed. Boston: Allyn, 2001.

Reiff, Judith C. *Learning Styles.* Washington, DC: NEA, 1992.

Resnick, David, and Lauren Resnick. "The Nature of Literacy: An Historical Exploration." *Harvard Education Review* 47 (1977): 370–85.

"Rhetoric and Technical Communication Policies and Procedures Manual." Michigan Technological University. <http://www.Hu.mtu.edu/hu_dept/RTC_manual/ManualCh4.html>. 27 July 1998.

Rice, William Craig. *Public Discourse and Academic Inquiry.* Garland Studies in American Popular History and Culture. New York: Garland, 1996.

Roberts, Paul. *The Roberts English Series: A Linguistics Program.* New York: Harcourt, 1970–71.

Rodgers, Paul. "A Discourse-Centered Rhetoric of the Paragraph." *CCC* 27 (1966): 2–11.

Rogers, Everett M. *Diffusion of Innovations.* 4th Ed. New York: Free, 1995.

Rogoff, Barbara. "Thinking and Learning in Social Context." Introduction. *Everyday Cognition: Its Development in Social Context.* Ed. Barbara Rogoff and Jean Lave. Cambridge: Harvard UP, 1984.

Rohman, D. Gordon, and Alfred O. Wlecke. *Pre-Writing: The Construction and Application of Models for Concept Formation in Writing.* U.S. Department of

Health, Education, and Welfare Cooperative Research Project No. 2174. East Lansing: Michigan State U, 1964.

Rose, Mike. "Remedial Writing Courses: A Critique and a Proposal." *College English* 45 (1983): 109–28.

Russell, David. "Activity Theory and Its Implications for Writing Instruction. Petraglia, *Reconceiving* 51–77.

———. "Rethinking Genre in School and Society: An Activity Theory Analysis." *Written Communication* 14 (1997): 504–54.

———. "Review Essay: Genre, Activity, and Expertise." *Rhetoric Society Quarterly* 26 (1996): 111–19.

———. *Writing in the Academic Disciplines, 1870–1990: A Curricular History.* Carbondale: Southern Illinois UP, 1991.

Sachs, Jacqueline. "Communicative Development in Infancy." Gleason 40–68.

Schell, Eileen E. *Gypsy Academics and Mother-Teachers: Gender, Contingent Labor, and Writing Instruction.* Portsmouth: Boynton, 1998.

Schell, Eileen E., and Patricia Lambert Stock, eds. *Moving a Mountain: Transforming the Role of Contingent Faculty in Composition Studies and Higher Education.* Urbana: NCTE, 2001.

Schroeder, Christopher L. *Reinventing the University: Literacies and Legitimacy in the Postmodern Academy.* Logan: Utah State UP, 2001.

Scribner, Sylvia, and Michael Cole. "Literacy Without Schooling: Testing for Intellectual Effects." *Harvard Educational Review* 48 (1978): 448–61.

———. *The Psychology of Literacy.* Cambridge: Harvard UP, 1981.

Seegars, J. C. "Form of Discourse and Sentence Structure." *The Elementary English Review* 10 (1933): 51–54.

Segal, Judy, et al. "The Researcher as Missionary: Problems with Rhetoric and Reform in the Disciplines." *CCC* 50 (1998): 71–90.

Shulman, Lee S. "Knowledge and Teaching: Foundations of the New Reform." *Harvard Educational Review* 57 (1987): 1–22.

Smagorinsky, Peter, and Michael W. Smith. "The Nature of Knowledge in Composition and Literary Understanding: The Question of Specificity." *Review of Educational Research* 62 (1992): 279–305.

Smart, Graham. "Genre as Community Invention: A Central Bank's Response to Its Executives' Expectations as Readers." *Writing in the Workplace: New Research Perspectives.* Ed. Rachel Spilka. Carbondale: Southern Illinois UP, 1993. 124–40.

Smith, Frank. *Comprehension and Learning.* New York: Holt, 1975.

———. *Writing and the Writer.* Hillsdale: Erlbaum, 1982.

Smith, Jeff. "Students' Goals, Gatekeeping, and Some Questions of Ethics." *College English* 59 (1997): 299–320.

Smith, Paul E., III. "Composing a Cultural Studies Curriculum at Pitt." Berlin and Vivion 46–65.

Snow, Catherine E., and Brenda F. Kurland. "Sticking to the Point: Talk about Magnets as a Context for Engaging in Scientific Discourse." *Discourse, Learning, and Schooling.* Ed. Deborah Hicks. Cambridge: Cambridge UP, 1996. 189–220.

Soliday, Mary. "From the Margins to the Mainstream: Reconceiving Remediation." *CCC* 47 (1996): 85–100.

Sowers, Susan. "A Six-Year Old's Writing Process: The First Half of First Grade." *Language Arts* 56 (1979): 829–35.

Spellmeyer, Kurt. "After Theory: From Textuality to Attunement with the World." *College English* 58 (1986): 893–913.

———. *Common Ground: Dialogue, Understanding, and the Teaching of Composition.* Englewood Cliffs: Prentice, 1993.

Stewart, Donald C. "What Is an English Major, and What Should It Be?" *CCC* 40 (1989): 188–202.

Stich, Steven P. *From Folk Psychology to Cognitive Science.* Cambridge: MIT P, 1983.

Stock, Patricia Lambert, and Janet Swenson. "The Write for Your Life Project: Learning to Serve by Serving to Learn." Adler-Kassner, Crooks, and Watters. 153–66.

Stotsky, Sandra. "On Planning and Writing Plans—Or Beware of Borrowed Theories." *CCC* 41 (1990): 37–57).

———. "Research on Reading/Writing Relationships: A Synthesis and Suggested Directions." *Language Arts* 60 (1983): 627–42.

Sullivan, Patricia A. "Writing in the Graduate Curriculum: Literary Criticism as Composition." *JAC* 11 (1991): 283–99.

Survey of the Profession. New York: MLA Commission on Writing and Literature, 1985.

Swales, John M. *Genre Analysis: English in Academic and Research Settings.* New York: Cambridge UP, 1990.

Tager-Flusberg, Helen. "Putting Words Together: Morphology and Syntax in the Preschool Years." Gleason 159–209.

Tate, Gary. "Empty Pedagogical Space and Silent Students." Fitts and France 269–73.

Tate, Gary, Amy Rupiper, and Kurt Schick, eds. *A Guide to Composition Pedagogies.* New York: Oxford UP, 2001.

Taylor, Denny, and Catherine Dorsey-Gaines. *Growing Up Literate: Learning from Inner-City Families.* Portsmouth: Heinemann, 1988.

Tchudi, Stephen N. *Teaching Writing in the Content Areas: College Level.* New York: NEA, 1986.

"Technical and Professional Communication." *English Department Masters Programs.* New Mexico State University. <http://www.nmsu.edu/~english/mtpc.html>. 27 July 1998.

Thaiss, Christopher. "The Future of Writing Across the Curriculum." McLeod, *Strengthening* 91–102.

Tierney, Robert J., and Margie Leys. "What Is the Value of Connecting Reading and Writing?" *Convergences: Transactions in Reading and Writing.* Ed. Bruce T. Petersen. Urbana: NCTE, 1986. 15–29.

Tobin, Lad. "How the Writing Process Was Born—and Other Conversion Narratives." Introduction. *Taking Stock: The Writing Process Movement in the 90s.* Ed. Lad Tobin and Thomas Newkirk. Portsmouth: Heinemann, 1994. 1–14.

Townsend, Martha. Personal Interview. 15 Nov. 2001.

Trimbur, John. "The Problem of Freshman English (Only): Towards Programs of Study in Writing." *WPA* 22 (1999): 9–30.

Tyack, David, and William Tobin. "The 'Grammar' of Schooling: Why Has It Been So Hard to Change?" *American Educational Research Journal* 31 (1994): 453–79.

Veal, L. Ramon, and Murray Tillman. "Mode of Discourse Variation in the Evaluation of Children's Writing." *Research in the Teaching of English* 5 (1971): 37–45.

Voss, James F. "On the Composition of Experts and Novices." *Thinking, Reasoning, and Writing.* Ed. Elaine P. Maimon, Barbara F. Nodine, and Finbarr W. O'Connor. New York: Longman, 1989. 69–84.

Vygotsky, Lev. *Mind in Society: The Development of Higher Psychological Processes.* Ed. Michael Cole et al. Cambridge, Harvard UP, 1978.

Walters, Kerry S. "Beyond Logicism in Critical Thinking." Introduction. Walters, *Re-Thinking* 1–22.

———, ed. *Re-Thinking Reason: New Perspectives in Critical Thinking.* Albany: State U of New York P, 1994.

Walvoord, Barbara E. "Getting Started." McLeod and Soven 13–21.

Walvoord, Barbara E., and Lucille Parkinson McCarthy. *Thinking and Writing in College: A Naturalistic Study of Students in Four Disciplines.* Urbana: NCTE, 1990.

Walvoord, Barbara E., et al. *In the Long Run: A Study of Faculty in Three Writing-Across-the-Curriculum Programs.* Urbana: NCTE, 1997.

Warren, Thomas H. "Critical Thinking Beyond Reasoning: Restoring Virtue to Thought." Walters, *Re-Thinking* 221–31.

Weese, Katherine L., Stephen L. Fox, and Stuart Greene, eds. *Teaching Academic Literacy: The Uses of Teacher-Research in Developing a Writing Program.* Mahwah: Erlbaum, 1999.

Wiley, Mark, Barbara Gleason, and Louise Wetherbee Phelps, eds. *Composition in Four Keys: Inquiring into the Field.* Mountain View: Mayfield, 1996.

Williams, Joseph M., and Gregory G. Colomb. "The Case for Explicit Teaching: Why What You Don't Know Won't Help You." *Research in the Teaching of English* 27 (1993): 252–64.

Wilson, Robin. "Universities Scramble to Find Teachers of Freshman Composition." *Chronicle of Higher Education.* On-line. <http://www.chronicle.com/colloquy/98/froshcomp/background.htm>. 26 Oct. 1998.

Winterowd, W. Ross. *The Culture and Politics of Literacy.* New York: Oxford UP, 1989.

———. "Transferable and Local Writing Skills." *JAC* 1 (1980): 1–3.

Witte, Stephen P. "Pre-Text and Composing." *CCC* 38 (1987): 397–425.

———. "Revising, Composing Theory, and Research Design." *The Acquisition of Written Language: Response and Revision.* Ed. Sarah Warshauer Freedman. Norwood: Ablex, 1985. 250–84.

Wittgenstein, Ludwig. *Philosophical Investigations.* 3rd ed. Trans. G. E. M. Anscombe. New York: Macmillan, 1958.

Wolcott, Willa, and Sue M. Legg. *An Overview of Writing Assessment: Theory, Research, and Practice.* Urbana: NCTE, 1998.

"WPA Outcomes Statement for First-Year Composition." *College English* 63 (2001): 321–25.

Young, Richard, and Maureen Daly Goggin. "Some Issues in Dating the Birth of the New Rhetoric in Departments of English: A Contribution to a Developing Historiography." Enos and Brown 22–43.

Zebroski, James Thomas. "The Syracuse Writing Program and Cultural Studies: A Personal View of the Politics of Development." Berlin and Vivion 87–94.

———. "Toward a Theory of Theory for Composition Studies." *Under Construction: Working at the Intersections of Composition Theory, Research, and Practice.* Ed. Christine Farris and Chris M. Anson. Logan: Utah State UP, 1998. 19–29.

Index

DAVID W. SMIT is a professor of English at Kansas State University, where for ten years he was the director of the Expository Writing Program. He teaches expository writing, modern drama, and Henry James. He has published numerous articles on literary style, portfolio assessment, and composition theory. His article "Hall of Mirrors: Antifoundationalist Theory and the Teaching of Writing" won the James L. Kinneavy Award for the best article in *JAC: The Journal of Advanced Composition* in 1995. His book *The Language of a Master: Theories of Style and the Late Writing of Henry James* is also published by Southern Illinois University Press.